EXTERNAL FINANCE IN THAILAND'S DEVELOPMENT

INTERNATIONAL FINANCE AND DEVELOPMENT SERIES
Published in association with the Institute of Social Studies

General Editor: E.V.K. FitzGerald, Professor of Economics, Institute of Social Studies, The Hague, and Director, Finance and Trade Policy Research Centre, University of Oxford

The *International Finance and Development Series* reflects the research carried out at The Hague and associated centres in Europe, Asia, Africa and Latin America on the relationship between international capital flows and the process of structural adjustment in less-developed economies. The studies in this series share a common analytical approach based on the use of advanced social accounting techniques and the explicit modelling of the economic behaviour of institutional sectors, which in turn permit a new approach to macroeconomic policy design.

Karel Jansen
EXTERNAL FINANCE IN THAILAND'S DEVELOPMENT

Karel Jansen and Rob Vos (*editors*)
EXTERNAL FINANCE AND ADJUSTMENT

Rob Vos
DEBT AND ADJUSTMENT IN THE WORLD ECONOMY

Rob Vos and Josef T. Yap
THE PHILIPPINE ECONOMY: EAST ASIA'S STRAY CAT?

External Finance in Thailand's Development

An Interpretation of Thailand's Growth Boom

Karel Jansen
Associate Professor of Economics
Institute of Social Studies
The Hague

in association with
INSTITUTE OF SOCIAL STUDIES

First published in Great Britain 1997 by
MACMILLAN PRESS LTD
Houndmills, Basingstoke, Hampshire RG21 6XS and London
Companies and representatives throughout the world

A catalogue record for this book is available from the British Library.

ISBN 0–333–72115–2

 First published in the United States of America 1997 by
ST. MARTIN'S PRESS, INC.,
Scholarly and Reference Division,
175 Fifth Avenue, New York, N.Y. 10010

ISBN 0–312–17714–3

Library of Congress Cataloging-in-Publication Data
Jansen, Karel.
External finance in Thailand's development : an interpretation of
Thailand's growth boom / Karel Jansen.
p. cm. — (International finance and development series)
Includes bibliographical references and index.
ISBN 0–312–17714–3 (cloth)
1. Investments, Foreign—Thailand.   2. Capital movements–
–Thailand.   3. Thailand—Economic conditions.   I. Title.
II. Series.
HG5750.55.A3J36 1997
332.6'73'09593—dc21   97–19874
                                                        CIP

This book is printed on paper suitable for recycling and made from fully managed and
sustained forest sources.

10   9   8   7   6   5   4   3   2   1
06 05 04 03 02 01 00 99 98 97

Printed and bound in Great Britain by
Antony Rowe Ltd, Chippenham, Wiltshire

Contents

List of Tables and Figures

Tables

viii

Figures

International Finance and Development Series

Series Editor's Introduction

At first sight, Thailand appears to be one more of the growing band of 'Asian miracle economies', the 'emerging markets' which have broken the development constraints to achieve sustainable high growth rates and attract increasing amounts of foreign investment. Indeed Thailand has achieved an average GDP growth rate of 7.5 per cent per annum since the mid-1960s, survived various external shocks through considerable entrepreneurial flexibility and sound economic policies, and has made a profound transition from a backward agricultural nation to the desirable status of 'newly industrializing country'.

However, as this contribution by Karel Jansen to the *International Finance and Development Series* shows, the story is rather more complex than appears at first sight. Thailand did not exhibit very high levels of saving, and relied to a greater extent than other Asian NICs on foreign investment. Nor did it appear to have either a dominant industrialization strategy or a very determined liberalization programme. In fact, Thai policy appears to have been highly pragmatic, and its response to external trade and capital shocks remarkably flexible. This in turn has serious implications not only for Thailand itself but also for interpretation by scholars and policy-makers – and not least by the international financial institutions entrusted with the transmission of the lessons of experience to other developing countries.

This volume is the result of over a decade of meticulous empirical research on the Thai economy by Karel Jansen. His original doctoral dissertation work at the Free University of Amsterdam focused on monetary policy, and was published as *Finance, Growth and Stability:*

Financing Economic Development in Thailand, 1960–86 (1990). That study made a number of important contributions to our understanding of the economy of Thailand, particularly concerning the relationship between sectoral behaviour and remarkable macroeconomic stability during a rapid growth period. Jansen's research then developed into a joint research project with the Thailand Development Research Institute as part of the research programme 'International Capital Flows and Economic Adjustment' at the Institute of Social Studies in The Hague, sponsored by the Netherlands Ministry for Development Co-operation. The results of that co-operative effort were reported by Akrasanee, Jansen and Pongpisanupichit in *International Capital Flows and Economic Adjustment in Thailand* (1993). Further work on general equilibrium modelling and foreign investment resulted in the present volume, which deepens the analysis and also updates the story to the mid-1990s.

This book is also the second country case study in the *Series*: the first was on the Philippines (R. Vos & J. Yap, *The Philippine Economy: East Asia's Stray Cat? Structure, Finance and Adjustment*, 1996) and should be followed by studies of Mexico, Colombia and Bolivia. Some of the key results are presented in a comparative framework in another volume in the *Series* which is at present in press: K. Jansen and R. Vos (eds), *External Finance and Adjustment: Failure and Success in the Developing World* (forthcoming).

The research team at The Hague (led by Karel Jansen, Rob Vos and myself) established a new approach to the relationship between capital flows and structural adjustment, which involves the careful disaggregation of macroeconomic behaviour by institutional sector. We set out three central hypotheses, which are in effect tested in this volume. The first of these hypotheses is that the impact of foreign capital inflows on the structural adjustment process depends critically on the type of flow involved. Official development assistance, international bank credit or direct foreign investment affect public and private expenditure in quite different ways. This is demonstrated very clearly by the Thai study, which indicates the radical shift from public borrowing from international commercial banks in the 1970s to direct foreign investment in the 1980s; this shift in turn reduced the role of the public sector and supported the increase in private investment. However, this shift was made possible not just by a flexible fiscal stance, but also by reliance on a highly concentrated and protected banking system, which could bear the strain of adjustment within wide profit margins.

Second, we have argued that the response of the economy to external shocks (whether on the current or capital account) depends critically upon the distinct investment and savings decisions of the main groups of economic agents (government agencies, parastatal enterprises, domestic and foreign firms, and households) and the relationship between them. Jansen demonstrates very elegantly, by careful examination of the flow of funds within a social accounting matrix, how the public sector was able to rectify its net wealth position in response to external shock. However, of even more interest is the way in which the effect of the gradual decline of household savings rates was checked by shifting household assets from informal capital markets into the banking system; and above all the way in which an increasing volume of corporate profits was complemented by inflows of private capital – inflows which increasingly became endogenous, responding to the needs of Thai business rather than decisions by foreign investors.

Third, our approach strongly suggests that economic policy is highly constrained by both this private sector response and current conditions of international trade and international capital markets. This hypothesis is certainly confirmed by the present volume. On the one hand, the Thai approach to policy-making appears to be a continuous pragmatic adjustment to these factors, rather than an autonomous objective function being maximized subject to the constraints of private and external sector behaviour. On the other hand, the computable general equilibrium model of the Thai economy constructed on the basis of the 1989 social accounting matrix clearly demonstrated how attempts to shift the policy variables very far from their observed values rapidly lead to severe macroeconomic disequilibria.

The Philippines provides an interesting contrast to Thailand because it had so little success with growth or foreign investment, failing to escape the debt trap or to make the breakthrough to manufactured exports. The first two case studies in the *Series* suggest at least four reasons for these differences: (i) the banking sector in Thailand was not obliged to channel as many resources towards the public sector, while the corporate sector was not credit-constrained and small firms were guaranteed a significant proportion of bank lending; (ii) private savings did not decline in Thailand under structural adjustment because firms reinvested their large profits, unlike in the Philippines where they were sent abroad; (iii) capital inflows to Thailand mainly took the form of direct foreign investment and thus contributed to the modernization of firms, rather than debt instruments in the case of the Philippines; and (iv) government policy in Thailand was geared to the provision of stable profit conditions for investors, and thus caused fewer abrupt changes than in the case of the Philippines.

In the 'Asian miracle' debate which contrasts the success of East Asian economies in achieving rapid industrialization and penetrating world markets for manufactures, with the failure of Africa and Latin America to do so, three schools of thought can be identified. The first, most traditional school, based on economic theory, suggests that in fact it is the high rates of capital accumulation (human capital – skills – as well as plants and equipment) which explain most of the high rates of growth, although it leaves the high rates of investment themselves unexplained. The second school argues that it is the market-friendly policies of governments in the region which have stimulated private investment and thus rapid productivity growth and technological modernization – this is a view notably espoused by the World Bank. The third school, which includes most Asian experts and indeed the Asian Development Bank itself, argues that it is the high degree of government intervention which has guided the private sector towards international competitiveness and high rates of investment. The debate is of considerable policy importance both for the rest of the region – particularly China and India, as they emerge into the global economy – but also for the semi-industrialized economies of Latin America and Africa.

Although Jansen does not address this debate directly, his study does throw valuable light on the issue. He agrees that most of the outstanding growth record of the past three decades can be attributed to accumulation of productive factors (particularly fixed investment) and that export expansion can be explained by world market growth and an appropriate real exchange rate. In other words, there is no 'miracle ingredient' here, nor even a particular attention to human capital formation. He attributes the high private investment rate (which rose from 17 per cent of GDP in the 1970s to 22 per cent in the 1980s and 30 per cent in the early 1990s) not to domestic savings, but rather to the demand for investment by firms of all sizes, supported by foreign capital inflows. As to market-friendly policies, it is true that corporate profitability was underwritten and credit kept freely available, but financial liberalization was gradual and there was no dramatic opening of the economy of the kind recommended by the World Bank. Nor was the government particularly proactive in the way it has been in Japan, Korea and Singapore. If anything, Thai economic policy was shaped by the private sector (through both political parties and a business-military alliance) and implementation delegated to technocrats.

Jansen concludes his thorough study of the Thai economy on a broadly optimistic note: high growth rates can be sustained because non-debt-creating private foreign investment will continue to flow in. However, there are a number of clouds on the horizon, two of which he identifies in the study: household savings rates are falling and portfolio flows can be affected by global capital market volatility. It seems possible to extend his argument further. On the one hand, financial liberalization would reduce the role of the banks (banks account for two-thirds of all financial intermediation) which at present act as a stabilizing factor and can be seen as transmitters – if not makers – of macroeconomic policy. This might lead to greater financial efficiency in the short run, but possibly to greater macroeconomic instability in the longer term. On the other hand, the present trend towards funding massive public infrastructure requirements through private sector bond issues apparently transfers all risk to the operating firms, but in fact generates a contingent government liability which would require fiscal bailout were payments schedules not met or Thai banks to fail.

In other words, financial structure still matters, and the new external capital flows may generate negative as well as positive shocks. The disaggregated behavioural economic analysis that Jansen sets out in this book – which is the hallmark of the research programme at The Hague in which he has been a leading figure – should allow both the Thai authorities and external observers to both foresee the policy problem and design an appropriate adjustment policy for the late 1990s.

E.V.K. FitzGerald
The Hague and Oxford
October 1996

Author's Preface

Several years ago I started my research on the Thai economy with a study on the financing of economic development, *Finance, Growth and Stability, Financing Economic Development in Thailand, 1960–86* (1990). That study concentrated on the investment and saving behaviour of the main institutional agents and on financial intermediation between them. The focus was very much on domestic finance and on the role of direct and indirect financial intermediation in financing growth and in changing the structure of the Thai economy. During this work it became clear to me how the importance of external finance had grown over the years. So this became a logical next topic for research.

My interest in the role of international finance fitted into the research programme of the *Finance and Development Research Group* at the Institute of Social Studies well. Together with my colleagues Valpy Fitz-Gerald and Rob Vos, I initiated the research programme *International Capital Flows and Economic Adjustment* (ICFEA), in which detailed country studies were made of Mexico (see Calderón & FitzGerald 1994), Pakistan (Naqvi & Sarmad 1993), the Philippines (Vos & Yap 1996) and Thailand. The Thailand study, *International Capital Flows and Economic Adjustment in Thailand*, was published by the Thailand Development Research Institute (Akrasanee et al. 1993). A volume with the comparative analysis of the various case studies will be published soon (Jansen & Vos, forthcoming).

After the ICFEA study I continued work in two directions. First, with the help of Luis Jemio, I constructed a general equilibrium model of the Thai economy to better understand the interactions between external finance, domestic financial intermediation and real variables (Jemio & Jansen 1993). Secondly, I made a more detailed analysis of the foreign investment boom that Thailand experienced in the late 1980s and early 1990s (Jansen 1995).

In this book, I have used these various lines of work to present a comprehensive and updated interpretation of the role of external capital in Thailand's economic development. Elements of the ICFEA study are used in Chapters 2, 3 and 4. Chapter 5 draws on Jansen (1995), and Chapter 6 on Jemio and Jansen (1993).

The history of this study as set out above indicates my intellectual debts. At the Institute of Social Studies, the many discussions with Valpy FitzGerald and Rob Vos helped to shape my ideas about the role of external finance; they also made many useful comments on earlier versions of the study. I am extremely grateful to my co-authors of the ICFEA study, Narongchai Akrasanee and Jeerasak Pongpisanupichit, who provided me with many well-informed insights into the Thai economy. A very special word of thanks goes to Luis Jemio, without whose help the general equilibrium model that is used in Chapter 6 would not have been constructed. Furthermore, three anonymous referees gave useful comments on an earlier version of the manuscript. I gratefully acknowledge the financial support for the ICFEA project from the Research Programme of the Directorate General for Development Co-operation of the Netherlands' Ministry for Foreign Affairs and a later research grant of the Institute of Social Studies that allowed me to update my research. Jacqueline de Vries and Joy Misa provided editorial assistance in the final stages of the production of this book.

Karel Jansen
Ho Chi Minh City
October 1996

1 Double-Digit Growth

1.1 Introduction

The years 1987 to 1990 stand out as a most remarkable period in Thai economic history. In these four years, the growth rate was at or above 10 per cent per year: double-digit growth. This made Thailand the fastest growing economy of the world at that time (World Bank 1991a). It also made Thailand one of the first developing countries to decisively and successfully recover from the debt crisis and the economic recession of the first half of the 1980s.

Even a superficial inspection of economic statistics is sufficient to reveal the main characteristics of the growth boom. The first of these is the unprecedented growth of inflows of direct private foreign investment (DFI). DFI inflows had always been relatively low in Thailand. Gross DFI inflows averaged around 0.6 per cent of GDP in the period 1970–86, and then increased to 2.1 per cent of GDP in the years 1987–90.

A second striking fact is the enormous increase in the private investment ratio. Private investment, as a percentage of GDP, had fluctuated in the 1970s and early 1980s around a level of 18 per cent, without showing a clear trend. By 1990 the ratio had almost doubled, to 34 per cent. Most of the foreign investment and a large part of the local investment were directed towards export activities. The export/GDP ratio increased from around 25 per cent in 1985–86 to 38 per cent by the early 1990s. However, the import ratio increased even more and the current-account deficit, which had fallen to about zero as a percentage of GDP in 1986–87, increased sharply in 1990–91, remaining high thereafter, at close to 6 per cent of GDP.

It will be argued in this study that exceptional growth is only possible in Thailand when external conditions are favourable and, in par-

1

ticular, when external finance is available to help finance high levels of investment. An earlier growth boom, around 1976–78, was also associated with a sharp rise in capital inflows. This dependence on external finance to generate high growth makes Thailand's experience different from those of earlier Asian miracles like Japan and, in later years, Hong Kong, Singapore, South Korea, and Taiwan.[1]

The role of international finance in Thailand's economic development is the central theme of this book. Over the last two decades, Thailand's relationship to the international financial markets has radically changed. Three main dimensions of this change can be identified. In the 1960s and early 1970s, capital flows to Thailand were relatively small and consisted mainly of aid and modest levels of direct foreign investment. A first change came in the mid-1970s, when international financial markets were awash with liquidity after the first oil shock. This increased the access of developing countries to international commercial borrowing. Thailand, like many other countries, seized this opportunity, and borrowing by the public sector increased sharply. The debt crisis of the early 1980s, however, closed this access for most developing countries.

A second radical change came in the late 1980s, when the re-alignment of the major world currencies (particularly the yen and the US dollar) and a worldwide process of industrial restructuring, or *globalization*, led to a sharp upsurge in DFI flows. The growing integration of financial markets led to a sharp rise in flows of foreign portfolio investment. Thailand became one of the 'emerging markets' on which these flows of direct and portfolio investment concentrated.

One might say that these sudden changes on the supply side of international financial markets came as 'external shocks' to Thailand, shocks to which the country had to adjust. In both periods, this adjustment was initially reflected in increased levels of investment and growth. International finance not only affected the rate of growth, but also the entire pattern of development. Sectoral balances shifted, for instance between public and private sector, between traded and non-traded activities, between manufacturing and the primary sector. Accompanying these shifts were significant changes in the income distribution, patterns of trade, and so on. All these shifts are explored in detail in the following chapters.

The third process of change was more gradual and culminated in the early 1990s in the full integration of Thailand's financial system with international financial markets. Over the years, Thailand's credit rating improved, also because in the 1980s a full-blown debt crisis was prevented by policy reforms. Increasingly, large and established domestic corporations could borrow on international markets. And since the early 1990s, off-shore banking (at the Bangkok International Banking Facility, BIBF) has provided direct and relatively cheap links to the international credit markets. International investors are attracted by the Stock Exchange of Thailand (SET) and by the high interest rate on domestic bank deposits. Thai banks are rapidly expanding regional and global networks. Thus, while initially, in the period 1987–90, capital inflows were dominated by foreign direct and portfolio investments, in more recent years a greater variety of inward and outward flows can be observed, including, in addition to inflows and outflows of foreign direct and portfolio investments, private sector short-term and long-term foreign borrowing, directly or through the BIBF, foreign borrowing by financial institutions, non-resident deposits, and so forth.

These developments bring about significant changes in the nature of capital inflows, and in their impact on the economy. Capital flows that used to flow to the public sector (in the 1970s) are now exclusively directed at the private sector. And short-term and volatile funds – such as portfolio investment and short-term loans and deposits – constitute a growing share of capital flows. This makes the capital flows more vulnerable to external shocks (such as the Gulf War or the Mexico crisis of 1994) and to domestic fluctuations.

The changes that occurred in the financial markets in the mid-1970s and since 1986 started as major shifts on the supply side of international funds, shifts that came as external or exogenous 'shocks' to which Thailand had to adjust. The integration of financial markets in recent years implies that 'international finance' has become more endogenous. Flows of international funds remain sensitive to shocks on the supply side, but domestic factors have become much more important in explaining the flows of international finance.

The large inflow of funds and the increasing integration with global financial markets posed a considerable challenge for economic policy-makers. How to manage the inflow of external finance, and how to ensure that a pattern of stable and economically sustainable growth evolves? It will be argued that economic policy was more successful in the late 1980s and early 1990s than in the period 1975–85.

These aspects will receive ample attention in the subsequent chapters. The study is mainly concerned with the macroeconomic impact of external finance, a topic that has figured prominently in the field of development economics from the early days. The central issue in this area is, of course, whether external finance can assist developing countries in their efforts at growth. Empirical studies on the link between capital inflows and growth give ambiguous results (see e.g. White 1992 for a survey). The debt crisis in many developing countries during the 1980s further demonstrated the dangers of excessive dependence on external funds. The recent experience of Thailand suggests a more positive interaction. The question will be addressed whether Thailand's recent spectacular growth boom is due to specific and incidental circumstances, or to a particular superior policy package from which other countries could learn.

Before that, however, this introductory chapter will place the recent growth boom in the historical perspective of Thai economic growth and in the comparative perspective of growth in Asia.

1.2 Economic Growth in Thailand

The process of economic development based on private sector initiative can be said to have started around 1960. In the 1950s there had been some attempts at industrialization through state enterprises. This strategy was not based on any state-oriented ideology, but on political leaders' fear that the Thai private sector was too weak and that, therefore, the free development of the private sector would lead to domination by foreign and Chinese businesses. In the late 1950s, disappointment set in when many state enterprises turned out to be quite inefficient (Ingram 1971). More importantly, the political leadership and local Chinese entrepreneurs found ways to accommodate each other (Skinner 1958). In the new strategy, initiated in the 1960s, the state looked after the investments needed for the infrastructure, while the private sector was allowed to take the initiative in the other sectors.

The success of this strategy has been spectacular. The average growth rate since 1960 has been over 7.6 per cent per year. In Figure 1.1 the pattern of the annual growth rate is presented; the horizontal line is the

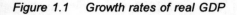

Figure 1.1 Growth rates of real GDP

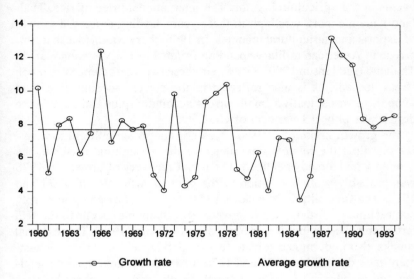

average growth rate over the entire period.

It should be noted, first of all, that Thailand's long-term average growth rate is exceptionally high. Of the hundred developed and developing countries listed in the 1992 *World Development Report* of the World Bank, only nine had a growth rate of GDP *per capita* higher than that of Thailand in the period 1965–90 (World Bank 1992). Figure 1.1 also shows the stability of Thai growth: in the crisis years of the early 1980s, when many developing countries experienced stagnation or decline, Thailand's growth rate fell, but remained at a respectable level, around 5 per cent per year. Stability can also be observed on the up-side: growth peaks have occurred over the years but tend to be short-lived.

Figure 1.1 illustrates that the recent growth boom is exceptional both in the level of the growth rate and in the duration of the boom. Earlier growth peaks occurred in 1966, in 1973 and in the years 1976–78, but they were not as high and were of shorter duration than the growth boom of 1987–90.

The earlier growth peaks of 1966 and 1973 were dominated by events in the agricultural sector. The international price of rice, Thailand's main export, was high in these years, leading to a rapid growth of exports and agricultural incomes. In 1966, there was also a sharp increase in American military spending (related to the Vietnam War) in Thailand (see Jansen 1990). Growth in these two years came very much 'from abroad', as is also reflected in the current-account deficit: in 1966 there was actually a small current-account surplus and in 1973 the deficit was only 0.3 per cent of GDP.

The growth boom of 1976–78 was not due to agricultural fortunes. By that time the relative importance of the agricultural sector in the economy had already declined. The initial recovery of growth in 1976 was probably more a reaction to the poor growth rates in 1974 and 1975. The first oil price shock of 1973–74 was followed by a sharply contractionary fiscal policy: government spending declined in real terms and the tax burden increased in 1973 and 1974. The external shocks also undermined private sector confidence. The private investment ratio declined in 1975 and 1976. In 1975–76, government spending and taxation returned to 'normal' levels, and investment by state enterprises started to rise rapidly, partly financed by foreign borrowing. These demand impulses led to a high growth rate in 1976, and to a gradual recovery of private investment.

The growth boom of 1976–78 can thus be ascribed to (i) catching up after the recession of 1974–75, (ii) expansionary public sector policies financed by rapidly increasing foreign borrowing, and (iii) a recovery of the world economy after the recession of 1975. The fact that the main impulse for this growth boom came from domestic demand and was financed by foreign borrowing also implied that the current-account deficit increased substantially.

This brief survey of earlier growth peaks points to two insights that will be useful in understanding the recent growth boom.

(a) Earlier growth peaks came after years of recession. This was particularly clear in 1973 and in 1976. The same observation applies to the 1987 recovery, which came after eight years of below-average growth. The extent of the recovery has to be considered in the light of the depth of the preceding recession.

(b) In general, growth spurts require external support. The 1966 and 1973 peaks are almost fully explained by external factors (good crops, good world prices for exports, US military spending). In later years, international financial conditions contributed to the growth spurts. In the period 1976–78, a substantial increase in foreign borrowing helped to finance the expansion. The current-account deficit had, in the period 1960–75, hovered around an average of 1.3 per cent of GDP, but in the three years 1976–78, the average deficit was 4.3 per cent of GDP. Here again, there appears to be a parallel with the later growth boom of 1987–90, which was accompanied by very high current-account deficits and huge inflows of foreign capital.

1.3   A Comparative Perspective on Thailand's Growth Record

In the years of double-digit growth, Thailand experienced growth rates like those associated with the success stories of East Asian industrialization, such as Japan (in the 1950s and 1960s), Korea and Taiwan. Immediately, it was suggested that Thailand would be the next Asian 'NIC' (newly industrializing country).

Table 1.1 provides some comparative information on growth in Asia. Over the entire period of 30 years, Thailand's growth performance has been better than the average for all developing countries. This above-average performance is common to the Asian countries included in Table 1.1, with the exception of the Philippines. The table also convincingly shows that the growth record of the final period, after 1987, is exceptionally good and cannot be rivalled by the other countries.

As Table 1.1 shows, the growth rate of Thailand in recent years resembles that of the Asian NICs, Singapore, Korea and Taiwan. However, the average growth rate of Thailand, over the entire period of 30 years covered in the table, is lower than that of the NICs. It also does not appear that Thailand is now starting a period of growth that will be comparable to the earlier experience of the NICs: after 1990, Thailand's growth rate fell back to a level just above its long-term average. Thus, although Thailand's growth record is strong, it is not as strong as that of the nearby Asian NICs.

Table 1.1   Growth rates of real GDP

	1961–70	1971–80	1981–86	1987–91	1961–91
All developing countries	6.6[a]	5.4	2.8	3.8	4.9
ASEAN					
– Indonesia	4.8[a]	8.0	4.9	6.4	6.3
– Malaysia	—	8.0	4.4	8.2[b]	7.0
– Philippines	5.0	6.3	-0.6	3.7	4.1
– Singapore	9.3	9.0	5.4	9.0	8.4
NICs					
– Korea	8.4	8.3	9.1	9.4	8.7
– Taiwan	9.6	9.7	6.7	8.1[b]	8.9
Japan	10.2	4.6	3.6	5.1	6.3
Thailand	8.1	6.8	5.5	10.4	7.5

[a] 1965–70   [b] 1987–90

Sources: IMF International Financial Statistics; for Taiwan: James, Naya & Meier 1989:
6 and Asian Development Bank *Annual Reports.*

The exceptional growth record of some Asian countries – Japan in
the 1950s and 1960s and, in later years, Korea and Taiwan[2] – has received ample attention in the literature (see e.g. Amsden 1989, Morishima 1982, Noland 1990, Porter 1990, Scitovsky 1986, Wade 1990).
These studies tried to understand the factors behind the rapid growth
of these countries. Although each individual country has its own history and characteristics, it is possible to identify a number of elements
that these countries had in common and that contributed to their rapid
growth. These elements may be summarized under four headings: culture, nature, accumulation behaviour and the role of government.

1.3.1   Culture

The Asian NICs share a culture strongly influenced by Confucianism,
which lays more emphasis on achievements in the present life than on
the afterlife. This is argued to have contributed to a psychology and a
social culture that stressed education, hard work, and social discipline
in labour relations, for example. The social discipline and the accept-

ance of co-ordination and co-operation may have facilitated the public acceptance of authoritarian governments. Many of these characteristics will have been strengthened by nationalistic feelings (after the Second World War) and by external security threats (in the case of Korea and Taiwan).

Thailand is a Buddhist country, where the accumulation of (moral) merit on the way to enlightenment is emphasized. This is said to lead to moderation in striving for material progress, to individualism, and to fatalism and the acceptance of one's position in life as being the result of deeds in past lives. In the anthropological literature Thailand has been characterized as a 'loosely structured society' (Embree 1950). Such notions have not gone unchallenged, however, and more recent studies seem to converge on the position that Thai society has a 'structure' and also an ability to cope with, and strive for, social and economic change (see e.g. Girling 1981, Klausner 1987, Mulder 1979, Potter 1976). At the same time, however, it is clear that Thai society lacks the co-ordination and sense of purpose of the NICs. This contrast is most sharply reflected in the differences in educational achievement and in the role of government in the process of development. Later, the role of government will be discussed in more detail; here some comments on the education record will be made.

Over the last few decades there has been considerable progress in educational development in Thailand. Participation in primary education is now almost universal. But beyond primary education, achievements are less convincing. The secondary school enrolment ratio of 28 per cent in 1987 compares to (1983) ratios of 89 per cent for Korea, 87 per cent for Taiwan, 49 per cent for Malaysia and 63 per cent for the Philippines (James et al. 1989, TDRI 1991). It is argued that the educational system of Thailand is weak and, in its present form, unable to adequately support future economic development (TDRI 1991).

1.3.2 Nature

The Asian NICs all have weak natural-resource bases. This implies that a development model based on the exploitation of natural resources is out of the question. Japan, Korea and Taiwan all implemented agrarian reforms early in their process of economic reform. These agricultural reforms consisted of redistributing land, and of setting limits to landownership. The outcome was an agrarian structure characterized by owner cultivation on small plots, leading to significant increases in land productivity. The reforms also implied that private wealth accumulation through large landownership, quite common in other Asian countries, was impossible. Private wealth was thus steered towards the industrial sector or financial assets.

Even with these reforms, the agricultural sector remained relatively weak in the NICs. To stimulate production and to keep the cost of food (and thus the industrial wages) low, the governments of the NICs had to resort to – often substantial – subsidies for the agricultural sector.

The weak agricultural base implied that the main impulse for economic development had to come from the industrial sector. It also implied that domestic demand for industrial goods from the still predominantly agricultural economy would be limited. Hence, rapid industrialization required an export orientation. The trade reforms of the early 1960s in Korea and Taiwan sought to create that orientation. Import tariffs were reduced to low levels and any anti-export bias that remained was neutralized by export incentives, such as import duty refunds for exporters, subsidized export credits, and other benefits.

The industrial sector that emerged was engaged in processing (imported) raw materials and intermediate goods into final goods for export. These exports were competing in international markets on the basis of cost advantages. Gradually, however, other competitive advantages were created. The NICs developed their own 'brand' names, with recognized quality, and based on technologies developed in the NICs. This was the outcome of a conscious and substantial effort of enterprises and of the state to develop indigenous technological capacity. The educational system emphasized education and training in technical subjects and engineering. Governments created research institutes and enterprises encouraged in-house 'Research & Development'.

The contrast with Thailand is striking, once again. Thailand has a strong natural-resource base. Agricultural growth has been rapid, based more on the expansion of acreage and the diversification of crops than on an increase in productivity (Jansen 1990: 154). This has given rise to a different pattern of industrialization (as will be argued in more statistical detail in Chapter 2). From an early stage onwards, industries emerged that were engaged in the processing of natural resources for the domestic market and for export. The more import-dependent industries initially produced, behind protective tariff walls, for the domestic market and only gradually (in the 1970s) diversified to produce for export markets.

The growth boom of 1987–90 was heavily based on import-dependent processing industries whose competitive edge derived from the relatively low production cost in Thailand. The question now is whether Thailand can turn this vulnerable and probably temporary cost advantage into a more durable competitive strength based on product quality and technical innovation, as the NICs did previously. It is generally argued that the present technological capacity is too weak to enable such a transition. In the same manner that the Thai performance is comparatively weak in post-primary education, it is also very weak in technical education and engineering. The availability of technical and scientific manpower lags very far behind the levels achieved in countries like Korea, Taiwan or Malaysia. Current educational programmes to create such manpower do not satisfy the existing demand. Expenditures on 'Research & Development' in Thailand are only a fraction of the expenditure levels in the NICs (TDRI 1991).

1.3.3 Accumulation

The high growth rates of the NICs were generated through high levels of investment. The investment/GDP ratio increased to levels around 25, and later even to more than 30 per cent. These high rates of investment were financed, in Taiwan, by own savings, as had been the case in the earlier period in Japan. Korea's savings were inadequate, and up to the early 1980s Korea had to borrow abroad to help finance its investments. In the second half of the 1980s, when its savings ratio increased, Korea was also able to close its resource gap.

In Thailand, as well, the investment ratio has been relatively high over the years, hovering around 24 per cent of GDP. In the 1960s, the Thai investment rate was comparable to that of the NICs, but when the NICs further increased their investment rates to over 30 per cent in the 1970s and early 1980s, Thailand lagged behind. Thailand could not finance a higher investment rate, because its savings ratio stagnated at a relatively low level, around 21 per cent of GDP. Thailand did borrow abroad to raise its investment ratio over the constraints of domestic savings, but it did not want to, and probably could not, borrow enough as to bring its investment rate to NIC levels.

The high growth rates of the last few years have been accompanied by a sharp increase in the savings ratio: the average savings ratio over the period 1970–86 had been around 21 per cent, in the last few years it increased to around 30 per cent. This increase is almost entirely due to the spectacular increase in public sector savings. Fiscal reforms and the financial reforms of state enterprises have pushed public sector savings to a level around 10 per cent of GDP. The reaction of private savings to the growth boom has, so far, been disappointing: the private savings ratio has not increased decisively. These patterns have created an unusual situation in recent years: the public sector, which throughout the 1970s and early 1980s ran a substantial investment-savings gap, has now turned this into a substantial surplus, while the private sector, which used to run savings surpluses, now faces a large deficit.

Despite the increase in the aggregate savings ratio, the investment-savings gap increased substantially. This gap was financed partly by non-debt-creating foreign capital inflows (direct and portfolio invest-ments), but the largest share was financed by long-term and short-term foreign borrowing by the private sector.

1.3.4 Role of the government

There has been much debate about the role of government in bringing about the success of the NICs. Initially there was a tendency to view the success as a triumph for market- and outward-oriented economic policies. The Asian NICs had, in varying degrees, reduced import pro-tection and introduced export incentives, liberalized financial markets (particularly in Taiwan), liberalized labour markets, created competitive industrial structures, and provided stable, and generally authoritarian, governments which implemented cautious macroeconomic policies. These policies fitted the neo-classical paradigm well and led to the assertion that the rapid economic growth was due to these policies. However, subsequent, more careful analysis has tended to emphasize the substantial role of the state in steering the development process.

Wade (1990) admits that there are many 'free-market' elements in the economic policies of the Asian NICs, but he also shows that the role of government has been much more important than is recognized in the neo-classical analysis. He shows that the state 'governed' the market through interventions like land reforms, through control of the financial system and of credit allocation, through selective export promotion measures, through initiatives in technological development, and through specific assistance to particular industries. These interventions significantly affected the outcomes in terms of the levels and the patterns of investment, production and exports.

Wade further counters the neo-classical argument that the state merely followed and supported private sector initiatives, i.e. supported actions based on private profit calculations, that would have taken place anyway. He shows that in Japan, Korea and Taiwan the governments drew up strategies, took initiatives and induced the private sector to take steps in directions that otherwise would most likely *not* have been followed. The state in NICs has been not a 'follower' but a 'leader' in the process of economic development.

This image of a strong government with its own independent long-term strategic vision does not extend to Thailand. The economic role of the Thai government should be interpreted against the background of the relationship between bureaucratic and military political power on the one hand, and business interests on the other (see e.g. Charoensino-larn 1988). The balance in this struggle has shifted. In the 1960s political leaders provided 'protection' for predominantly Chinese businesses, in exchange for financial rewards. Later, in the 1970s and 1980s, business interests took more control over politics by establishing political parties. Most of these parties are dominated by one or a few leading politician-*cum*-entrepreneurs, with their own specific economic agendas. In the patron-client relationships that have emerged in this context, it is not always clear which party decides on relevant economic policies, but it would appear that in specific policy decisions, specific private interests can and do interfere. Policy-making thus becomes strongly *ad hoc* and lacks strategic design. On the whole, one could conclude, in Wade's terminology, that the government of Thailand has been much more a 'follower' of private sector initiatives and interests than a 'leader' of the development process.

To this observation may be added that the size of state activities in Thailand is relatively small. The tax ratio (the ratio of government revenue to GDP) averaged 16 per cent in the 1980s, compared to 18 per cent in Korea, 24 per cent in Taiwan and even 26 per cent in Malaysia.

The high growth rates in the successful Asian industrializing countries have thus been explained by factors including the Confucian social dis-

cipline, the emphasis on education and on the building up of technological capabilities, the poor natural-resource base leading to a co-ordina-
ted industrialization drive governed by state intervention, and high
savings and investment ratios. As most of these factors do not apply to
Thailand, it may not be surprising that Thailand did not, in the long
run, grow as fast as these star performers. Still, Thailand did grow fast,
much faster than most other developing countries. Three general factors
can be mentioned as underlying Thailand's good long-term performance (see Jansen 1991, Falkus 1995).

(a) The dynamic agricultural sector. Agricultural growth has been high,
     with a long-term average over the last three decades of around 4
     per cent per year. This growth is based on the expansion of the
     area cultivated and on the diversification into higher value crops.
     The sector provided ample and cheap food for the workers, inputs
     for the processing industries, and export crops to earn foreign ex-
     change. In these ways it supported the industrialization drive.

(b) A dynamic entrepreneurial class, which was able to diversify from
     agriculture and trade into industry and finance, unhampered by the
     state, which was relatively weak.

(c) Macroeconomic stability. Traditionally, and with few exceptions,
     Thailand adhered to cautious fiscal and monetary policies. As a
     result, inflation remained low and the exchange rate exceptionally
     stable. This environment inspired confidence among domestic and
     foreign investors. It should also be mentioned that Thailand always
     maintained an outward orientation in its policies. Domestic industry
     was protected, but never to the extreme. Export growth was high
     throughout the decades and supported economic growth.

The long-term growth rate of Thailand is lower than that of the Asian
star performers because its growth generating capacity is limited by the
relatively low savings ratio, the lack of indigenous technological
capability, and perhaps also the absence of a directed and coherent
development strategy. The medium-term growth booms that occurred
in 1976–78 and 1987–90 were thus based on external impulses and
were dependent on substantial inflows of foreign capital.

1.4   The 1987–90 Growth Boom: Double-Digit Growth and Beyond

A number of conclusions may be drawn from the historical and comparative analysis of the Thai growth record presented in sections 1.2 and 1.3. Thailand's economic growth is, on average, relatively high. The boom of 1987–90 should be viewed, to some extent, as a recovery from the depression in the preceding years. Such rebounds occurred previously and are well in line with investment and growth models based on the accelerator mechanism. In the 1979–86 period, the growth rate was below the long-term average for eight years in a row. One could thus hypothesize that there was a large stock of pent-up investment demand.

But such a 'catch up' scenario is an incomplete explanation. The 1987–90 boom had a number of characteristics that make it necessary to analyse it as more than just a welcome recovery. The first of these characteristics is the extremely high level of investment. The rate of investment before 1987 hardly ever exceeded 25 per cent, even during growth peaks. By the early 1990s it had increased to around 40 per cent. Equally dramatic is the increase in the private investment ratio: historical peaks had been around 18 or 19 per cent, but by 1990 the private investment ratio increased to 34 per cent.

As was often the case in Thai economic history, the growth boom was induced by external factors. In this case the main external event was the 'endaka', the appreciation of the Japanese yen, and to a lesser extent the currencies of the Asian NICs, after the 'Plaza Agreement' of 1985 (see Das 1993). This reduced the cost advantage of exporters in Japan and in the NICs. These firms then started to shift the more labour-intensive and technologically simpler parts of their production processes to low-cost countries. This led to a substantial upsurge of outflows of direct investment from Japan and the Asian NICs, for which Thailand became one of the favoured destinations. These foreign investments, coming from Asian exporters looking for cheaper production platforms, were almost entirely export-oriented. However, these foreign investments are an indicator of a more comprehensive process of globalization of industrial production, a process in which Thailand participates through affiliates of, and joint ventures with, multinationals, as well as through local corporations. This broader process explains why private investment in export-oriented manufacturing increased by much more than the increase in DFI flows did.

This boom in global DFI flows found Thailand ready. The stabilization and adjustment policies that had been implemented since the early 1980s had, more or less, achieved their targets by 1986. The period between 1979 and 1986 was one of external shocks and domestic adjustment. The main dimensions of structural adjustment in Thailand had been (i) public sector financial reform and (ii) a devaluation in 1984. Since 1985, the public sector borrowing requirement (PSBR) had decreased, leading to a decline in the domestic interest rates (by 1987 the PSBR was zero). Thai exports became competitive due to the devaluation. This coincidence, around 1986, of the changes on the global scene and the successful completion of the domestic adjustment programme probably explains why Thailand was one of the first developing countries to benefit from the upsurge in global DFI flows. This coincidence further explains why the Thai economy benefitted so much from this external impulse that it was for some years the fastest growing economy in the world.

The DFI flows helped to finance the increase in private investment, but they were not sufficient to finance the entire domestic private investment-savings gap. Nor was the rapidly growing public sector savings surplus enough to fill that gap, although it made a substantial contribution. The remainder of the gap was filled by foreign borrowing by the private sector.

The investment boom changed the nature of Thai industrialization. Up to the mid-1980s, industrial growth had been driven by both natural-resources processing industries and import-dependent industries. Since 1987, there has been a significant shift towards import-dependent industries. Thailand has become more integrated in the Asian distribution of labour, led by Japan and the NICs. Regional networks of investment, production and trade are developing in which Thailand emerges as a reliable basis for the simpler and labour-intensive parts of the production process. Whether Thailand can maintain or extend that position will depend mainly on the development of production cost. This will depend fundamentally on the availability of infrastructure and public utilities and on the ability to contain wage increases.

The growth boom came to an end after 1990, when the growth rate dropped back to levels just above its long-term average despite the fact that capital inflows remained high. This appears to confirm the conclusion of the previous section, that it is difficult for the Thai economy to grow at double-digit rates over the medium or longer term, like the NICs did. It should also be noted that the nature of the capital inflows gradually changed: directly productive investments (DFI) constitute a smaller share, and short-term funds constitute growing shares.

1.5   The Rest of this Book

This book aims to study the role of international finance in Thai economic development. It will do so by concentrating on two periods in recent Thai economic history when international financial flows were particularly high: 1975–85 and 1987–94. In both cases, the initial impulse for the upsurge in capital inflows is to be found outside Thailand. Developments in international financial markets rather suddenly increased the supply of external funds.

The two finance booms differ from each other radically in many respects. A first and fundamental difference is the nature of the external capital that became available. In the 1970s, this consisted of loans for the public sector, and in the 1980s of foreign direct and portfolio investments and loans for the private sector. This difference was reflected in the structure of economic growth that emerged: in the 1970s the share of public investment increased, and in the 1980s the share of private investment increased.

A second difference is that the 1970s boom was associated with a growing public sector deficit, with a rising debt burden, and with a deteriorating export performance, all of which made the boom unsustainable in the end, and necessitated a period of structural adjustment. The 1980s boom also subsided, in the early 1990s, but in this case the large public sector surpluses and the strong export performance helped to avoid debt problems.

The chapters that follow will analyse these patterns in detail. Chapter 2 traces the process of structural change of the Thai economy and highlights in particular the long-term shifts in the relationship with the world economy. In recent decades, Thailand has become increasingly integrated with the world economy, in terms of both trade and finance. This integration has affected all economic sectors and institutions, and is reflected in, for instance, radical changes in the composition of ex-p,orts. At the end of Chapter 2 the structure of the Thai economy that emerged from this process of structural change is summarized in the Social Accounting Matrix for 1989.

Chapter 3 gives a statistical presentation of the trends in the flows of the various types of international finance. The familiar macroeconomic identity equation states that total net capital inflows (F) are equal to the current-account deficit (CAD) and equal to the gap between domestic investment (I) and savings (S), or:

$$CAD = F = I - S$$

Any increase in capital inflows will thus be reflected in adjustments in either investment or savings or in both. But Chapter 3 goes beyond these macroeconomic aggregates, and distinguishes different types of capital inflows (DFI, portfolio investment, loans to public and private sector) and disaggregates total investment and savings by main economic agents (households, private corporations, government, state enterprises). The chapter then relates each type of capital flow, in the first instance, to the agent that receives it. Such a disaggregation gives a much better impression of the impact of capital flows, and allows an analysis of the interaction between capital inflows, sectoral investment-savings balances, and domestic financial intermediation.

Using the background information of Chapters 2 and 3, Chapter 4 then analyses the first foreign finance boom, the 'loan boom' of 1975–85. The chapter traces the background of the first growth boom in the years 1976–78. International finance started to flow in 1976, and reached very high levels around 1980. Most of it consisted of commercial loans for the public sector. Initially, this upsurge was associated with an increase in the investment ratio and an acceleration of growth. But the external shocks of 1979–80 (when oil prices went up and international interest rates reached very high levels) put an end to this growth boom, and led to a prolonged growth recession and a period of structural adjustment. By 1986 capital inflows had dropped to a very low level. The chapter shows how the boom in foreign borrowing led to a rise in the public sector investment ratio, but a decline in its savings ratio. The public sector investment-savings gap (or: the PSBR) rose sharply, creating tensions on the domestic financial markets, which translated into high real interest rates.

The capital inflows had an expansionary effect on aggregate demand, and this was reflected in an increase in inflation. The oil shock further added to inflation, and the real exchange rate appreciated. The devaluation of 1981 could not fully correct for this appreciation, and export performance slackened, also because of poor world market prices for primary exports. The build-up of external debt, together with the poor export performance, made the debt-carrying capacity an issue of concern for Thai policy-makers and international observers.

By the early 1980s it was clear that the situation was becoming untenable. Structural adjustment policies were implemented, focusing on the restoration of public sector financial balances and on the recuperation of export growth. By 1986 the economy was 'stabilized', though still weak.

Structural adjustment was completed in Thailand by 1986–87, just when the new wave of DFI came up. In a short period of time, foreign investment inflows shot up to levels never experienced before. The patterns of DFI differed from historical trends in level, origin (most of it came from Asia) and destination (predominantly export-oriented manufacturing). As Chapter 5 accounts, the impact on the economy was radical. There was a sharp upsurge in private investment and growth, but not in private savings, so that the private sector savings-investment gap turned decisively negative for the first time. It helped that the public sector balances, after the financial reforms under structural adjustment, turned strongly positive. But even the substantial public sector savings surplus could not fill the private sector gap, and private sector external borrowing increased rapidly, leading to a new accumulation of external debt. The DFI boom further changed the structure of the economy. There was a sharp acceleration in the process of industrialization. As much of the foreign investment was export-oriented, the export ratio increased sharply. But the new pattern of development was also very import intensive: the import ratio increased as well, leaving a large current-account deficit. External debt burdens remained quite manageable thanks to the strong export performance.

The economic policy challenge in this period was quite different: how to stabilize the economy in the face of such large inflows of foreign finance? On the whole, this was done effectively: the rate of inflation remained low. But the period of double-digit growth revealed a number of structural weaknesses in the Thai economy. The first of these is its low savings ratio, which implies that rapid growth can only be financed with the help of foreign capital. But there is also increasing concern regarding the inadequacy of the existing infrastructure, the lack of technical personnel and the inability of the educational system to provide it, the growing income inequality, and the environmental degradation that has accompanied development. These weaknesses pose important challenges for economic policy-making, that go beyond the scope of this book.

The final chapter first summarizes the main findings of Chapters 4 and 5 and uses them to compare the two booms in foreign finance: the loan boom of 1975–85 and the foreign investment boom of 1987–94. As the above summary of the two chapters already indicated, the contrasts between the two periods are sharp. This suggests that different types of international capital flows have quite different impacts on the receiving economy, so that the question of the macroeconomic impact of international finance cannot be answered at the aggregated level, but only for each type of capital flow separately. However, when comparing the two periods, one must recognize that external conditions and policy regimes also differed substantially. It is thus uncertain how much of the difference in economic performance should be attributed to the type of capital inflow and how much to differences in accompanying external conditions and policies. To provide some insight into this topic, Chapter 6 uses a Computable General Equilibrium model (CGE) of the Thai economy. The CGE model, built on the 1989 Social Accounting Matrix introduced in Chapter 2, is applied in a number of dynamic simulations. In such simulations, changes in one variable (e.g. DFI flows) can be introduced while external conditions and policy regimes are kept unchanged, so that the effects of the various variables can be separated. The model simulations strongly confirm the findings of Chapters 4 and 5, and suggest that the inherent characteristics of the different types of capital flows are an important determinant of the contrasts between the two foreign finance booms that Thailand experienced.

2 The Integration of Thailand in the Global Economy

2.1 Introduction

The discussion in the previous chapter led to two important conclusions. Firstly, economic growth has been comparatively rapid in Thailand. With an average growth rate of real GDP of around 7.5 per cent per year over the last three decades, Thailand ranks among the fastest growing economies in the world. The second conclusion was that short-term and medium-term fluctuations in the growth rate have been strongly influenced by external factors. In particular, the growth booms, as they occurred over the years, could all be traced to external impulses. In the 1960s and early 1970s, when agriculture was still the dominant sector, such external impulses often came from shifts in international prices of Thailand's main primary commodity exports. In later years, the share of the agricultural exports declined and external price shocks became less important. Increasingly important among external impulses in these later years, has been international finance. The growth booms of 1976–78 and the one since 1987 have both been supported by foreign capital. This observation leads to the hypothesis that Thailand can grow rapidly, i.e. at above average rates, only if external finance is available. This hypothesis will be explored in more detail in Chapters 4 and 5.

Whereas the previous chapter analysed the historical trends in the rate of growth, this chapter will analyse the patterns of growth and structural change. Over the years, Thailand has gone through the standard process of structural change, with a declining share of agriculture and an increasing share of manufacturing in value added. The substantial overall growth rate is based on a strong performance of the agricultural sector and on an even higher pace of industrialization. The pattern of agricultural development will be traced in section 2.3, and the main dimension of the industrialization process will be analysed in section 2.4.

A striking feature of structural change in Thailand is the rapidly increasing openness of the economy, or the increasing integration of Thailand with the global economy. This integration has been reflected in, and supported by, patterns of agricultural development and industrialization, but also by the development of an export-oriented services sector (see section 2.5). These patterns are reflected in sharply increased export and import ratios and in the rapidly changing composition of exports and imports (see section 2.6). The integration with the global economy is also reflected in increased financial linkages. The financing of trade and investment depends increasingly on foreign capital, as is reflected in growing levels of current-account deficits and capital inflows. Virtually all productive sectors and all institutional agents in the Thai economy have developed financial linkages with international financial markets, as will be discussed in Chapter 3.

The final section of this chapter will summarize the economic structure that has emerged from these processes of structural change and global integration in the form of a Social Accounting Matrix (SAM) for 1989. The advantage of the SAM format is that it shows, within one consistent accounting framework, the interdependencies and interactions among the processes of production and the processes of income generation and income spending. Domestic production and expenditure are linked to the rest of the world through international trade. The SAM includes capital accounts, showing how the investments of each agent are financed from own savings, domestic financial intermediation and international finance. The 1989 SAM provides the basis on which the general equilibrium model, used in Chapter 6 for some simulation exercises, has been constructed.

The next section will first sketch a brief account of the long-term background of recent economic development.

2.2 Background

The modern economic history of Thailand is generally said to have started with the signing of the Bowring Treaty in 1855. This treaty allowed Thailand to maintain its political independence, but it helped to integrate the country into the regional colonial economy. Before the treaty, Thailand's international trade had been minimal, but after 1855 it increased. The food needs of the workers on the colonial plantations and in the mines in Southeast Asia were satisfied by rice exports from Thailand. The export of tin and teak increased as well. The increasing imports of industrial consumer goods had a negative effect on local cottage industries (Nartsupha & Prasartset 1981).

The Bowring Treaty also established rules for trade and for public revenue. The fear of more active foreign intervention, should Thailand depart from those rules, led Thai authorities to adhere very strictly to the treaty: public investment was hardly undertaken, and fiscal and monetary policy was passive and cautious. The low levels of private and public investment kept the economic growth rate low: it was basically determined by the growth of the rural population and by the availability of new land. The low level of import duties and the absence of government assistance prevented the emergence of an industrial sector (Suehiro 1989). In the years between 1855 and 1940, Thailand systematically ran a trade surplus. These surpluses were necessary to finance the remittances made by local Chinese and European traders (Ingram 1971: 203–4).

After the Second World War, a new era set in. In the post-war decolonization period the development of backward areas became a central concern of new governments in the now independent countries and of international agencies. Thailand had never been a colony, but it was touched by the new ideas of development, also because a more modern leadership had replaced the traditional monarchy after the Revolution of 1932. Of great importance was also the success of the Communist Revolution in China in 1949, which cut off the Chinese merchant class in Thailand from its motherland. Capital remittances to China dropped sharply, and the resident Chinese became more interested in investing in Thailand (Siamwalla 1975).

However, the same Chinese revolution also led to some apprehension in Thailand about the role of the local Chinese, and the early 1950s were characterized by a nationalistic economic policy, including the establishment of a number of state enterprises, aiming at developing a Thai business class (see e.g. Girling 1981). Rather quickly, however, this strategy was abandoned. The state and the local bourgeoisie of mainly Chinese origin formed a close coalition that steered economic development policy (Skinner 1958).

The rapid integration of the Chinese into the Thai society since then has further changed the political conditions. The breaking point was the 1973 student-led uprising, which temporarily discredited the military, and which, more permanently, increased the role of political parties. Almost all political parties are run by businessmen and represent business interests. Thai political affairs are, therefore, increasingly dominated by private sector business groups. This has been reflected in a political atmosphere strongly supportive of the private sector. Two aspects deserve mention.

First, government policies have favoured the modern industrial sector over the agricultural sector. Through investment incentives and through import controls and tariffs, the establishment and growth of industrial firms have been supported. Furthermore, the government controlled food prices (through the rice premium) so that the industrial real wage level could remain low. Trade union action was strongly discouraged, to prevent wage demands.

At the same time, macroeconomic management was largely delegated to economic technocrats at the central bank and the ministry of finance. They implemented conservative and cautious policies aimed at defending the price level and the exchange rate. With the exception of some years, these policies were highly successful: inflation was generally low and mainly driven by world inflation. Up to the late 1970s, the current-account deficit was relatively small, and during the last three decades, the exchange rate of the baht has been exceptionally stable.

In summary, the integration of Thailand into the global economy started after 1855, with its role as rice exporter in the Southeast Asian colonial economy. After the Second World War, a more forceful development policy was undertaken by a political leadership dominated by commercial and industrial interests. The process of development that emerged from this policy will be analysed in some detail in this chapter. The next section will describe the development of the agricultural sector, historically the backbone of the economy and the source of the investable surplus, but also increasingly a relatively backward sector.

2.3   Agricultural Development

Rapid economic growth, as it occurred in Thailand, is only possible when (i) the productivity in each of the main economic sectors increases; and (ii) the production structure shifts towards the more productive sectors. Both processes did indeed occur (see Table 2.1).

In 1950 Thailand's economy still had many of the characteristics of the pre-war period. Agriculture was the dominant sector, accounting for about half of all GDP, and within the agricultural sector rice was the dominant crop. Close to 90 per cent of the area cultivated was devoted to paddy cultivation (Ingram 1971: 238), and rice exports accounted for half of total exports. Agricultural products accounted for more than 80 per cent of all exports (Ingram 1971: 94).

But the change since 1950 has been rapid and dramatic. By 1994 the share of agriculture in GDP had fallen to only 10 per cent and the share of unprocessed agricultural commodities in exports fell to 15 per cent. However, these dramatic declines in the shares of the agricultural sector in output and in exports are combined with an impressive growth of the agricultural sector. Over the period 1950–94, the average growth rate of the sector was around 4 per cent per year, considerably higher than population growth. Also, the volume and value of agricultural exports increased continuously, and helped to finance the foreign exchange needs of the emerging industrial sector.

Agricultural growth was based on the expansion of cultivated acreage, and on the introduction of new crops, rather than on the intensification of production and increases in yields (World Bank 1982). The growing population cultivated available new land, first growing paddy, the main staple, but also diversifying into remunerative cash crops (e.g. maize, kenaf, cassava, sugar-cane). In this way, output could increase without the larger financial investment outlays that intensification of agriculture would have required: Thai agriculture uses relatively little capital (Panayotou 1985).

The low level of investment resulted in relatively low and stagnant yields: from a comparative perspective, yields in Thai agriculture are very low. Compared to yields in other Asian countries, paddy yields in Thailand are low and have shown slow growth over time. The proportion of land used for high-yielding varieties and under irrigation is small, and fertilizer use is limited (Wong 1979, Douglass 1984,

Table 2.1   *Growth and structural change*

	Growth rates (%)				Share in GDP (%)			
	1970–80	1980–86	1986–90	1991–94	1970	1980	1986	1992
Agriculture	4.2	3.6	3.9	3.7	24	19	17	10
Mining	6.3	21.0	9.6	8.9	3	1	2	2
Construction	4.3	6.2	18.0	10.3	5	5	5	6
Manufacturing	9.7	5.7	16.5	10.8	19	25	25	32
Trade	7.2	4.0	13.3	6.5	17	18	16	16
Public utilities	12.4	11.2	16.3	11.5	2	4	5	7
Public administration	8.8	5.6	4.1	3.2	4	4	4	3
Services	7.3	5.8	9.7	8.2	25	26	26	24
Total GDP	6.8	5.5	11.7	8.3	100	100	100	100

Note: The shares and growth rates in the table have been calculated on the basis of GDP at constant market prices. The National Accounts estimates have, over the years, been revised and rebased. Public utilities include public transport and communications, and electricity, water and gas. Services include private transport and communications; banking, insurance and real estate; ownership of dwellings; and services.

Osotsapa 1987). On the other hand, Thailand has experienced a faster increase in acreage than these other countries have (Osotsapa 1987). These patterns continue in the 1990s. In 1991 rice yields in Thailand remained much lower than yields in other Asian countries.[1]

The fact that new land was available meant that output could increase rapidly without much financial investment, that a comparatively large part of the population remained active in agriculture, and that the concentration in landownership is still limited.

The fact that landownership is not strongly concentrated should not be taken to imply that rural incomes are also equally distributed: they are not. Available studies show a highly unequal distribution of income in the rural areas, with a small group of richer households owning the most productive land and engaging in non-agricultural activities (such as rice milling, money-lending and trade), earning a disproportionate share of rural income (see e.g. Douglas 1984, Pongphaichit 1982, Potter 1976, Visser 1978). Most of the agricultural 'surplus' is thus concentrated in the few hands of such rich farmers, traders (e.g. rice exporters), or processors (e.g. rice millers and sugar factories). The fact that these groups decided not to reinvest this surplus in the agricultural sector itself implies that these funds became available for investment in other sectors of the economy. Some of these funds were directly channelled to other uses, but many of them were channelled through the financial system (see Jansen 1989).

2.4 Industrialization

The strong and diversifying agricultural sector also had an impact on the pattern of industrialization in Thailand. In his excellent study of industrial development in Thailand, Suehiro identifies two main types of industrialists. The first type, which he calls 'domestic industrialists', is made up of groups that have moved from the import business into the local production of previously imported goods. This trend was stimulated by promotional and protective policies after 1960. The growth of these groups depended strongly on technical and financial support from (mainly Japanese) multinationals. The second type, which Suehiro calls the 'agro-business groups', emerged more on the export-business side: the growth of these groups was based on the diversification of agricultural export crops and on the increased processing of these crops prior to their export. From the start, these groups were export-oriented, depending less than the domestic industrialists on multinationals (Suehiro 1989).

The two types of industrialists correspond to two types of industries. Import-dependent (ID) industries emerged as local assembly plants for previously imported consumer goods. They are import dependent because they typically import the raw materials and intermediate inputs for local assembling. Examples are textile, petroleum, chemical, metal, and electrical machinery and appliances industries. These import-substitution industries needed protection on the domestic market. The second type of industries is natural-resource based (NR): they process domestically produced primary commodities for export or for domestic consumption. In this group one finds, for example, food manufacturing, leather, and rubber products industries.

Table 2.2 describes the pattern of industrialization in Thailand along the lines of these two types of industries. The ID and NR industries are further subdivided in Table 2.2 on the basis of whether they are oriented towards foreign or towards domestic markets. This two-way classification shows directly the linkages among the various sectors of the economy (i.e. the link between agriculture, as supplier of natural resources, and processing industries). Further, it shows the balance-of-payments consequences of industrialization (i.e. the relative growth of import-dependent and export-oriented industries).

It should be noted that the classifications in Table 2.2 are based on the 1985 Input-Output Table, and thus reflect the structure of the manufacturing sector at that time. In particular, many manufacturing subsectors that were export-oriented in 1985, were not yet export-oriented in 1960 or 1970. For instance, the gross value of the export of garments in 1970 was equivalent to only 0.8 per cent of the value added of that subsector. In 1994 the export of textiles and garments was equivalent to 75 per cent of the sector's value added. The growth rates of some of the export-oriented sectors in the 1960s, and even in the 1970s, must therefore be read as growth rates of subsectors that were eventually to become export-oriented. Similarly, the export drive of recent years will have turned some industries which were still domestic market-oriented in 1985, into export-oriented industries since then.

This becomes clear in Table 2.3, which illustrates the composition of exports. Available statistics allow only a rough classification of exports

Table 2.2 Pattern of industrialization

Type of industry	Growth rates of mftg value added* (%)				Shares of mftg value added (%)				
	1960–70	1970–80	1980–86	1986–94	1960	1970	1980	1986	1994
Natural-resource based									
Export-oriented	13.1	7.8	7.9	10.6	43	40	29	33	27
Domestic-demand oriented	14.8	8.3	3.8	14.0	13	14	13	12	12
Total	13.5	7.9	6.7	11.6	56	54	42	45	39
Import-dependent									
Export-oriented	20.2	16.2	8.8	16.6	6	11	17	20	25
Domestic-demand oriented	13.2	9.1	3.1	13.3	38	35	41	35	36
Total	14.5	11.1	4.9	14.6	44	46	58	55	61
Total manufacturing	13.9	9.5	5.7	13.3					
Share of total manufacturing in GDP					13	`16	22	24	32

* at constant prices

Note: The classification is based on the Input-Output tables for 1985. ID-industries import more than 25 per cent of their total intermediate inputs, and NR-industries import less than 25 per cent. In export-oriented sectors, exports account for at least 15 per cent of total final demand.

On the basis of the 1985 Input-Output table, manufacturing subsectors have been classified, and for these subsectors growth rates and shares have been calculated with National Accounts data. It is likely that sectors that were ID or NR in 1985 were also ID or NR in 1960 and 1994. But that will not apply to the other breakdown: some manufacturing sectors that were export-oriented in 1985 were not (yet) so in 1960 or 1970.

Table 2.3   Composition of exports (% distribution)

	1970	1980	1994
Natural-resource based industries			
Primary commodities	70.6	50.9	16.7
Processed primary commodities	4.4	6.7	10.5
Import-dependent manufacturing exports			
Main manufactures	0.1	10.5	15.2
Other manufactures	0.8	3.7	44.9
Other merchandise exports	11.3	16.5	1.4
Tourism	12.8	11.8	11.3
Total exports & tourism	100.0	100.0	100.0
Exports & tourism as % of GDP	12.5	22.0	35.6

Note: The classification used for merchandise exports in the Quarterly Bulletin changes over the years, becoming more detailed towards the end of the period (hence the decrease in the category 'other merchandise exports' in 1994).

The extent of processing may be underestimated: for instance, goods like sugar and rubber have been consistently classified as unprocessed 'primary commodities', although in fact some processing took place and, possibly, the extent of processing increased.

Main manufactures are textiles, garments and integrated circuits. Tourism exports are taken from the entry 'receipts from travel' from the balance-of-payments statistics.

Source: Bank of Thailand, Quarterly Bulletin.

into (i) unprocessed primary commodities, (ii) processed primary commodities, (iii) main import-dependent manufactured exports (textiles, garments, integrated circuits), and (iv) other manufactured exports. Tourism is added to the table to show the relative significance of this important foreign-exchange earner. The available statistics may fail to record the full extent of processing of primary commodities, and may underestimate the shift from unprocessed to processed exports. But it is clear from the table that the exports of manufactured goods started with processed primary commodities.

Tables 2.2 and 2.3 lead to a number of conclusions. First, the growth rates of the ID industries surpassed those of the NR industries in most periods presented. As a result the share of the ID industries in the total manufacturing sector has risen over time. This is one reason for the increase in the overall import propensity of the Thai economy, that will be analysed in more detail further on.

Second, Thailand does not fully fit the typical pattern of industrialization that is often suggested for developing countries, a sequence starting with import substitution for the domestic market, and later on extending to export production. From the beginning of the industrialization process in Thailand, there was a significant export orientation. The basis for this was the ample supply of primary commodities suitable for simple processing for export markets. As early as 1970, a significant proportion of exports was manufactured, mainly due to an increase in the processing of exported primary commodities. In 1980 more than 24 per cent of merchandise exports was manufactured goods. Some of the ID industries had also shifted to export markets at this time: exports of textiles and integrated circuits accounted for 12 per cent of total commodity exports. By 1994 exports had come to be dominated by manufactured goods: more than two-thirds of commodity exports were manufactured goods, and more than half of all the commodity exports were produced by ID industries. While the late 1980s were characterized by an increase in exports by ID industries, NR industries also continued to grow and to contribute to exports, as Table 2.3 clearly shows.[2]

Ajanant et al. (1986) trace the sources of growth in manufacturing output and come to the same conclusion. They found that in the 1966–75 period domestic demand and import substitution constituted the main sources of growth, but that since 1975 export demand has become much more important.

Other studies of Thai industrialization use different classifications, but give similar results. Dahlman and Brimble divide the manufacturing sector into (i) resource intensive, (ii) labour intensive, (iii) scale intensive, (iv) differentiated, and (v) science based activities. In 1970 resource intensive activities accounted for 54 per cent of manufacturing value added and 87 per cent of manufactured exports. By 1987 these shares had dropped to 40 and 37 per cent respectively. In 1987 labour intensive activities had increased their share in value added to 39 per cent, from 23 per cent in 1970, and their share in manufactured exports to 39 per cent, up from 11 per cent in 1970 (Dahlman & Brimble 1991). The same study also lists 37 manufacturing subsectors that had a revealed comparative advantage in 1987. Some natural-resource based industries are included in this list (e.g. tin, leather products, rubber products), but most of the sectors on the list are import-dependent activities (Dahlman & Brimble 1991: 106).

In another study, the export-output ratios of manufacturing subsectors are listed. The average ratio for the entire manufacturing sector increased from 13 per cent in 1977 to 21 per cent in 1987. The ratios are particularly high for the sectors apparel, leather products, footwear and electrical machinery, all of which had export-output ratios of more than 50 per cent in 1987. For the sectors food manufacturing, wood products, furniture, plastic products, non-electrical machinery, and professional and scientific goods, the export-output ratios exceeded 25 per cent in 1987 (see UNIDO 1992: 147). It is clear that the strongly export-oriented sectors provide a combination of natural-resource based and import-dependent activities.

The pattern of industrialization that emerges from these figures can be summarized as follows. At the outset, the industrialization strategies were double-edged: the processing of local natural-resource products and the substitution of imports of consumption goods. The NR industries had a natural comparative advantage in the rich natural-resource base of Thailand, and they could, almost from the start, compete on export markets. In a sense, the tourism industry can also be characterized as a natural-resource based export activity. The ID industries initially produced for the domestic market, where they needed protection against competing imports. Quite soon, however, some of the ID industries became efficient enough to be able to compete on export markets. In the last decade, such ID industries, competing on the basis of cost advantages, became the engine of Thailand's industrial development and overall economic growth.

A third observation arising from Table 2.2 concerns the time trend in the industrialization process. The high growth rates for all categories in the 1960s mainly reflect the very narrow basis from which industrialization started. The 1970s show a balanced pattern of growth, with comparable growth rates for most categories of industries, the only exception being the higher growth rate for export-oriented ID industries, reflecting the entry of these industries to the export markets. In the early 1980s, low growth rates for the domestic-demand-oriented industries indicate a growth recession though export-oriented industries continued to grow. The years after 1986 show spectacular growth for all groups of industries, growth caused by unprecedented levels of private investment.

An interesting parallel with agricultural growth is the extensive nature of industrialization. Paitoon Wiboonchutikula carried out growth accounting for Thai industrial growth between 1963 and 1979, and concluded that 92 per cent of growth is accounted for by increases in real inputs (such as labour and capital) and only 9 per cent by the increase in total factor productivity. The contribution of productivity growth is significantly lower than it is in the Asian NICs (see Wiboonchutikula 1987). This confirms the point made in Chapter 1 about Thailand's technological capacity being limited.

The balance of ID and NR industries also had an impact on the trade policies accompanying the industrialization process. The initial efforts at industrialization were, of course, accompanied by protection against imports, but protectionism was never excessive. The *World Development Report 1987* (see World Bank 1987: 83) classifies the trade strategies (i.e. tariffs and import controls, export incentives and exchange rate policies) of a sample of 41 developing countries in four categories: strongly outward-oriented, moderately outward, moderately inward, and strongly inward-oriented. Two periods are studied (1963–73 and 1973–85). About three-quarters of the countries are classified as inward-looking, but Thailand is included in the moderately outward-oriented group for both periods. Verbruggen (1985) shows that, in comparison to other Southeast Asian countries, protection was moderate in Thailand. Apparently, the primary commodity exporters and the emerging export-oriented processing industry provided some countervailing pressure against the domestic-market-oriented import substitution interests. There was protection for some industries, but this did not result in a strong anti-export bias. At a relatively early stage, in the 1970s, Thailand gradually shifted to an export orientation: the import protection remained, but was accompanied by a more active export promotion policy. A recent report on Thai trade policies summarizes the findings as follows:

> Over the past two decades, the policy trend in Thailand has been towards greater liberalization and greater reliance on the private sector. Emphasis on exports has increased. Import substitution policies have become more selective . . . Through a more realistic exchange rate and a series of import liberalization measures, Thailand has reduced the anti-export bias which was the earlier hallmark of Thai economic policies. (GATT 1991: 5–6)

The precise impact of trade policies, and other public policies, on the industrialization process is difficult to assess. The UNIDO report on industrialization in Thailand asserts that the government has been a 'facilitator' or a 'promoter', rather than a 'regulator', operating more through incentives than through controls (UNIDO 1992).

Investment incentives, managed by the Board of Investment (BoI), are provided to both foreign and local investors. The BoI, established in 1960, initially concentrated on supporting import-substituting industries through trade protection measures. In the early 1970s a shift occurred towards export promotion through a redirection of investment incentives, import duties rebates and subsidized credit. In recent years, investment incentives have shifted further to export industries, to industries that utilize domestic inputs (so as to stimulate inter-industry linkages), and to industries that establish outside the Bangkok region (GATT 1991).

The declining importance of trade protection can also be seen in the decrease in the relative value of import duties collected. Total import duties collected fell from 20 per cent of total merchandise imports in 1970 to 10 per cent in 1980 and 9 per cent in 1994.

The process of industrial accumulation has certainly also been supported by the income policies of the government. Up to the mid-1980s, a relatively overvalued exchange rate and agricultural price policies on some crops, such as rice, kept the local price of basic wage goods relatively low, shifting incomes in favour of urban groups (Siamwalla & Setboonsarng 1987). The low cost of living helped to keep wage levels down. Government policies to discourage labour militancy and to control trade union movement further contributed to a low wage cost.[3] A recent report observes the relatively high share of gross profits in manufacturing value added: in 1990 77 per cent of manufacturing value added accrued to profits, and only 23 per cent to wages and salaries (these proportions were 75 and 25 per cent in 1975). This distribution compares to an average of the profit share of 66 per cent in a sample of 28 developing countries in the late 1970s (see UNIDO 1992: 45).

The present industrial structure of Thailand is thus dominated by import-dependent, labour-intensive manufacturing activities, oriented to export markets. Such industries compete internationally on the basis of cost advantages and are thus vulnerable to increases in the cost of production in Thailand and to the emergence of new countries with lower production costs. The growth boom of the last few years has generated tensions on the labour market and led to upward pressures on the wage levels. The rapid growth of production has also outpaced the supply of infrastructure (e.g. roads, electricity supply, communications). Infrastructural bottlenecks are emerging, leading to a higher cost of production (see Chalamwong 1993).

To strengthen Thailand's industrial structure, the *Seventh National Development Plan (1992–96)* seeks to promote inter-industry linkages. New basic and intermediate industries should also help to reduce the import dependency (UNIDO 1992). It is also suggested that Thailand move into the higher quality segments of industrial sectors and into more skilled and technology-intensive activities.

There is, however, widespread concern that the present science and technology basis is too narrow to sustain continued diversification and innovation in the manufacturing sector. Expenditures on research and development (R&D) in Thailand are negligible. In 1987 such expenditures were estimated to be equivalent to 0.2 per cent of GDP, compared to 2 per cent in South Korea, for instance. Even 15 years ago, when Korea's level of development was comparable to that of Thailand today, Korea spent 0.5 per cent of GDP on R&D (UNIDO 1992: 29–30). Neighbouring, and competing, countries also spent more on R&D: Malaysia's research and development activities account for 0.8 per cent of its GDP. For Singapore the figure is 0.9 per cent (Tiralap et al. 1993). The research and development infrastructure in Thailand is small and fragmented. There is an inadequate supply of technical manpower, both in terms of number and in terms of quality (Vongpanitlerd 1992).

A consequence of the absence of local technological capability is that Thailand remains dependent on other countries for new technologies. Such new technologies come through direct foreign investment and through licences. The technological dependence is one of the causes of the growing import intensity.

Table 2.4   Value added per worker (labour productivity, '000 baht)

Sector	1960	1970	1980	1991
Agriculture	2.6	3.5	3.9	5.9
Industry	21.0	34.2	46.0	53.4
Services	18.3	27.5	33.1	40.6
Total	5.2	8.7	13.5	23.8

Note: Value added per worker at constant 1972 prices; calculated by dividing the
sectoral value added by sectoral employment.

The patterns of agricultural growth and industrialization, as described
in this and the preceding section, fundamentally changed the Thai economy, from an agricultural economy in the 1950s to an emerging industrial economy in the early 1990s. The pattern of development has also
led to serious imbalances within the economy, as is shown in Table 2.4.

Value added per worker has increased in all sectors, and, in terms of
growth rates, the performance of the agricultural sector is not poorer
than that of the other sector. But the absolute gap between the sectors
has widened substantially, and the size distribution of income has become more unequal. Available data confirm that impression. Household
surveys conducted in 1962–63, 1968–69, 1975–76, 1980–81, 1985–86,
1988–89 and 1990–91 showed that the income distribution has become
increasingly unequal. In the same period the proportion of the population living below the poverty line has tended to decrease. The rapid
economic growth in Thailand ensured that many people could improve
their standard of living, but the gains were very uneven, favouring
those in the urban modern sector. The surveys show that the households which experienced the slowest rate of increase in income were
those in rural locations, involved in agriculture and with members who
have had little education (see Krongkaew 1985 & 1993 and Hutaserani
& Jitsuchon 1988).

The richest 20 per cent of households increased its share in total income from 49 per cent in 1975–76 to more than 56 per cent in 1990–
91. The poorest 40 per cent saw its share drop from 16 per cent to 11
per cent in the same period (TDRI 1993, Table 2). The highly unequal

Table 2.5   *Contribution of services sector to GDP (% of GDP)*

	1970	1980	1994
Education & health	3.0	4.1	4.4
Hotels & restaurants	4.9	4.2	5.3
Banking, insurance & real estate	2.3	3.1	7.9
Private transport	4.8	5.1	4.3
Ownership dwellings	5.6	4.7	2.5
Other services	4.2	4.5	2.9
Total	24.8	25.7	27.3

Note: This table gives the breakdown of the contribution of the services sector to GDP at current prices. The category 'other services' includes the National Accounts categories 'recreation & entertainment', 'business services' and 'other services'.

Source: National Accounts of Thailand.

income distribution is a major social problem. The gap between the top 20 per cent of the population, which in the 1990–91 survey earned 56 per cent of all income, and the bottom 20 per cent, that earned only 4 per cent of total income, is becoming too large.[4]

2.5   The Services Sector

Analyses of growth and structural change usually concentrate on agriculture and the patterns of industrialization. In the case of Thailand it is relevant to give some explicit attention to the services sector.

Table 2.5 presents a further breakdown of the contribution of the services sector to GDP at current prices. The contribution of the entire services sector to GDP has been relatively stable over the years (see also Table 2.1 above, which shows the shares in GDP at constant prices). Within the services sector, the share of the subsector 'Hotels & Restaurants' is exceptionally high, due partly to the importance of the tourism industry.

Another striking element in the services sector is the sharp growth of financial services. By 1994 the finance sector contributed almost 8 per cent of the total GDP, approaching the level of the contribution of the agricultural sector. The rapid growth of the share of financial services in GDP reflects the rapid pace of financial development, which will be analysed in greater detail later on.

In economic analysis the services sector is generally classified as a 'nontradeable' sector. In the case of Thailand, that classification is unjustified. As Table 2.3 above indicates, tourism, as an 'exporter' of services, is a major foreign exchange earner. As a matter of fact, in 1994 receipts from tourism were estimated at 145 billion baht, compared to export earnings from textiles and garments at 150 billion, and export earnings from rice exports at 39 billion. Since 1982, tourism has been a more important foreign exchange earner than rice. Since 1989, annual tourist arrivals have exceeded 5 million. The sector has a strong effect on the domestic economy because it is labour-intensive, decentralized and has a relatively low import content (Ratanakomut 1995).

The financial services of banks and non-bank financial institutions are also increasingly outward-oriented. Thai financial institutions are increasingly active on international financial markets and are establishing networks of branches in the region around Thailand.

2.6   Trade Linkages

Several references have already been made to the changing composition of exports, from primary commodities to manufactured goods and services. This section examines in some detail the growth and structural change of external trade.

It should be pointed out, first of all, that the trade ratios of Thailand are relatively high. According to the usual pattern in developing countries, the export and import ratios increase as *per capita* income rises. For a country at its level of development, Thailand has an exceptionally high export ratio.[5] The Thai export/GDP ratio of 38 per cent in 1994 is lower than the export ratio of Malaysia (73 per cent), but higher than the ratios of Indonesia (26 per cent), the Philippines (19 per cent) and South Korea (26 per cent).

Equation 2.1 defines the current account of the balance of payments:

Current Account Balance = X + T – M – NFP   (2.1)

The current account is the balance of export earnings *(X)*, net current transfers received *(T)*, payments for imports *(M)* and net factor payments *(NFP)*. In Table 2.6 the variables of this equation are further disaggregated. The trends in merchandise trade, services payments and receipts (including tourism), net factor payments (including investment income payments and workers' remittances receipts) and net private and public transfers are all expressed as percentages of GDP. The table presents the various ratios for a number of benchmark years. It should be noted that 1986 is a special year, at the worst of the recession of the early 1980s, with very low levels of investment and economic activity.

2.6.1 Exports

The longer-term role of exports in the Thai economy may be seen in the share of merchandise exports in total GDP. In 1970, the share of merchandise exports was 10 per cent of GDP. It increased to 20 per cent in 1980, stagnated at that level in the early 1980s, and experienced a sharp increase after 1986, reaching a level of 31 per cent in 1994. If trade in non-factor services is included, in 1994, the share of goods and service exports was as high as 39 per cent.

In the first half of the 1970s the increase in export value was due mainly to the commodity boom which increased the price of Thailand's major export items such as rice, rubber, maize, tin and sugar. The export value decreased by about 10 per cent in 1975, but gradually increased throughout the second half of the 1970s. In the early 1980s, Thai merchandise exports slumped again due to the second oil crisis, the worldwide economic recession, the depressed commodity prices of Thailand's major exports and the increasingly overvalued exchange rate. Still, despite these adverse factors, the average annual growth rate of the export volume in the period 1980–85 was 8 per cent per year. The growth rates of the export value were lower, as international prices were stagnating or decreasing. After 1986 the growth rate of the export volume increased (to 14 per cent per year) and export prices improved, so that the growth rates of the export value increased sharply.

In the past two decades, Thailand has gone through a period of rapid growth and structural change. Not only have exports expanded, the export composition has also changed radically, as Table 2.3 indicates. Manufactured goods play an increasing role in Thailand's merchandise exports: its share increased from virtually zero per cent in 1960 to

Table 2.6   Current-account balance (% of GDP)

	1970	1980	1986	1994
Trade				
Merchandise exports	9.7	19.9	20.2	31.0
Tourism earnings	1.5	2.7	3.3	4.0
Other services received	5.1	3.2	2.8	4.0
Total exports of goods & serv.	16.3	25.8	26.3	39.0
Merchandise imports	-19.9	-28.7	-21.4	-37.3
Services payments	-1.9	-2.3	-2.2	-7.5
Total imports of goods & serv.	-19.8	-31.0	-23.6	-44.8
Balance goods & services	-3.5	-5.2	2.7	-5.8
Net factor payments				
Investment income payments				
– Interest payments: private	-0.3	-1.3	-1.0	-1.2
– Interest payments: public	-0.2	-0.9	-2.1	-0.6
– Profits and dividends	-0.4	-0.3	-1.0	-0.9
Workers' remittances		1.2	1.8	0.9
Net other factor services	0.7	0.5	0.3	0.9
Total net factor payments	-0.2	-0.8	-2.0	-0.9
Net transfers				
Net private transfers	0.0	0.2	0.1	0.7
Net official transfers	0.6	0.4	0.4	0.0
Total net transfers	0.6	0.6	0.5	0.7
Current-account balance	-3.1	-5.4	1.2	-5.9

Source: Bank of Thailand.

more than two-thirds of total commodity exports in 1994. In 1985 manufactured exports surpassed agricultural exports as the main foreign
exchange earner for the first time. In Table 2.2 it has been observed
that since the 1970s both the natural-resource based and the import-

dependent industries had increasingly shifted to production for export markets. The manufacturing sector has become more export-oriented, and the ratio of exports over output increased in many sectors. The share of non-factor services exports to GDP was relatively high during the Vietnam War era, decreasing after that. The share of tourism earnings to GDP has increased from 1.5 per cent of GDP in 1970 to 4.0 per cent in 1994.

To sum up, the Thai economy has become more export-oriented, judging from the higher exports to GDP ratio. The growing importance of exports has been seen in both merchandise and services. For merchandise exports, there was structural change from a dependence on primary commodities to manufactured goods with a great variety of products.

2.6.2 Imports

Accompanying the rapid growth of exports, there has been an equally rapid growth of imports. The value of merchandise imports increased from 26 billion baht in 1970 to 1370 billion baht in 1994. A drastic increase in merchandise import values occurred between 1973 and 1981 because of the skyrocketing price of oil. The value of merchandise imports increased at a rate of 22 per cent per year between 1970 and 1980, although the import volume increased by only 6 per cent per year. During the recession of the early 1980s, the growth rate of import volumes declined further, to only 2 per cent per year. As a result, there was *decrease* in the import/GDP ratio between 1980 and 1986. As the Thai economy picked up after 1986, and achieved dramatic growth rates during the late 1980s, import volumes and values also increased rapidly. Between 1986 and 1994 the average annual growth rate for the volume of imports was 16 per cent per year. Merchandise imports increased from 18 per cent of GDP in 1970 to 29 per cent in 1980. After 1981 the share decreased, to 22 per cent in 1986. The economic boom after 1986 has resulted in a sharp rise in the merchandise import ratio, to 37 per cent of GDP in 1994.

As Table 2.7 indicates, the composition of merchandise imports changed radically over the years. Oil imports rose very rapidly in comparison to non-oil imports between 1970 and 1980, due to the two oil crises. However, after 1985 the weakening price of oil and the growing reliance on alternative energy sources led to a rapid fall in the share of oil imports in GDP.

Chapter 2

Table 2.7   Merchandise imports by type of commodity (% of GDP)

	Con-sumer goods	Intermed. prods & raw mat.	Capital goods	Vehicles & parts	Fuel & lubri-cants	Others	Total
1960	6.2	3.2	4.4	1.4	1.9	0.7	17.8
1970	3.6	4.6	6.4	1.5	1.6	0.8	18.3
1971	2.9	5.1	5.6	1.4	1.8	0.7	17.5
1972	2.9	5.4	5.8	1.3	1.8	1.0	18.2
1973	2.8	6.1	5.8	1.5	2.1	0.6	19.0
1974	2.9	6.6	7.1	1.5	4.5	0.4	22.9
1975	2.8	5.3	7.3	1.5	4.7	0.4	22.0
1976	2.7	5.8	5.6	1.5	4.8	0.6	21.0
1977	2.8	6.7	6.0	2.0	5.2	0.7	23.3
1978	2.7	6.1	6.4	1.6	4.7	1.0	22.3
1979	2.9	7.8	7.1	1.3	5.8	1.3	26.2
1980	2.9	6.9	7.0	1.1	8.9	1.9	28.7
1981	2.4	7.6	7.5	1.3	8.6	1.2	28.5
1982	2.2	6.5	5.9	0.9	7.4	1.1	24.0
1983	2.5	7.3	7.7	1.3	6.3	1.1	26.0
1984	2.3	7.2	7.6	1.2	5.9	1.0	25.2
1985	2.4	7.5	7.4	0.9	5.6	1.0	24.8
1986	2.2	7.7	7.2	0.8	3.0	1.2	22.0
1987	2.7	9.6	8.5	1.2	3.5	1.2	26.7
1988	2.6	11.9	13.5	2.0	2.6	1.5	34.1
1989	3.1	13.1	13.4	2.2	3.3	1.6	36.7
1990	3.3	13.1	15.0	2.6	3.6	1.1	38.7
1991	3.3	13.1	15.4	1.9	3.5	1.0	38.2
1992	3.7	11.8	15.2	2.1	3.0	0.9	36.8
1993	3.6	11.0	15.8	2.6	2.7	1.0	36.7
1994	4.0	11.0	17.0	2.6	2.5	0.9	38.0

Source: Bank of Thailand, Monthly Bulletin, various issues.

As Thailand developed its manufacturing sector over the past decades, the composition of imports changed. The import ratio of final consumer goods decreased rapidly in the 1960s with the growth of local industry. By the early 1970s the ratio had dropped to a low level, where it stabilized, rising again in recent years. It seems that by the early 1970s, the import substitution of consumer goods had been completed.

At the same time, however, the share of intermediate products and raw materials increased from 3.2 per cent of GDP in 1960 and 4.6 per cent in 1970 to 7.5 per cent in 1985. The further increase to 11 per cent of GDP in recent years is spectacular, and shows the import-intensive nature of the current investment boom. In the Thai manufacturing sector, industries with a high import propensity are: machinery, transport equipment, and electrical machinery and appliances. Low import ratios are found in labour-intensive or natural-resource based industries, including the food, leather, beverage, tobacco, wood product, rubber, ceramic, plastic, and other nonmetal industries (see Wattananukit & Bhongmakapat 1989: 13). In addition, the share of capital goods imports also showed an increasing trend, from 6.4 per cent of GDP in 1970 to 7.4 per cent in 1985 and 17 per cent in 1994, reflecting the increasing level of investment activities.

Although imports of non-factor services have been relatively low compared to merchandise imports, the value has increased steadily and the ratio of services imports to GDP has risen slowly over the past two decades. This growth accelerated in the last few years, however, particularly due to rising expenditures of Thais travelling abroad, a sign of the new wealth. Expenditures on outward travel were equivalent to 3.3 per cent of GDP in 1994.

2.6.3 Net factor payments

Table 2.6 gives data on the major items of factor payments: gross payments of investment income and receipts of workers' remittances. Payments of interest, and transfer of profits and dividends and other investment income accounted for a minor share of GDP in the 1970s. By the early 1980s, however, the effects of debt accumulation became clear: investment income payments accounted for 2.5 per cent of GDP in 1980 and for 4.1 per cent in 1986. The restrictive policy on external debt after the mid-1980s stopped the rapid growth of the outstanding debt. This policy, together with the rapid growth of GDP, helped to reduce the debt/GDP and the investment-payments/GDP ratio. The outward remittances of profits and dividends increased sharply in the 1980s. In the 1970s such outflows averaged around 0.4 per cent of GDP. The increase started in the early 1980s and accelerated in the second half of the decade. Given the present high level of foreign investment, further increases are to be expected.

The remittances from workers overseas, particularly those in the Middle East, increased from 1977 onwards, but became significant only in the early 1980s. The ratio of remittances to GDP increased until 1985, when it reached a peak, at 2.3 per cent of GDP. Although the absolute amount of remittances received continued to increase slowly after that year, their share in GDP dropped to a level of around 1 per cent of GDP in 1994.

2.6.4 Net unrequited transfers

The last item on the current account of the balance of payments, included in Table 2.6, is the unrequited transfers received from and paid to the rest of the world. The high level of the official transfers received in the early 1970s was caused by payments related to the US military presence in Thailand. After the end of the Vietnam War these payments quickly decreased. Since then, the net private and public transfers received by Thailand have been a small share in GDP.

2.6.5 Direction of trade

There have been significant changes in the origin of Thailand's imports and the destination of its exports over the years. Table 2.8 sketches the broad patterns.

Up to 1986, Thailand's exports were mainly directed towards the European Union countries, the USA, and the NICs. The share of the NICs is strongly influenced by the significant exports to Singapore, a large part of which may be shipped on to other countries from there. In the period covered by the table, the share of exports to Japan decreased. As manufactured goods became more important in Thailand's export package, the destination of these exports shifted away from Japan, and towards the United States and the EC. After 1986 the share of Japan recovered, while the share of the USA continued to increase.

Table 2.8   Direction of trade (% distribution)

	1970	1980	1986	1994
Destination of merchandise exports				
USA	13.4	12.6	18.1	21.0
Japan	25.5	15.1	14.2	17.1
Asian NICs	19.3	14.9	17.2	22.3
ASEAN	7.9	8.6	5.4	4.0
EC	18.3	25.3	20.0	14.9
Others	15.6	23.5	25.1	20.7
Total	100.0	100.0	100.0	100.0
Origin of merchandise imports				
USA	14.9	14.4	14.3	11.8
Japan	37.4	21.2	26.4	30.2
Asian NICs	4.6	11.7	14.1	16.3
ASEAN	2.0	5.5	7.6	6.7
EC	22.3	12.5	13.9	13.6
Others	18.8	34.7	23.7	21.4
Total	100.0	100.0	100.0	100.0

Note: The Asian NICs include Hong Kong, Korea, Singapore and Taiwan. ASEAN includes Brunei, Indonesia, Malaysia and the Philippines. Singapore is also member of ASEAN, but has been classified with the NICs here.

Source: Bank of Thailand.

On the import side, Thailand is strongly oriented towards Japan. The sharp drop in the share of Japanese imports between 1970 and 1980 is related to the increasing cost of oil imports, which pushed up the share of imports from 'other' countries and thus reduced the other shares. But throughout the period, Japan remained the main supplier of imports for Thailand. After 1986 the share of imports from Japan and the Asian NICs increased. This increase is related to the strong rise in direct foreign investments by these countries in Thailand, and will be discussed in more detail in Chapter 5.

In 1970 and 1980 trade between Thailand and the USA was more or less balanced, with the share of the USA in Thai exports matching the share of US imports. Since then, a growing imbalance has emerged: Thailand is exporting much more to the USA than it is importing from there. A similar imbalance can be observed between Thailand and the EC. The opposite pattern holds for Japan. Thailand is importing much more from Japan than it is exporting to Japan. The Japanese investments in Thailand may largely explain these differences. Affiliates of Japanese firms in Thailand and joint ventures produce exports for the United States and the EC using imported inputs from Japan. There is, of course, no need for Thailand's trade with each individual trading partner to be balanced, but the imbalances noted here imply, unfortunately, that Thailand is caught in the trade disputes that rage between the major economic powers.

The unbalanced trade patterns also make Thailand vulnerable to fluctuations in the values of the major world currencies. The imports consist mostly of capital goods, intermediate goods and raw materials required by the manufacturing sector, and they come, to a considerable extent, from Japan, while exports, mainly manufactured goods, concentrate on the United States. In 1994 Thailand's trade deficit with Japan accounted for 95 per cent of its total trade deficit. Due to this imbalance, the strength of the US dollar in the first half of the 1980s and the strong yen in the second half of the 1980s had important implications for Thailand's import values and export earnings and for its balance of trade.

It appears that after 1986 trade patterns start to shift considerably. Imports are increasingly coming from Asian countries (Japan and the NICs), countries from which most of the foreign investments also came after 1986. The share of exports to Japan is rising too, after a long period in which it had been decreasing. It would appear that the trade patterns are shifting somewhat to a more regional orientation.

2.7 The Structure of the Thai Economy: a SAM approach

The foregoing sections have described the main trends of structural change in the Thai economy. In this section, the economic structure that emerged from this process of change in the late 1980s is summarized in a Social Accounting Matrix for 1989 (SAM89). The Social Accounting Matrix (SAM) has become popular in socio-economic analysis, because it enables the combination of various types of data within one consistent framework. Statistical information obtained from National Accounts, input-output tables, household surveys, flow-of-funds statistics and balance-of-payments accounts can be brought together; the resulting framework can be seen as a complete and consistent description of the economic and social structure of the country.

The disadvantage of the SAM is that a lot of work has to be done to obtain one static picture, valid only for that particular moment in time, of an economic and social structure that is constantly, and sometimes very rapidly, changing. There are some ways to overcome this disadvantage. The first is to construct and compare SAMs for various moments in time to obtain insight into the structural changes that occurred in the time between them.[6] The second method, which will be applied in Chapter 6, is to make the SAM the basis of a dynamic general equilibrium model, which can then be used for dynamic simulation. The behavioural equations of the CGE model then determine how the assumed changes in the exogenous variables affect the endogenous variables and how, in this process of adjustment, the structure of the economy changes.

The Social Accounting Matrix is a summary table that integrates the accounts of production and income generation with accounts of income distribution to social groups, and with accounts for the major elements of final expenditures. This presentation has the great advantage that the interrelations between the structures of production, income generation and distribution, employment, capital accumulation and financial intermediation can be identified. The concept of the SAM and the basic structure of the SAM are set out in the Appendix to this chapter, and the SAM for 1989 is presented in Table 2.9.

The SAM emphasizes the links between the principle economic agents in the process of production, income formation and capital accumulation. The economic agents identified in the SAM89 are (1) households and unincorporated businesses, (2) private corporations, (3) government enterprises, (4) government, (5) financial institutions, and (6) the rest of the world. These agents are involved in six production activities and in the use of six types of commodities: (a) agriculture, (b) mining, (c) light manufacturing, (d) other manufacturing, (e) construction and public utilities, and (f) services. Most SAMs that have been prepared for developing countries provide more detail, e.g. by breaking down households into many subgroups and specifying production sectors with much more disaggregation. In contrast, the presentation here gives more weight to the processes of capital accumulation and financial intermediation, where most other SAMs are highly aggregated. The advantage of this is that it allows the explicit analysis of flows of external and domestic finance and their interrelationships with the structures of production, income distribution and accumulation. It also makes it possible to include fully specified portfolio behaviour in the CGE model of Chapter 6.

In Table 2.9 the SAM for 1989 (SAM89) is presented. Production in the six sectors can be read in columns 11 to 16; it is composed of domestic intermediate deliveries (rows 11 to 16) and imported intermediate inputs (row 24), to which is added the contributions of the production factors labour (row 17) and capital (rows 18 and 19). Adding indirect taxes (row 23) gives the total supply at market prices.

The factor incomes are distributed among institutions (households, corporations, etc.) in the block between columns 17 to 19 and rows 20 to 22. The institutions use this income (in columns 20 to 23) to pay for consumption (rows 11 to 16), to finance inter-institutional transfers (rows 20 to 23, for instance dividend payments and direct tax payments) and to save (rows 26 to 29).

These savings indicate the transition from the current account of the SAM to the capital account part. In the capital account the sources of funds can be read in the rows, and the uses of funds in the columns. For instance, private corporations (row 27) obtain funds from their own savings (column 21), from capital transfers from households (column 26), from other corporations (column 27), public enterprises (column 28) and from government (column 29). These transfers will consist of new equity capital and of other capital transfers and direct credits. Moreover, private corporations receive indirect finance from commercial banks (column 31), from other financial institutions (column 32), from the stock market (column 33) and from international financial markets (column 34). The uses made of these funds by the corporations are reflected in column 27. Corporations purchase investment goods (rows 11 to 16) and imported investment goods (row 24), and make capital transfers to, and obtain financial assets from households, other corporations, government (rows 26 to 29), and financial institutions (rows 30 to 33).

It should be noted that the SAM concept includes only the flows of income and expenditures, and the flows of financial transactions. To be able to model portfolio behaviour of the various agents in the model, it is necessary to add the estimates of the stocks of real and financial assets and liabilities to the table. In Table 2.9, the block between the rows 1 to 10 and the columns 26 to 35 records the stocks of the various assets and liabilities of the different institutions (including the financial institutions) at the beginning of the period (i.e. 1 January 1989). The rows 37 to 47 and columns 26 to 35 provide the same information at the end of 1989 (i.e. 31 December 1989). The differences in the stocks are explained by savings during the period, by the acquisition of real and financial assets and the incurrence of liabilities, and by revalorization of assets or liabilities.

The most striking feature of the Thai economy, as reflected in the SAM89, is the still prominent role of the unincorporated sector. This is the sector of small-scale family businesses. The share of 'unincorporated profits', i.e. the operating surplus of this sector (see row 18 of Table 2.9), in total factor income is still around 40 per cent. In another study, similarly structured SAMs were constructed for 1975 and 1985 (see Akrasanee, Jansen & Pongpisanupichit 1993). Those SAMs showed that the share of unincorporated profits had been 62 per cent in 1975 and 45 per cent in 1985. The unincorporated profits accrue directly to the household sector; they constitute the capital income from the household firms. This highlights immediately the special nature of the household sector in a developing country like Thailand. Households are not primarily wage-earning consumption units: most households are engaged in self-employment on farms or in small, family businesses in trade, repairs, manufacturing and services. A comparison of the subsequent SAMs shows that production is rapidly becoming formalized, with large-scale corporate units taking over from small-scale family businesses. But that process is far from complete, and a majority of the Thai labour force still earns its income in the unincorporated sector. Typically, such household businesses are small, use simple technologies with few imported inputs, face competitive input and output markets and have a restricted access to formal credit.

. The corporate sector is growing rapidly. It consists of large domestic firms, of affiliates of multinationals, and of joint ventures between local and foreign capital. Large Thai companies are generally controlled by one of a handful of powerful family groups. The biggest of these groups also control local banks and other financial institutions. The ownership interlinkages among corporations and financial institutions ensure corporations access to domestic credit. The larger corporations also have increasing access to foreign credit, and certainly affiliates of foreign firms and joint ventures will find it easy to borrow on international financial markets.

The state enterprise sector is relatively small in Thailand, and restricted mainly to the public utilities sector. In the 1970s and early 1980s this sector depended rather heavily on foreign loans to finance investments. The public sector reforms of the 1980s enabled state enterprises to follow a cost-based pricing strategy, which helped to increase their profits and savings, and to reduce their dependence on foreign capital.

The government sector in Thailand is comparatively small: in 1989 the ratio of total government expenditure to GDP was 15 per cent. After the public sector reforms of the 1980s the government's budget has shown a growing surplus. Government revenue is recorded in row 23, its current expenditure and savings are recorded in column 23, and its capital expenditure in column 29.

The financial sector is dominated by Thai commercial banks: they hold about two-thirds of all the assets of financial institutions. The 'other financial institutions' include finance companies, which provide credit along very much the same lines as the commercial banks, and the Bank for Agriculture and Agricultural Cooperatives (BAAC), which specializes in rural credit, including credit to small farmers. All banks have to meet a mandatory lending quota (20 per cent of all deposits) for lending to agriculture and rural businesses. This requirement ensures the unincorporated household sector access to formal credit, and, as the SAM89 shows, the household sector figures prominently in the balance accounts of the commercial banks.

The main trends observed in the earlier sections, such as the process of industrialization, the growth of the export-oriented services sector, and the growing openness of the economy to international trade and to international finance, are all fully reflected in the SAM89. Thus, the

SAM89 provides an up-to-date and statistically consistent summary of the economic structure of Thailand. The Computable General Equilibrium Model that is introduced later, in Chapter 6, is based on the structure of the SAM89. The CGE model combines structural characteristics as laid down by the SAM with behavioural equations determining, for instance, consumption and investment demand, imports and exports, and the demand for financial assets and liabilities. The dynamic nature of the CGE model is due to the incorporation of production functions for each of the six activities that combine intermediate and factor inputs to change production. Investments, financed by own savings and by financial intermediation, are an important determinant of the growth of output. The CGE model will be used in Chapter 6 to simulate the effects of some external shocks and policy interventions.

Table 2.9   Social Accounting Matrix for Thailand 1989
             (billions of baht)

			11	12	13	14	15	16	CURRENT Total	17
I N I T I A L A S S E T S	1	Households & unincorp.								
	2	Private corporations								
	3	State enterprises								
	4	Government								
	5	Bank of Thailand								
	6	Commercial banks								
	7	Other fin. institutions								
	8	SET								
	9	Rest of the World								
	10	Physical capital								
		TOTAL								
C U R R E N T A C C O U N T S	11	Agriculture	32	0	253	1	1	18	304	
	12	Mining	0	16	1	15	75	0	107	
	13	Light manufacturing	28	0	242	21	21	96	408	
	14	Other manufacturing	17	14	35	94	87	65	311	
	15	Construction	1	2	20	19	35	26	102	
	16	Services	19	8	101	59	68	102	358	
		SUBTOTAL Production	98	41	651	209	286	307	1590	
	17	Labour	44	22	117	56	52	282	572	
	18	Unincorp. capital income	205	0	82	33	33	259	612	
	19	Corporate capital income	0	39	102	58	35	83	316	
		SUBTOTAL Factors	248	60	301	147	120	624	1501	
	20	Households								593
	21	Private corporations								
	22	Public corporations								
	23	Government	1	3	69	30	8	143	254	
		SUBTOTAL Institutions	1	3	69	30	8	143	254	593
	24	Rest of the World	15	7	81	148	42	65	357	
		Imports	15	7	81	148	42	65	357	
		Other								
C A P I T A L A C C O U N T S	25	Changes in com. stock								
	26	Households & unincorp.								
	27	Private corporations								
	28	State enterprises								
	29	Government								
	30	Bank of Thailand								
	31	Commercial banks								
	32	Other fin. institutions								
	33	SET								
	34	Rest of the World								
		TOTAL								
F I N A L A S S E T S	35	Depreciation								
	36	Capital gains (period)								
	37	Households & unincorp.								
	38	Private corporations								
	39	State enterprises								
	40	Government								
	41	Bank of Thailand								
	42	Commercial banks								
	43	Other fin. institutions								
	44	SET								
	45	Rest of the World								
	46	Physical capital								
	47	Capital gains (accum.)								
		TOTAL								
GRAND TOTAL			362	111	1103	532	456	1139	3703	593

Table 2.9 (Continued)

18	19	Total	20	21	22	23	Total	24	ACCOUNTS		
									Households & unincorp.	1	I N I T I A L A S S E T S
									Private corporations	2	
									State enterprises	3	
									Government	4	
									Bank of Thailand	5	
									Commercial banks	6	
									Other fin. institutions	7	
									SET	8	
									Rest of the World	9	
									Physical capital	10	
									TOTAL		
		51				0	52	17	Agriculture	11	C U R R E N T A C C O U N T S
		0				0	0	8	Mining	12	
		289				3	292	373	Light manufacturing	13	
		48				6	55	115	Other manufacturing	14	
		100				4	104		Construction	15	
		433				136	569	128	Services	16	
		922				150	1071	642	SUBTOTAL Production		
								21	Labour	17	
									Unincorp. capital income	18	
									Corporate capital income	19	
								21	SUBTOTAL Factors		
612		1205		71	0	3	74	2	Households	20	
	221	221	17			43	60	17	Private corporations	21	
	96	96				6	6		Public corporations	22	
			33	42	20		95	6	Government	23	
612	316	1522	50	113	20	52	235	25	SUBTOTAL Institutions		
			128	27	18	39	211		Rest of the World	24	
			127			25	152		Imports		
			1	27	18	14	59		Other		
									Changes in com. stock	25	C A P I T A L A C C O U N T S
		182					182		Households & unincorp.	26	
			158				158		Private corporations	27	
					64		64		State enterprises	28	
						115	115		Government	29	
									Bank of Thailand	30	
									Commercial banks	31	
									Other fin. institutions	32	
									SET	33	
								64	Rest of the World	34	
		182	158	64	115		518	64	TOTAL		
									Depreciation	35	F I N A L A S S E T S
									Capital gains (period)	36	
									Households & unincorp.	37	
									Private corporations	38	
									State enterprises	39	
									Government	40	
									Bank of Thailand	41	
									Commercial banks	42	
									Other fin. institutions	43	
									SET	44	
									Rest of the World	45	
									Physical capital	46	
									Capital gains (accum.)	47	
									TOTAL		
612	316	1522	1282	297	102	355	2036	753	GRAND TOTAL		

Table 2.9   Social Accounting Matrix for Thailand 1989
              (billions of baht) (continued)

			25	26	27	28	29	30	31	32	33	34	35	Total	GRAND TOTAL
INITIAL ASSETS	1	Hshlds & unincorp.			87				372	61			1232	1752	1752
	2	Private corp.		172	13	8	14		424	144	224	134	279	1411	1411
	3	State enterp.					54		14	5		171	245	490	490
	4	Government		31	13			42	124	116		134	68	529	529
	5	Bank of Thailand		95	4	3	15		32	1		17	127	294	294
	6	Commercial banks		617	32	39	30	58	18	25		114	202	1135	1135
	7	Other fin. inst.		177	37	13	3	15	53	15		22	32	366	366
	8	SET		129	42					53				224	224
	9	Rest of the world						179	45				367	592	592
	10	Physical capital		531	1182	427	413							2552	2552
	TOTAL			1752	1411	490	529	294	1135	366	224	592	2552	9345	9345
CURRENT ACCOUNTS	11	Agriculture	-17	5										5	362
	12	Mining	-5											0	111
	13	Light manufac.	20		9	1								9	1103
	14	Other manufac	-4		52	4								56	532
	15	Construction	-8	115	66	44	33							258	456
	16	Services	43		38	3								41	1139
	Subtotal Production		30	120	165	51	33							369	3703
	17	Labour													593
	18	Unincorp. cap. inc.													612
	19	Corp. cap. income													316
	Subtotal Factors														1522
	20	Households													1282
	21	Private corp.													297
	22	Public corp.													102
	23	Government													355
	Subtotal Institutions														2036
	24	Rest of the world			171	13								184	753
		Imports			171	13								184	694
		Other													59
CAPITAL ACCOUNTS	25	Changes in com. stock			30									30	30
	26	Hshlds & unincorp.			29				169	35			182	414	596
	27	Private corp.		55	4	1	2		77	51	56	112	158	517	674
	28	State enterp.					5		0	2		5	64	76	140
	29	Government		-6	-1			-15	-13	8		-12	115	76	191
	30	Bank of Thailand		18	2	0	31		-1	0		-10		40	40
	31	Commercial banks		183	51	11	8	-16	2	5		60		304	304
	32	Other fin. inst.		31	59	0	-2	1	8	14		4		116	116
	33	SET		13	6				37					56	56
	34	Rest of the world						70	25				64	160	224
	TOTAL			294	151	12	43	40	304	116	56	160	583	1758	2341
FINAL ASSETS	35	Depreciation		-39	-148	-43	-30						-259	-519	-519
	36	Cap. gains (period)		221	71				88		380	88		849	849
	37	Hshlds & unincorp.			116				541	96			1596	2349	2349
	38	Private corp.		227	17	9	16		501	195	279	246	359	1850	1850
	39	State enterp.					59		15	7		176	267	523	523
	40	Government		26	12			28	111	124		122	154	576	576
	41	Bank of Thailand		112	6	4	46		32	1		7	127	335	335
	42	Commercial banks		800	83	50	38	42	20	30		263	202	1527	1527
	43	Other fin. inst.		208	96	13	1	16	60	29		26	32	482	482
	44	SET		363	120				177					659	659
	45	Rest of the world						249	70				520	839	839
	46	Physical capital		612	1400	448	416							2876	2876
	47	Cap. gains (accum.)									380			380	380
	TOTAL			2349	1850	523	576	335	1527	482	659	839	3256	12016	12016
GRAND TOTAL			30	2349	1850	523	576	335	1527	482	659	839	2876	12016	20059

3 Financing Economic Growth

3.1 Introduction

The high rate of growth in output in recent years has been generated by a high level of investment. As can be seen in Figure 3.1, the investment ratio was relatively stable, around 23 per cent, in the first half of the 1970s. After 1976 the ratio increased to a level around 26 per cent, and with this increase the growth rate improved. The economic crisis of the early 1980s resulted first in a stagnation in the investment ratio and then to a drop in 1985–86.[1] After 1987 the investment ratio, and with it economic growth, rose to unprecedented levels, reaching a peak of 41 per cent in 1991.

It is also clear from Figure 3.1 that savings have, on average, been inadequate to finance investments. Only in three years (1973, 1974 and 1988) did savings exceed investments while in two more years (1987 and 1989) they were close to doing so. The patterns of aggregate savings and investment, as given in Figure 3.1, hide significant sectoral differences. A first insight in this can be obtained from Figures 3.2a and 3.2b, which present the savings and investment ratios of the private and public sectors. These figures indicate that the gap between total investment and savings in the period 1975–85, that was shown in Figure 3.1, was entirely due to the public sector gap, whereas the widening gap after 1989 is entirely due to the private sector gap. In fact, the public sector has a large savings surplus in these years.

But the total investment-savings gap was substantial in most years. In the 1970s this gap averaged around 2 per cent of GDP, but in the early 1980s and the early 1990s a considerably larger gap emerged, of around 5 to 6 per cent of GDP. This gap was filled by external finance. According to the National Accounts definitions:

55

Figure 3.1   Investment and savings (% of GDP)

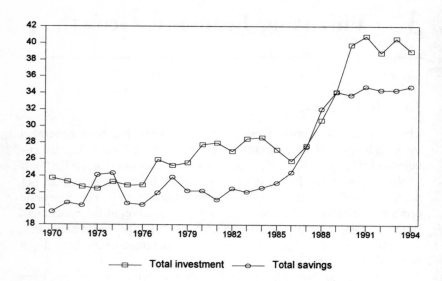

— □ — Total investment   — ○ — Total savings

National Savings – Investment = Current Account Balance

or:

$S - I = CAB$ *(3.1)*

and, according to the balance-of-payments identity:

Current Account Balance + Net Capital Flows = zero

or:[2]

$CAB + F = 0$ *(3.2)*

Inserting equation 3.2 into equation 3.1 and rearranging somewhat gives:

$I = S + F$ *(3.3)*

Figure 3.2a Private investment and savings (% of GDP)

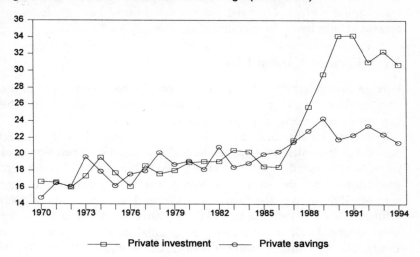

Figure 3.2b Public investment and savings (% of GDP)

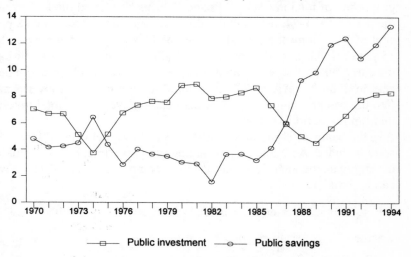

or, investments are equal to, and financed by, national savings and foreign capital inflows. Over the years, capital flows have made an increasing contribution to investment financing.

3.2   Foreign Capital Flows

Foreign capital has played an important role in the development of the Thai economy. As Figure 3.1 above showed, foreign capital filled the gap between domestic savings and investment in the country.

In Figure 3.3 the total capital inflows, as measured by the capital account of the balance of payments, and expressed as a percentage of GDP, are presented. The figure shows that in the early 1970s the capital inflows from abroad were relatively low, at between 1 and 2 per cent of GDP, as was the case in the 1960s. The importance of such inflows started to increase in 1974, increasing further to a very high level around 1980, and remaining substantial in the first half of the 1980s. The structural adjustment policies of the mid-1980s resulted in a reduction of the inflows of external capital, but after 1986 a new boom of external finance occurred, this time at levels never experienced before.

The importance of foreign capital inflows may be deduced from the proportion of total investment financed through external funds. During the period 1970–74, net capital inflows accounted for a moderate 8 per cent of Thai domestic capital formation. This proportion increased to 15 per cent during the years 1975–79, and to about one-quarter during the early 1980s. Subsequently it dropped to a lower level, around 6 per cent in 1986–87. After 1987 substantial foreign capital inflows came into the country, equivalent to 24 per cent, on average, of total investment in the period 1988–94.

In the balance-of-payments equation 3.2 above, net capital flows *(F)* were included. As in the case of savings and investment, it is useful to disaggregate the total flow into its major component parts. Total flows can be broken down into

$$F = DFI + PFI + NFL_{pr} + NFS_{pr} + NFL_{se} + NFS_{se} + NFL_g \qquad (3.4)$$

where:

DFI = net inflow of direct foreign investment
PFI = net inflow of portfolio investment

Figure 3.3   Total capital inflows (% of GDP)

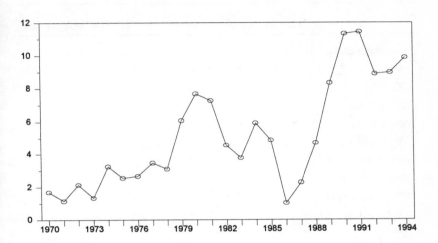

NFL = net inflow of long-term loans
NFS = net inflow of short-term loans

and the subscripts '*pr*', '*se*' and '*g*' refer to the receiving 'private', 'state enterprise' and 'government' sectors.

Table 3.1 expresses the net inflows of the various types of funds as percentages of GDP for six periods since 1970. The available balance-of-payments statistics split up the total loan inflow into long-term and short-term loans directed towards the private sector, the state enterprises and the government.[3] The table confirms that from the early 1970s to the late 1970s and the early 1980s there was a steady and rapid increase in the level of capital inflows from abroad. After a slight decline in the period 1983–86, there was another burst in recent years.

In the first period the current-account deficit and the capital-account balance were relatively small. Capital inflows were dominated by flows aimed at the private sector *(DFI, NFL$_{pr}$)*. Only 14 per cent of all capital inflows was directed towards the public sector. In the second and third period this picture changed drastically. The size of the total capital inflow, and its share in GDP increased dramatically, and the share of the public sector in these inflows rose to over 50 per cent.

Table 3.1   International capital flows to Thailand

Period	I 1970–74	II 1975–79	III 1980–82	IV 1983–86	V 1987–90	VI 1991–94
Percentage of GDP						
DFI	0.8	0.4	0.6	0.7	1.9	1.2
PFI	0.1	0.1	0.1	0.2	0.9	1.5
NFL private	0.4	0.4	1.7	0.5	1.0	
NFS private	0.3	0.8	0.5	1.0	2.5	
Total private	1.6	1.7	2.9	2.4	6.3	7.1
NFL state enterp.	0.2	1.1	2.4	1.2	-0.1	
NFS state enterp.	0.0	0.0	0.3	-0.2	0.0	
NFL government	0.1	0.7	1.0	0.6	-0.2	-0.0
Total public	0.3	1.9	3.6	1.6	-0.4	—
Grand total	1.9	3.6	6.5	4.0	5.9	9.8
Percentage distribution						
DFI	42.7	11.1	9.9	18.5	31.3	12.2
PFI	5.8	2.3	1.2	4.0	15.7	15.3
NFL private	22.8	12.2	25.9	11.7	16.7	
NFS private	14.6	22.2	7.6	25.0	42.8	
Total private	86.0	47.7	44.6	59.2	106.5	72.5
NFL state enterp.	9.3	31.9	36.5	29.6	-1.9	
NFS state enterp.	0.0	0.0	4.0	-4.6	-0.5	
NFL government	4.6	20.4	14.9	15.8	-4.0	0.0
Total public	14.0	52.3	55.4	40.8	-6.5	—
Grand total	100.0	100.0	100.0	100.0	100.0	100.0

Note: After 1992 the balance-of-payments classifications change, so that NFL_{pr}, NFL_{se}, NFS_{pr} and NFS_{se} have to be grouped together.

Source: Bank of Thailand.

Table 3.1 also shows that these shifts were caused by the rapid rise in the inflow of long-term loans. The inflow of long-term loans from international financial markets rose from less than 1 per cent of GDP in the early 1970s to over 5 per cent of GDP in the period 1980–82. Most of these loans were taken by the public sector, in particular by state enterprises.

The main explanation for this drastic change can be found on the supply side. Traditionally, developing countries had limited access to the market for commercial international loans. But after the first oil crisis, the international financial markets were very liquid, with the deposits of oil dollars, and the demand for credit from the rich countries was limited due to a recession. Against that background, lending to developing countries became attractive. Instruments like consortium loans and variable interest rate loans reduced the risks of Third World lending (for a full account of changes in the international financial markets see Vos 1994).

International banks concentrated their lending on the public sector. Two reasons for this bias may be suggested. The first of these is that the international financial markets only deal in large loans. The capacity to manage and absorb such large amounts is concentrated in the public sector of developing economies. The second reason is that the international banks demanded a government guarantee on the loan servicing to reduce the sovereign risk involved in international loans. In most countries such a guarantee is only provided for public sector agencies loans.

Obviously, the changes in the international financial markets only made the trends observed in Table 3.1 and Figure 3.3 possible. The actual occurrence of these trends is a result of the fact that Thai economic agents decided to make use of these new opportunities. Capital inflows to the public sector started to increase in 1975, and increased rapidly from then on until 1981. The capital inflows to the private sector show more fluctuations and less clear trends, at least until 1987. Since then, the situation has changed drastically, with capital flows to the public sector becoming negligible and private sector inflows rising very rapidly, to an average of 7.6 per cent of GDP over the last period.

Thailand's import substitution policy in the 1960s and early 1970s attracted a significant amount of foreign direct investment (DFI). In the years 1970–74, DFI accounted for over 40 per cent of the total foreign capital inflow and was equivalent to 0.8 per cent of GDP. However, the contribution of DFI levelled off in the second half of the 1970s and the early 1980s. It was not until 1987 that a new wave of DFI from Japan and Asian NICs came to Thailand. As in the case of the 'loan boom', the upsurge in DFI flows in recent years also can only be understood in connection with developments on the international financial markets. The sharp appreciation of the Japanese yen after 1985 is generally seen as one of the main reasons for the upsurge in DFI in Southeast Asia (see e.g. Das 1993). The trends and patterns of DFI will be analysed in detail in Chapter 5.

The contribution of foreign portfolio investment in Thai corporate securities (PFI) to the total foreign capital inflows has never been significant (see Table 3.1). Only in the most recent years, when the capital market in Thailand became more developed, and overall economic growth and the rate of return on investment were attractively high, did PFI increase very rapidly. However, PFI inflows have been very volatile over the years. They increased from a low level (e.g. 2.6 billion baht in 1986), to 13 billion and 11 billion baht in 1987 and 1988, and to a high of 37 billion baht in 1989. After 1989 there was a decline to 11 billion in 1990, and even further to only 1 billion baht in 1991. A recovery occurred in 1992, when the net inflows returned to a level of 11 billion baht, and 1993 was a peak year, with a net inflow of 67 billion baht. But this was followed by a sharp drop in 1994, with a net outflow of 10 billion baht. With the fluctuations in the net inflows, the index of the Security Exchange of Thailand also fluctuated strongly. The reasons for the volatility are external (the Gulf War, conditions on international capital markets) as well as internal (political instability in 1991 and early 1992).

In the 1980s, for which period meaningful data are available, the share of short-term loans increased from more than 10 per cent of all capital inflows during the first half of the decade, to over 40 per cent in the most recent years. The public sector tended to rely mostly on long-term loans, so that almost all of the short-term loan inflows were directed to the private sector.

Among the inflows to the public sector, official development assistance loans also played a role. Since the early 1970s, however, the role of official development assistance loans has become less significant, as has the role of the official grants.[4] This is not surprising. Once a country becomes more developed, the need for foreign development assistance becomes relatively smaller. Of the outstanding public sector debt in the early 1970s, the largest part derived from official sources: multilateral and bilateral sources accounted for 90 per cent of all public and publicly guaranteed debt in 1970 and 1975, with private sources (such as commercial bank loans, bond market issues and suppliers' credit) accounting for only 10 per cent. But after 1975, funds from private sources started to flow, and as early as 1980, 40 per cent of the then outstanding debt came from such private sources. Capital inflows to the public sector that came on concessional terms (i.e. had an aid component) accounted for 74 per cent of the total debt in 1970. By 1980 that proportion had fallen to 31 and by 1988 to 27 per cent. This decrease is due to two processes: firstly, the increase in the share of funds obtained from private sources, and secondly, with Thailand's increasing income level, the country qualified less for concessional funds from official sources. In addition to these two factors, it can also be observed that the end of the USA military presence in Thailand after the Vietnam War was accompanied by a decrease in American aid to Thailand.

The destination of the foreign loans within the Thai economy is not easy to trace. As Table 3.1 shows, most loans go to the public sector, and within the public sector to state enterprises. State enterprises in Thailand are mainly found in the public utilities sectors.

Table 3.2 reproduces World Bank data on the sectoral allocation of the long-term public and publicly guaranteed debt. It may be assumed that debt has accumulated from the loans made to government and state enterprises, because as a rule the Thai government does not give a guarantee on private sector loans. The table shows that the debt concentrated on the sectors 'electricity, gas & water' and 'transport & communications' – i.e. the typical public utilities sectors – and, at a much lower level, on 'agriculture' and 'manufacturing'.

Non-guaranteed, private sector foreign loans reached a high level in the first few years of the 1980s (see Table 3.1). In the last years there was another increase in foreign long-term loans to the private sector, and an even greater increase in short-term capital, reflecting the private sector needs for funds to finance its investment boom.

Complete information on the sectoral allocation of foreign long-term loans to the private sector is not available. The data available suggest

Table 3.2 *Sectoral distribution of long-term publicly guaranteed debt (in million US dollars)*

	1970	1975	1980	1985	1988
Agriculture, forestry, fishing	34	37	272	851	1 226
Construction	0	0	0	0	27
Petroleum, natural gas	0	0	138	272	0
Electricity, gas & water	126	270	1 060	2 863	3 580
Manufacturing	18	46	151	880	889
Mining	0	0	14	3	12
Financial institutions	0	0	0	0	25
Services	4	9	186	281	341
Transport & communication	116	233	933	2 090	2 900
Trade	0	0	0	18	41
Public admin. & defence	7	2	65	284	386
Balance-of-payments support	0	0	166	288	478
Debt reorganization	0	0	0	300	1 576
Other uses	18	19	1 085	1 807	1 918
Grand total	323	616	4 070	9 937	13 399

Source: World Bank.

that the sectoral distribution closely resembles the sectoral distribution of direct foreign investment (see later), with the greatest share going to the 'manufacturing' sector and with significant amounts going to the sectors 'financial institutions', 'trade' and 'real estate'. Sectors like mining, construction and agriculture received only minor proportions of the loan inflows.

The sectors that particularly benefitted from the various forms of capital inflows from abroad were, in the public sector, 'electricity, gas & water' and 'public transport & communications' and, in the private sector, predominantly 'manufacturing' and to a lesser extent 'financial institutions', 'trade', and 'real estate'. The analysis of the changes in the production structure in Chapter 2 showed that most of these sectors, the main receivers of foreign capital, did increase their share in value added. These are also the sectors with the highest levels of productivity. These observations suggest that international finance contributed to the increasing segmentation of the economic structure, by enabling the modern sectors to draw in funds and grow fast. Of course, it is to be expected that international finance is attracted by and directed towards the most dynamic sectors of the economy.

The above analysis of trends in the various types of capital inflows in Thailand has shown the importance of changes in the international financial markets for the development of the Thai economy. The main feature of the 1970s and early 1980s has been an increase in flows of international loans to the public sector. The accumulated net inflow of funds that the Thai public sector received from the various international sources during the public sector lending boom in the period 1975 to 1985, was equivalent to 31 per cent of total public sector investment in that period. These proportions are substantial, and they suggest strongly that the increased access to international funds made significant additional resources available to the public sector, which may have financed a higher level of public sector investment than otherwise would have been the case. This 'loan boom' period, and its consequences for the stability and growth of the Thai economy, will be analysed in greater detail in the next chapter.

The total net capital inflows to the private sector (including DFI, PFI and long-term and short-term loans) were also significant. In the period 1970 to 1986 the net capital inflows received by the private sector were equivalent to about 15 per cent of total private corporate investment. In recent years (1987–94) this proportion increased to about one-third. Of course, these proportions are somewhat misleading: not all foreign funds finance investments, some foreign funding finances trade and working capital requirements. Still, the size of the proportions suggests a very significant impact of capital inflows on the Thai economy.

3.3 Domestic Financial Intermediation: The Capital Market of Thailand

Equation 3.3 $(I = S + F)$ stated that, for the economy as a whole, investments are by definition equal to national savings and foreign capital inflows. However, such an aggregated view does not allow an investigation of the interaction between external finance and domestic investment and savings. In the SAM 1989 that was presented in Chapter 2, four institutional sectors were distinguished. Total savings and investments can be broken down into savings and investments of households *(h)*, private corporations *(c)*, state enterprises *(se)* and government *(g)* and total capital inflows are separated according to the receiving sector: F_c, F_{se} and F_g. Equation 3.3 then becomes:

$$I_h + I_c + I_{se} + I_g = S_h + S_c + S_{se} + S_g + F_c + F_{se} + F_g \qquad (3.5)$$

where net capital inflows, investments and savings are split up over the four main economic agents, and where it is assumed that the household sector does not receive any direct capital inflows from abroad.[5]

However, equation 3.5 does not give the complete picture of the patterns of sectoral accumulation and their interaction with foreign finance. By definition, the macroeconomic balance identity, $I = S + F$, holds at the level of the economy as a whole. But at the level of the individual disaggregated sector, it need not hold. For instance, the private corporate sector can finance its investments from its own savings and from capital inflows from abroad, but also from funds obtained at domestic financial markets.

Of course, in principle, each sector's sources of funds should equal its uses of funds. The sources of funds for each of the sectors can be listed as:

- own savings;
- increase in credit from financial institutions;
- increase in other domestic liabilities;
- foreign liabilities incurred.

And the uses of these funds can be divided into:

- own investments;
- acquisition of financial assets with financial institutions;
- acquisition of other domestic financial assets;
- acquisition of foreign financial assets.

This listing of sources and uses indicates the importance of domestic financial intermediation. In the period under study, the domestic financial market of Thailand has grown rapidly. The term 'capital market' in the title of this section refers to a wide concept, including all channels of direct and indirect financial intermediation. Direct financial intermediation refers to transactions between institutional sectors, e.g. households providing share capital to corporations, corporations providing trade credit to households or state enterprises, or government making capital transfers to the state enterprises (these are all part of what above was called 'other' domestic financial assets or liabilities). Indirect domestic financial intermediation refers to intersectoral transfers channelled through financial institutions.

Direct financial transfers between sectors are generally difficult to trace. For the SAM89 in Chapter 2, flow-of-funds accounts estimates were used to fill in these cells (the block between rows/columns 26 to 29). For instance, the flow-of-funds account records a direct capital transfer from the household sector to the private corporate sector of 55 billion baht. This is the direct transfer of share capital by owners to the firms. Corporations obtained another 56 billion baht in new shares issued at the stock market. The amount of funds from the issue of new share capital, totalling 111 billion baht in 1989, compares to an increase in outstanding loans of domestic financial institutions to the corporations of about 129 billion baht and to flows of international finance to the private sector of around 112 billion baht (all these figures can be read from the SAM89: see Table 2.9 of the previous chapter). The debt-equity ratio (or gearing ratio) of Thai corporations has, on average, been relatively high. Estimates for the late 1970s and early 1980s range from 2.5:1 to 4:1 (see Vongvipanond 1980, World Bank 1983). It might be expected that the ratio would have decreased in recent years, since the boom at the Stock Exchange of Thailand (SET) made it more feasible and attractive to expand share capital, but available studies do not support this expectation (see Chapter 5).

The SET was established in 1975, but remained relatively small until 1986.[6] In recent years, the booming economy and the inflow of foreign portfolio investment gave a major impulse to the development of the market. The total market capitalization of private corporate stock was valued at 29 billion baht in 1982 and at 49 billion in 1985. By the end of 1994 the market capitalization at the SET had increased to over 3,000 billion baht, or 92 per cent of GDP. This rapid increase is the result of an increase in the number of listed corporations (from 81 in 1982 to 389 in 1994), a growing number of new share issues, and a strong increase in the share prices as reflected in the SET index (which increased from 135 in 1985 to 1360 in 1994).

Financial intermediation through financial institutions has increased very rapidly. The domestic financial institutions have not been a main channel through which external finance entered the economy. Banks and other financial institutions did borrow abroad, but mainly to cover temporary imbalances between the demand for and the supply of funds, and not to systematically increase their reserves for credit expansion. On balance, the financial system accumulated foreign assets in excess of its foreign liabilities. Thus, the main role of the financial system has been domestic financial intermediation. In that role, it has been rather successful. The broad money supply (or M2, i.e. currency in circulation, demand deposits, and time and saving deposits at commercial banks) amounted to 78 per cent of GDP in 1994. This is quite high. Of the about 80 developing countries listed in the *World Development Report 1994* (World Bank 1994), only four had a higher ratio than Thailand. There has been a longstanding process of financialization of savings in Thailand. Figure 3.4 expresses financial savings (i.e. the increase in M2 balances and the increase in M3 balances – M2 plus holdings of promissory notes of finance companies) as a percentage of total savings. The M3/savings ratio was between 30 and 40 per cent during most of the 1970s, but has increased significantly in the 1980s.

The rapid growth and the comparatively high level of money holdings, or financial savings, can be explained by three factors (see Jansen 1990, Chapter 4, for a more detailed analysis). The major factor is, of course, the rapid growth of incomes that occurred. Secondly, the rapid growth of the financial system, in particular the extension of the branch network of banks throughout the country, has made access to banking services much easier. A third factor is Thailand's consistently modest inflation, which did not make people adverse to holding money balances. In general, the real interest rates on deposits were positive.

One factor that may have contributed to the rapid growth of the official financial system is the gradual replacement of informal financial markets and transactions by official financial institutions. The informal or unregulated financial market was certainly important in Thailand, as in many other developing countries. It can be divided into an urban and a rural segment. There is little information available on the urban segment. The Household Savings Survey conducted by the Bank of Thailand in 1980 concluded that households in municipal areas obtained 61 per cent of their total liabilities from official financial institutions, and

Figure 3.4   Financial savings (% of total savings)

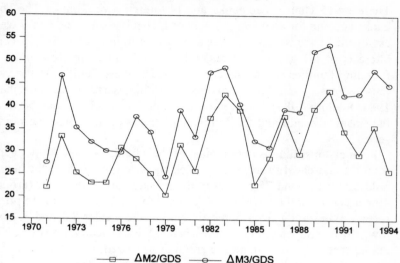

39 per cent from informal sources (Kirakul 1986).

The rural credit market in Thailand has been the subject of more research (see Thisyamondol, Arromdee & Long 1965, Onchan, Chalamwong & Aungsumalin 1974 and Kirakul 1986). The Agricultural Economic Research Division (AERD) of the Office of Agricultural Economics has also collected data on farmers' loans. From these studies it may be concluded that the size of the informal money market, relative to the formal financial system, has been decreasing rapidly. There are even indications that the value of transactions on the informal money market, when corrected for inflation, is hardly increasing. The unregulated money market appears to be relatively stagnant and a rapidly expanding official credit market is taking care of a growing share of credit. It is likely that in more recent years this trend has been further extended. Some crashes of loan schemes on the informal financial market have undermined public confidence, and access to the official institutions has become easier and more attractive (see for further analysis Jansen 1990, Chapter 4).

The official financial system is dominated by the commercial banks. There are 15 Thai-owned banks, and 14 foreign-owned banks. The Thai banks account for about 95 per cent of all bank assets. The banks were established by business families and groups to look after the financial interests of the group. The major banks still maintain close links to founding families and to the corporations of these families in the various sectors of the Thai economy (see Phipatseritham & Yoshihara 1983, Suehiro 1989). This factor accounts for the close links between the financial sector and the dominant elements of the private corporate sector.

Financial institutions obtain most of their funds (around 80 per cent) from the household sector, and use their funds to give credit to the household sector (around 25 per cent), the private corporate sector (around 40 per cent) and the government (around 35 per cent). State enterprises receive little credit from domestic banks (see Tables 3.3 and 3.4 below). In recent years this picture changed dramatically, however. The public sector claim on domestic credit disappeared, so that all domestic financial resources could be allocated to support the private sector boom.

The commercial bank system is highly concentrated. The four largest banks account for about 65 per cent of all bank assets. The other main element of the official financial system, the finance and security corporations, are really no competition for the banks. Their resources are smaller and some of the major finance companies are affiliated with domestic banks.

The concentration is characteristic of not only the financial system itself, but also of its relations with the rest of the economy. The major share of bank resources comes from household deposits. But these are not the pooled savings of a large number of small savers. The many accounts of small savers bring in only a small share of total funds. The top 1 per cent of accounts brings the banks more than half of all their deposit funds. Thus, most of the resources of the financial institutions are obtained from a very small number of very rich households. On the credit side of the banks' books there is also a strong concentration. In 1980, 5590 customers accounted for 58 per cent of total loan value (World Bank 1983). The Thai financial system is thus part of a closely knit network of wealthy business families, corporations and financial institutions in which relations of business, finance and kinship interact.

The importance of this observation for the study of intersectoral flows is that there is intense interaction between the wealthy top of the household sector, private corporations and financial institutions. In terms of financial intermediation this interaction may exist in transfers of equity capital, trade credit, bank deposits and loans.

In the last few years, however, this closely knit network has been increasingly exposed to competition. The Thai capital market is relatively 'open'. There had previously been official controls on capital outflows, but in the early 1990s these controls were strongly reduced, rendering international capital flows in and out of the country virtually free. The domestic capital market has become increasingly integrated with world markets and increasingly sensitive to market conditions. Direct investments and portfolio investment came to Thailand in recent years when prospects for returns were comparatively attractive. Large public and private corporations have taken long-term and short-term loans on international financial markets when domestic credit was in short supply or relatively expensive. Financial institutions too are in contact with international markets in order to manage the foreign exchange reserves (Bank of Thailand) or to borrow reserves to expand the domestic credit supply (banks and other financial institutions).

3.4   External Capital and Domestic Adjustment

This section will seek to determine the interaction between, on the one hand, external finance and, on the other, the saving and investment patterns of the different economic agents, as well as the financial intermediation among those agents.

It is often asserted that the main structural macroeconomic problem of Thailand is its low savings ratio. Indeed, compared to high-growth countries of Asia (e.g. Hong Kong, Korea, Singapore and South Korea) the average level of the Thai aggregate savings ratio is low (see James, Naya & Meier 1989: 64). It seems that in the 1960s the Thai savings ratio was at a level comparable to that in other Asian countries, but when growth accelerated in these countries, their savings ratios increased, whereas in Thailand growth has been accompanied by a stagnating savings ratio. One would therefore expect that the greater access to international finance, as it occurred in the 1970s, would relax this savings constraint and would allow an increase in the level of the investment ratio. This is indeed what happened: the aggregate investment ratio increased from the first to the second and third periods, and declined in the fourth period when the access to international finance became less easy. It increased again sharply in recent years, influenced by private capital inflows. In this period the savings ratio increased to far above historical levels, mainly due to the sharp rise in public sector savings.

The justification for the disaggregation of savings, investment and external finance in equation 3.5 over the four institutions is, first of all, that the savings and investment patterns and behaviour of each of the sectors are quite different. But is also important to note that the four sectors have different relationships with external finance and trade. Household firms and private corporations produce for the domestic market and for export. State enterprises and government produce mainly non-traded goods and services. Private corporations and state enterprises are strongly dependent on imported inputs (both intermediate and capital goods) for their production process, whereas the household firms and government use less imports. These differences have important implications for the foreign-exchange balance of the economy: for instance, external-debt-financed investment by state enterprises will increase the demand for foreign exchange for imports and debt service, but may do little directly to increase the earnings of foreign exchange through exports.

In Tables 3.3 and 3.4 the main sources and uses of funds of the four institutional sectors are presented as percentages of GDP. The definition of the variables and the sources of data are discussed in the Appendix to this chapter. The tables contain the capital flows and the savings and investment estimates for each institution. The sources-and-uses of funds picture in the tables is completed by the financial intermediation variables.

The data of Table 3.1, together with those of Tables 3.3 and 3.4 (and Appendix Table A.3.1), can be used to investigate the relationship between external finance, domestic finance and the level of the sectoral savings and investment. As argued above, the shocks in the availability of external finance were strongly influenced by developments on the international capital markets. One would expect that an increase in access to international finance would be translated into an increase in the level of investment. But this increase in access occurred in a period that was characterized by multiple international shocks.

Table 3.3　Public sector sources and uses of funds (% of GDP)

Period	I 1970–74	II 1975–79	III 1980–82	IV 1983–86	V 1987–90	VI 1991–94
Central and Local Government						
Sources of funds						
Savings	2.1	2.0	0.8	0.4	5.5	9.0
Total financial liabilities	3.6	3.2	5.4	5.1	0.5	—
– Domestic liabilities thru fin. institutions	2.6	2.3	3.8	2.9	-0.2	-1.0
– Other domestic liabilities	0.9	0.2	0.7	1.6	0.9	—
– Net foreign inflows	0.1	0.7	1.0	0.6	-0.2	-0.3
Total sources	5.7	5.2	6.2	5.5	6.0	—
Uses of funds						
Investment	4.2	3.9	3.8	3.0	2.2	4.3
Domestic financial assets	1.6	0.8	1.7	1.9	3.2	—
– Financial assets with fin. institutions	0.7	-0.0	0.2	0.4	1.7	1.8
– Other financial assets	0.9	0.8	1.5	1.6	1.4	—
Total uses	5.8	4.7	5.5	4.9	5.4	—
Statistical discrepancy	-0.1	0.5	0.8	0.6	0.6	—

(Continued)

Table 3.3 Public sector sources and uses of funds (% of GDP) (continued)

Period	I 1970–74	II 1975–79	III 1980–82	IV 1983–86	V 1987–90	VI 1991–94
State Enterprises						
Sources of funds						
Savings	2.7	1.7	1.7	3.2	3.7	3.2
Total financial liabilities	1.5	2.8	4.4	2.1	1.5	—
– Domestic liab. thru fin. institutions	0.0	0.2	0.4	-0.0	0.2	—
– Other domestic liabilities	1.2	1.4	1.4	1.2	1.5	—
– Net foreign inflows	0.2	1.1	2.6	1.0	-0.1	0.3
Total sources	4.2	4.4	6.1	5.3	5.3	—
Uses of funds						
Investment	1.6	3.0	4.8	5.1	3.1	3.4
Domestic financial assets	0.7	1.0	1.5	0.9	1.6	—
– Fin. assets with fin. institutions	0.1	0.3	0.2	0.3	0.6	1.1
– Other financial assets	0.6	0.7	1.2	0.6	0.9	—
Total uses	2.3	4.0	6.2	6.0	4.7	—
Statistical discrepancy	1.9	0.4	-0.1	-0.7	0.6	—

(Continued)

Table 3.3 Public sector sources and uses of funds (% of GDP) (continued)

Period	I 1970–74	II 1975–79	III 1980–82	IV 1983–86	V 1987–90	VI 1991–94
Public Sector						
Sources of funds						
Savings	4.8	3.7	2.5	3.7	9.2	12.1
Total financial liabilities	5.1	5.9	9.8	7.2	2.0	—
– Domestic liab. thru fin. institutions	2.6	2.5	4.2	2.9	-0.1	0.1
– Other domestic liabilities	2.1	1.6	2.0	2.7	2.4	—
– Net foreign inflows	0.3	1.9	3.6	1.6	-0.3	0.0
Total sources	9.9	9.6	12.3	10.9	11.3	—
Uses of funds						
Investment	5.9	6.9	8.6	8.1	5.3	7.7
Domestic financial assets	2.3	1.8	3.1	2.8	4.7	—
– Fin. assets with fin. institutions	0.8	0.3	0.4	0.7	2.4	—
– Other financial assets	1.5	1.5	2.7	2.1	2.4	—
Total uses	8.1	8.7	11.7	10.9	10.0	—
Statistical discrepancy	1.7	0.9	0.6	-0.0	1.2	—

Note: The data for savings and investments are based on the national accounts, the data for net foreign capital inflows are based on the balance-of-payments statistics, and the data on domestic financial intermediation on the Flow-of-Funds Accounts. The statistical discrepancy covers the gap between sectoral total sources and total uses. For the final period no complete Flow-of-Funds Accounts were available, hence the gaps in the table. The data on 'domestic liabilities through financial institutions' are based on the Financial Survey, published in the *Quarterly Bulletin* of the Bank of Thailand.

Table 3.4   Private sector sources and uses of funds (% of GDP)

Period	I 1970–74	II 1975–79	III 1980–82	IV 1983–86	V 1987–90	VI 1991–94
Household Sector						
Sources of funds						
Savings	10.1	10.3	11.7	11.2	12.7	9.2
Total financial liabilities	1.4	4.0	3.0	4.9	9.1	—
– Domestic liabilities thru fin. institutions	1.3	3.7	2.6	3.2	7.2	—
– Other domestic liabilities	0.0	0.3	0.4	1.7	1.9	—
– Net foreign inflows	0.0	0.0	0.0	0.0	0.0	0.0
Total sources	11.5	14.3	14.8	16.1	21.8	—
Uses of funds						
Investment	3.3	3.3	5.1	6.8	8.3	8.0
Domestic financial assets	8.8	8.5	10.4	12.2	17.0	—
– Financial assets with fin. instutitions	5.5	6.3	8.9	9.0	13.5	—
– Other financial assets	3.3	2.2	1.5	3.1	3.6	—
Total uses	12.1	11.8	15.5	18.9	25.3	—
Statistical discrepancy	-0.6	2.5	-0.7	-2.8	-3.5	—

(Continued)

Table 3.4   Private sector sources and uses of funds (% of GDP) (continued)

Period	I 1970–74	II 1975–79	III 1980–82	IV 1983–86	V 1987–90	VI 1991–94
Corporate Sector						
Sources of funds						
Savings	6.9	7.8	7.6	8.1	9.9	13.2
Total financial liabilities	10.4	9.3	11.8	11.8	21.6	—
– Domestic liab. thru fin. institutions	3.4	3.9	3.6	4.7	10.2	—
– Other domestic liabilities	5.4	3.7	5.3	4.8	4.7	—
– Net foreign inflows	1.6	1.7	2.9	2.3	6.8	9.8
Total sources	17.3	17.1	19.4	20.0	31.5	—
Uses of funds						
Investment	14.0	14.2	13.9	12.6	19.5	24.4
Domestic financial assets	3.4	3.1	5.3	4.3	5.9	—
– Fin. assets with fin. institutions	0.7	0.9	0.7	0.5	2.3	—
– Other financial assets	2.8	2.2	4.5	3.8	3.6	—
Total uses	17.4	17.4	19.2	16.9	25.4	—
Statistical discrepancy	-0.1	-0.3	0.2	3.1	6.1	—

(Continued)

Table 3.4   *Private sector sources and uses of funds (% of GDP) (continued)*

Period	I 1970–74	II 1975–79	III 1980–82	IV 1983–86	V 1987–90	VI 1991–94
Private Sector						
Sources of funds						
Savings	17.0	18.1	19.4	19.4	22.6	22.4
Total financial liabilities	11.8	13.3	14.8	16.8	30.7	—
– Domestic liab. thru fin. institutions	4.8	7.6	6.2	7.9	16.8	22.3
– Other domestic liabilities	5.4	4.0	5.7	6.5	6.7	—
– Net foreign inflows	1.6	1.7	2.9	2.3	6.8	9.8
Total sources	28.8	31.4	34.2	36.1	53.3	—
Uses of funds						
Investment	17.2	17.6	19.0	19.4	27.8	32.4
Domestic financial assets	12.3	11.6	15.7	16.4	22.9	—
– Financial assets with fin. institutions	6.2	7.2	9.7	9.5	15.8	—
– Other financial assets	6.1	4.3	6.0	6.9	7.1	—
Total uses	29.5	29.2	34.7	35.8	50.6	—
Statistical discrepancy	-0.7	2.2	-0.5	0.3	2.7	—

Note: See note to Table 3.3.

The differences in the external conditions provide the basis for the definition of the periods. In the analysis of the impact of international finance, the last two decades can be divided into six periods. The external shocks will be analysed in more detail in the next chapter. Here a brief description will suffice.

In the first period (1970–74) the external shocks related mainly to prices: the average annual growth rates of export and import prices were phenomenal. Capital inflows in this period were still modest: the average current-account deficit of 1.5 per cent of GDP is still well in keeping with the longer-run average as observed over the 1960s.

The second period, 1975–79, was the period in which access to international financial markets opened up for countries like Thailand. International borrowing expanded rapidly, as is reflected in the rapid rise of the average level of the current-account deficit, or, in other words, the rapid growth of capital inflows.

The third period, 1980–82, again shows high rates of growth for import prices (second oil shock) and a substantial increase in the average level of international interest rates, while world trade stagnated.

The period 1983–86 was one of debt crisis and adjustment: international lending became more costly after the increase in international interest rates after 1979, and access to international finance became more difficult after the Mexican debt crisis of 1982. The growth of world trade was very modest and terms of trade for developing countries worsened.

The period after 1987 was again one of a sharp increase in the supply of external finance. The composition of the capital inflows shifted dramatically from public sector borrowing to private sector capital inflows, with direct foreign investment taking the leading role. In the period 1987–90 foreign investment, together with rapidly growing levels of domestic investment, generated double-digit growth. In the final period, after 1991, DFI flows tapered off, and private loans, for the private sector, became the dominant type of capital inflow. Investment remained high, but growth rates decreased somewhat.

One would expect, from the identity in equation 3.3, that capital inflows are used to finance a higher level of investment. But they may also be used to reduce savings. The negative shocks, as they occurred in 1973–74 and 1979–80, had an immediate effect on the current account of the balance of payments and on the real incomes of economic agents: one would expect that the access to international financial markets would be used to compensate for some of these 'trade' shocks, i.e. to maintain a high level of consumption (and thus reduce savings). The impact of external finance is thus uncertain.

The data for the first period (1970–74) show that the first oil shock had less adverse effects than might have been feared. The saving grace was that in 1972 export prices had reached very high levels, inducing a sharp increase in the household savings ratio (compared to that of the late 1960s). Household investments remained rather stable. The private corporate savings ratio also increased somewhat, and corporate investments continued the increasing trend of the 1960s. It would appear that in this first period the household sector was more affected by the external shocks than the private corporate sector: household savings increased rather sharply, whereas the corporate ratios more or less continued trends that had started in the 1960s.

Since the 1960s, there had been a trend for the government savings to decline steadily. The external shocks provided an incentive for strong fiscal action that halted this trend. The government investment ratio declined sharply in this period, and in 1974 there was even a small budget surplus. The state enterprise sector hardly seemed to be affected by the shocks in this period: its savings and investment ratios remained rather stable. The result of the forceful fiscal policy was that the gap between public investment and savings in this period remained relatively small. It was financed mainly by the domestic financial markets.

The main change that characterized the second period (1975–79) was the opening up of international financial markets to borrowers from developing countries. Thailand also participated in this process, as is reflected in the rising capital inflows. Table 3.1 showed that the government and the state enterprises were the main recipients of these additional flows. The accumulation balance of the household sector was hardly affected by this. That is not surprising, given the fact that households have no access to international financial markets. The private corporate accumulation balance also did not change much, and a small private sector savings surplus remained.

Big changes occurred, however, in the public sector balances. The increase in the capital inflows can be seen in the increased public sector deficit. The state enterprise investment ratio almost doubled, while the state enterprise savings ratio dropped. The government investment ratio did not change much in this period, but the government savings ratio decreased after its peak in 1974. It would thus appear that the shock of this period, i.e. the increased access to international finance, was used to finance both a higher level of public investment and a lower level of public savings.

In this period the gap between public investment and savings was already widening by more than the increase in capital inflows to the public sector. This pattern continued up to the mid-1980s, resulting in ever growing claims by the public sector on the domestic financial markets. Table 3.3 shows the details: the government sector's savings gap was largely filled by funds from the domestic financial system. Government liabilities with financial institutions increased sharply in the early 1980s. The state enterprise sector has never drawn very heavily on the domestic financial system: the domestic liabilities through the financial intermediaries have always been quite modest. The main domestic source of funds has been the 'net other domestic liabilities', which in this case consisted mainly of government transfers.

Period III (1980–82) again showed sharp increases in import prices (the second oil shock), and this time the effects were not so strongly cushioned by simultaneous increases in export prices, as had been the case in period I. In 1979 international interest rates increased substantially. Furthermore, world trade stagnated in this period. One would thus expect that in this period the sharp increase in external borrowing served, at least in part, to accommodate the negative impact of the external shocks.

Household savings remained strong, benefitting from the mild increase in export prices that occurred in 1979 and 1980. Household investments also increased, so that the household sector savings surplus showed a small decrease. Private corporations reacted to the negative developments in the external environment as one might have expected: investments were reduced and the corporate savings ratio fell. The outcome was that the overall private sector savings surplus remained positive, but small.

The fiscal reaction to the second oil shock was quite different from the reaction to the first oil shock. Government savings decreased, and government investments were maintained. The fiscal deficit increased sharply. State enterprises continued to increase the investment ratio, largely financed by external funds. The public sector savings gap increased to over 6 per cent of GDP, far in excess of the private sector surplus. The gap was filled by external borrowing. Whereas the first oil crisis of the early 1970s had invited a sharp contractionary fiscal response, it appears that the government borrowed its way out of the second oil shock. However, the patterns in the public sector contained elements that were unsustainable in the longer run. State enterprise investments, financed by external funds, increased despite the higher lending cost. Apparently, the access to funds was more important than the cost of the funds. And public sector savings fell to a very low level. Attempts by the government to cushion the domestic effects of the external shocks (e.g. subsidizing oil prices to mitigate the inflationary effect of the oil shock) led to a significant decrease in government savings and to an increase in the fiscal deficit.

Period IV was a period of adjustment. World trade recovered somewhat and the international interest rate fell back to a moderate level. The 1982 Mexican debt crisis made clear, however, that access to international finance was going to be more difficult. And that crisis warned of the dangers involved in excessive external borrowing.

How did Thailand react to that challenge? Not so well, to judge from the tables. Two negative elements stand out: the continued decline of the government savings ratio and the continued increase of the state enterprise investment ratio. But the debt crisis had some effect on the public sector as the government investment ratio was reduced and the state enterprise savings ratio increased substantially. On balance, however, the overall public sector savings gap remained very high, far in excess of the private sector savings surplus.

The household sector savings ratio decreased, and its investment ratio increased somewhat. The decrease in savings may be related to the poor performance of the agricultural sector in this period: the value added of the sector at current prices in 1986 was lower than it had been in 1983, due to poor prices and bad weather. The corporate investment ratio fell further, due to the uncertain external environment and the growing internal imbalances, but the corporate savings ratio recovered somewhat from the very low level of the previous period. On balance, the private sector savings and investments were more or less in balance in this period.

The external shocks of this period were not so much felt in concrete changes in prices, interest rates or world trade growth. Rather, they were felt in the general uncertainty of the international environment and in the growing awareness that debt-financed growth was unsustainable. A significant indicator is also that the exports/GDP ratio that had continuously increased throughout the earlier periods decreased somewhat in this period. Thus, the export growth necessary to reduce the dependence on external finance could not be achieved. The private corporate sector's confidence in the economy was affected negatively by these factors: its investment ratio decreased. The public sector's response to the external changes was mixed. Some adjustments were made (a slight reduction government investments, and a significant increase in state enterprise savings), but the overall public sector savings gap remained high. The continued large public sector resource gap, together with the fall in external capital flows to the public sector in this period, implied a continued high level of the claims of the public sector on the domestic financial market. This created tensions on the capital market that were reflected in very high real interest rates.

In the most recent periods (1987–94), the sectoral accumulation balances in the Thai economy have taken a dramatic turn. The public sector reforms, hesitantly initiated in the foregoing period, were more vigorously executed. This resulted in a dramatic shift in public sector balances. State enterprise investments decreased drastically, and the savings ratio improved further, so that the dependence on foreign funds totally disappeared. Even more striking is the move to the fiscal surplus. The public sector, which had always had a savings deficit, now showed a savings surplus. In the most recent years, there has been a recovery of government investment and state enterprise investment, reflecting the urgent demand of the rapidly growing economy for public utility services and for social and physical infrastructure, but as public savings remain strong, this has not affected the overall public sector savings surplus.

An important aspect of the public sector financial reforms is that the claims by the public sector on the domestic financial market almost disappeared. The domestic financial system could thus direct all its resources to help finance the private sector boom.

The capital inflows shifted totally towards private-sector oriented flows. As a consequence the investment ratio of private corporations almost doubled, to an unprecedented level. The private corporate savings ratio also increased, but to a far lesser extent, so that the savings gap widened. The booming economy also induced a higher level of household investments. The result was that the private (i.e. corporate plus household) sector's savings-investment balance, which over the years had fluctuated but had been just positive on average, now turned into a large deficit (equivalent to about 10 per cent of GDP around 1990–91).

The above analysis suggests that in the last two decades there has been a close relationship between the level of sectoral savings and investment ratios on the one hand, and capital inflows and external conditions on the other. It is also clear that the nature of that interaction can only be grasped if the accumulation balances are disaggregated. The stability of the average aggregate savings ratio from period I to periods II and III was the outcome of significant short-term fluctuations (see Figure 3.1), which reflected large sectoral shifts: a decreasing public sector savings ratio and an increasing private sector ratio. The increase of the aggregate savings ratio in period IV, however, was the result of the recovery of the public sector savings. The private savings ratio stagnated in these years.

The fluctuations of the aggregate investment ratio in periods I to IV are the outcome of considerable changes in the composition: the share of the public sector, and in particular of state enterprises, increased in periods II, III and IV, while the private corporate investment ratio decreased in these years. The most recent periods, V and VI, turned these patterns upside down. The sharp rise in the aggregate investment ratio was entirely due to the recovery of private investment; the public sector investment ratios decreased sharply in period V and recovered slowly in the years after that. The sharp rise of the aggregate savings ratio was due to a recovery of private sector savings and a dramatic rise of public sector savings.

In all periods, one can discern a relationship between the trends in the sectoral savings and investment ratios, and the external capital flows received by the sector. The sharp rise in capital inflows in periods II and III was related to a rise in public sector investments and a decline in the public sector savings ratio. The increase in the private sector capital inflows in the most recent period gave rise to a quite different pattern: private sector investments increased substantially and the private savings ratio increased to a lesser extent.

The years 1975–82 can be called the public sector's 'foreign loan boom period'. In those years the public sector investment ratio increased to a high level. This increase was financed by the capital inflows, but also by an increased claim on domestic financial resources. This aggregate picture was the result of the state enterprise sector doing most of the foreign borrowing and accounting for most of the investment growth, and the government sector doing most of the domestic borrowing.

In the adjustment period, 1983–86, capital inflows were cut, but investment remained high and the improvement in the savings ratio was not sufficient to compensate for the loss of foreign funds. The result was a high claim on domestic financial resources. Only in the last period did the public sector boom come to a definite and spectacular end. In those years public sector investment, by both government and state enterprises, fell substantially and the savings ratios improved dramatically. The result was that the public sector showed a savings surplus.

Foreign capital inflows to the private corporate sector started to increase slightly in periods III and IV. In contrast to the public sector pattern, the rise in capital inflows to the private sector was not accompanied by an increased corporate investment ratio: the corporate investment ratio fell during these years. It is likely that the corporations took recourse to borrowing abroad in these years, as domestic borrowing became more costly due to the high local interest rates.

The periods V and VI showed a sharply different pattern. Foreign capital inflows increased further and reached a very high level. In these periods the increase in capital inflows was indeed accompanied by a sharp recovery of the corporate investment ratio. The corporate savings ratio improved as well, in contrast to the public sector's experience, where the capital inflow boom had been associated with a decrease in the savings ratios. The provisional flow-of-fund data for this final period suggest that the investment boom led to a sharp increase in the demand of private corporations for domestic credit.

The main source for this credit was the financial assets (financial savings) that the household sector accumulated. The intersectoral flows of funds contained in Tables 3.3 and 3.4 are from the household sector and from the rest of the world to the private corporate sector and, in the 1970s and early 1980s, to the public sector as well.

The last few years have thus shown a radical turnabout in the traditional sectoral balances of the Thai economy. Capital inflows shifted towards the private sector. The private sector savings surplus disappeared and made way for a substantial savings gap. The public sector deficit that had been large and increasing was turned into a savings surplus in a relatively short time.

Two main factors are responsible for these recent changes. The first of these relates to the changing international environment which opened up opportunities for Thailand. Changes in the alignment of major currencies induced an outflow of export-oriented direct investments from Asian countries to Thailand. The second factor is the radical change in public sector policy. In the Thai development philosophy priority had always been given to the private sector. The increasing share of the public sector in total investment in the period 1975–86 had not fundamentally changed that position. Most of the public sector investments were made in the standard public utilities sectors, supporting private sector accumulation. The drastic cutback of public sector activities in the last few years may be seen as a reconfirmation of the basic philosophy. When the growing public sector deficit and the rising debt burden started to endanger private sector growth, the reaction was probably somewhat slow in coming, but quite effective once it took hold. Not only were the investment ratios of government and state enterprises significantly reduced, current government spending was also curtailed. The ratio of current government spending to GDP had been around 16 per cent in the mid-1980s; by 1990 it had dropped to 12.1 per cent, and in 1994 the ratio was 11 per cent. Chapter 4 will provide a more detailed analysis of the structural adjustment policies in these years.

The data in Table 3.4 show a worrisome trend in the last few years. The household savings ratio drops sharply in the 1990s, while the household investment ratio remains high. One of the possible explanations for the decrease in the savings ratio, in the face of rapid growth of income, is the negative wealth effect. The boom in foreign investment has been accompanied by a boom in the stock market and increases in values of land and real estate, resulting in an increase in the value of household wealth. In studies of Thai saving behaviour, a negative wealth effect has been found (see e.g. Sussangkarn et al. 1991, Jansen 1995).

The longer-term trend in the household savings ratio will be determined by more structural factors. Studies have found that self-employed households (or own-account workers), particularly in the agricultural sector, have a higher saving propensity than other households (Jansen 1990, Sussangkarn et al. 1991). The decreasing share of agricultural households in the population, and of agricultural income in total household income, and in general the decreasing share of income of unincorporated household enterprises that was observed in Chapter 2, might explain the declining trend in the household savings ratio. On the other hand, the average household size and the dependency ratio are decreasing, and this in turn may help to increase household savings (Campbell et al. 1993). It is likely that the household investment ratio will continue to increase. With the growth of the number of households, the declining average household size, and the growth of household incomes, expenditures on residential construction as percentage of GDP may be expected to continue to rise (Campbell et al. 1993).

The prospects for the household savings-investment balance are thus uncertain, but it is possible that the large surpluses of the past will not recur. In the years covered by Table 3.4, households used their substantial savings surplus to obtain financial assets from financial institutions (deposits and promissory notes) and other domestic financial assets (shares, trade credit, etc.). In that way, the surplus could be used to finance investments in other sectors. But the recent trends imply that such financial intermediation may not be possible in the future. This would increase the need for external finance to fill the large private corporate resource gap.

4 Debt-Financed Growth and Structural Adjustment, 1975–86

4.1 Introduction

The previous chapters have shown that the role of international finance in the Thai economy has increased over the last two decades. It has been argued, in particular, that Thailand can finance high levels of investment only with the aid of external capital. This chapter sets out to investigate this financial dependence in more detail, and will analyse the impact of external finance on the Thai economy, concentrating on the period 1975–86.

In this period the inflows of foreign capital significantly increased. In the years 1970–74, total net capital inflows averaged around 1.9 per cent of GDP, a level that had also characterized the 1960s. First there was a modest increase, to a level equivalent to 3.6 per cent of GDP, over the period 1975–79, but in subsequent years there was a dramatic rise to a level of over 6 per cent of GDP in the early 1980s (see Table 3.1 of Chapter 3). By 1986–87 the inflows had dropped back to a low level, around 1.5 per cent of GDP. The years 1975–86 thus capture the period of the rise and fall of Thailand's foreign 'loan boom'.

The characteristics of this period, which will be analysed in more detail below, may be summarized in five points.

(a) The 1970s brought sharp external shocks in export and import (including oil) prices, in international interest rates and in world trade growth. In developing countries, where the import capacity is one of the main determinants of growth, such shocks provided major policy challenges. International finance provided an obvious opportunity to soften the impact of the shocks or to postpone painful adjustment (see section 4.2).

(b) However, international finance did more than just assist in the adjustment to shocks. The high liquidity at international financial markets led to an increased access of developing countries to international commercial loans. These loans were particularly available for public sector agencies in developing countries, and this led to an increase in public sector investment, also in Thailand (section 4.3.2).

(c) The macroeconomic impacts of these capital inflows were rather complex, but three aspects stand out. Firstly, they seriously affected public sector financial balances: public investments increased, while the public sector savings ratio decreased. In fact, the public sector investment-savings gap increased by more than the foreign capital inflows, so that the domestic public sector borrowing requirement also increased. Secondly, the capital inflows initiated an increase in domestic demand which was reflected in an acceleration of inflation and an appreciation of the real exchange rate, with negative effects on the export performance (section 4.3.3). A third effect was that the capital inflows accumulated in a rapidly growing external debt and in a sharp increase in the debt-servicing burden, particularly after international interest rates rose in 1979 (section 4.3.4).

(d) The increase in public sector investment, the expanding public sector investment-savings gap, and the growing claims by the public sector on domestic financial markets, all affected, in their own ways, the desire and the ability of the private sector to invest. The growing external debt burden and the associated balance-of-payments problems further affected private sector expectations. The impact of all these various effects on private investment goes beyond simple notions of crowding in or out (as will be argued in section 4.4).

(e) By the early 1980s it had become clear that this form of debt-financed growth was unsustainable under the then current conditions of the world economy. Public sector imbalances undermined the confidence of the private sector, private investment fell to low levels, and so did the growth rate. The growing debt-servicing

burden and the stagnating export earnings undermined the balance
of payments. As further financing of the gaps became impossible,
'structural adjustment' became unavoidable (section 4.5).

4.2   Adjusting to an Unstable World Economy

As Chapter 2 has argued in some detail, one of the major elements of
structural change in the Thai economy over the last four decades has
been its growing integration into the world economy. This is, first of
all, reflected in the growing relative importance of international trade:
both export and import ratios increased substantially. There has also
been a growing integration with international capital markets.

The result of this is that virtually all sectors of the Thai economy
have intensive links with world markets, either through the import of
intermediate or final goods, through the export of output, or both. The
growing openness has made the Thai economy more vulnerable to external trade shocks.

Such 'shocks' arise from fluctuations in world market prices and in
the growth of world trade. The prices of Thailand's primary commodity
exports and the prices of all imports are determined on the world markets. The growth of world trade reflects the strength of demand for
Thailand's exports. The 1950s and 1960s was a period of relatively
stable commodity prices and of rapid growth of world trade, but this
was to change after 1970. In the 1970s and early 1980s there were
sharp fluctuations in both import and export prices and in the growth
of world trade. The volatilities of the international markets also extended to financial markets. In the 1950s and 1960s, countries like
Thailand received relatively stable flows of official development aid
and foreign investment. Around the mid-1970s, access to borrowing on
commercial markets increased until, after the Mexican debt crisis of
1982, the willingness of banks to lend to developing countries, as well
the desire of these countries to borrow more, declined sharply. After
1986, Thailand experienced another external financial 'shock' when,
rather suddenly, foreign investment increased to unprecedented levels.

These shocks have affected the balance of payments and the entire
economy in a substantial way. The effects may be analysed by starting
from the balance-of-payments identity:

$$X + WR + CT - M - NFP + F - RES = 0$$

The receipts from exports of goods and non-factor services *(X)*, from workers' remittances *(WR)*, from net current transfers from the rest of the world *(CT)*, and from net capital inflows *(F)* have to pay for imports of goods and non-factor services (*M*), for net factor services payments (*NFP*, mainly payments of investment income), and for the accumulation of foreign financial assets *(RES)*. In principle, the various items included in the equation should add up to zero, since the balance of payments is an identity. In the measurement of the actual balance of payments of Thailand, measurement errors occur and a term 'errors and omissions' *(E&O)* has to be added to make the items indeed add up to zero.[1]

$$X + WR + CT - M - NFP + F - RES + E\&O = 0 \qquad (4.1)$$

Like all open economies, the Thai economy is vulnerable to shocks on the global commodity and financial markets. In the appendix to this chapter, a methodology is developed to measure the external shocks. The method consists of disaggregating the change in the import volume into (i) the impact of exogenous changes in world market prices, world trade, and other exogenous factors and (ii) the impact of policy decisions with respect to external borrowing and export promotion. To do this, the balance-of-payments equation 4.1 is rephrased:

$$p_m M' = p_x X' + WR + CT - NFP + F - RES + E\&O \qquad (4.2)$$

where p_m and p_x are the prices of imports and exports, and M' and X' their volumes. Equation 4.2 focuses on the volume of imports. The capacity to import is a crucial determinant of growth. The growth of production requires the growth of imports of investment goods, of raw materials and of intermediate inputs, and the growth of income will generate an additional demand for imported consumer goods. In countries where the capacity to import is severely constrained, growth stagnates.

Two further identities

$$X' = \frac{X'}{WX} * WX$$

and

$$NFP = i_w * D + NOFP$$

define the volume of exports as the share in the volume of world export *(WX)*, and the net factor payments as the interest payments on external debt (the international interest rate, i_w, times the outstanding external debt, *D*) and net other factor payments *(NOFP)*. Inserting the identities into equation 4.2 and taking first differences gives:

$$\Delta(p_m M') = \Delta(p_x \frac{X'}{WX} WX) + \Delta WR + \Delta CT - \Delta(i_w * D)$$

$$- \Delta NOFP + \Delta F - \Delta RES + \Delta E\&O \qquad (4.3)$$

This equation can be used to trace the factors behind the changes in the import volume (M'). It should be remembered that equation 4.3 is an identity, derived from the balance-of-payments equation. By necessity, all terms contained in the equation have to add up to zero. The identity, in itself, says nothing about causality. If one term of the identity changes, others have to change as well to maintain the identity. Still, it is possible to identify variables in the equation which are exogenous, i.e. variables on the level of which Thailand cannot exert any influence, and variables that are endogenous, i.e. determined by the state of the Thai economy and by Thai economic policies.

Equation 4.3 shows that the change in the volume of imports can be related to five types of factors:

(a) Terms of trade shocks: changes in the level of p_m, p_x, or i_w. The levels of these prices are fully determined on international markets, and any change in them comes as an external shock to Thailand. As equation 4.3 is measured in the domestic currency, any change in the exchange rate affecting the domestic currency prices of exports and imports is included as a terms of trade shock.

(b) Changes in current external transfers: Changes in the level of workers' remittances and in other current transfers do also, to a considerable extent, depend on factors beyond Thailand's control. The level of, and the fluctuations in, workers' remittances have been strongly influenced by the events in the Middle East: for instance, there was a dip in such remittances in 1986, probably related to the drop in oil prices in that year. In the late 1960s and early 1970s, the level of current transfers was strongly influenced by American military transfers related to the Vietnam War.

(c) World trade: The growth of Thailand's exports depends on the strength of demand on the world market. Fluctuations in the growth of world exports are determined mainly by the economic conditions in the OECD countries.

(d) Trade policies: Thai exports are, however, not fully determined by the growth of world demand. Over the years, the volume of Thai exports grew faster than world exports. The share of Thailand in world trade increased with the improving competitiveness of Thai producers and with the effectiveness of export promotion policies.

(e) Financial policy: The change in the level of external financing is the outcome of a complex process. It depends on the conditions on the international financial markets and on financial policies of Thailand.

Of these five effects, the first three are totally or largely beyond Thailand's control. The changes in import volume that can be ascribed to these factors may thus be labelled as 'exogenous shocks'. It should be noted that such shocks can be positive as well as negative. The last two effects are also influenced by exogenous factors, but here policy decisions do play a much larger role.

In the Appendix, the detailed algebraic decomposition of the change in the import volume is provided. In Figure 4.1 the three exogenous external shocks calculated with that method, and expressed as percentages of GDP, are presented. The different lines indicate the size of terms-of-tradè shocks, of shocks related to current transfers (including workers' remittances) and of fluctuations in the growth of world trade. It should be noted that the method measures changes from one year to the next and thus provides a very short-term view. For instance, when export prices rise substantially in one year, this is measured as a (positive) shock, and when export prices drop to a normal level the following year, this is measured as a further (negative) shock, while if export prices had remained at the unusually high level, this would not have been seen as a shock.

Figure 4.1 shows that Thailand suffered substantial external shocks in the early 1970s. In 1972–73 these shocks were largely positive, due to the sharp increase in the world's prices of Thailand's commodity exports and to the strong growth of world trade. But in 1974 the first oil price shock hit the world, increasing the cost of imports substantially.

Figure 4.1   External shocks (% of GDP)

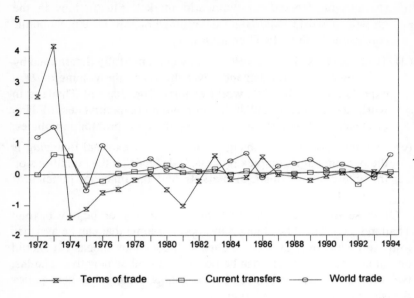

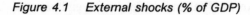
—×— Terms of trade   —□— Current transfers   —○— World trade

This shock was followed by a slowdown in world trade in 1975. From 1974 on, there was also a decline in the current transfers, largely caused by the decrease in American transfers related to the Vietnam War. In later years the current transfers increased with the remittances of Thai workers abroad, mainly in the Middle East. After 1974 the terms of trade remained poor, and in 1979 the second oil price shock hit Thailand. In 1979–80 the international interest rate also increased substantially. Although export prices were also relatively good in 1979–80, on balance the terms-of-trade shocks were strongly negative.

It is remarkable that the external trade shocks were quite substantial in the 1970s, but considerably less dramatic in the period after 1981. Two reasons can be given for this. The first is that the world economy calmed down in the 1980s after the hectic shocks of the 1970s. The second, very important, reason is the structural change in the Thai economy. In the 1970s Thailand exported primary commodities and imported industrial goods and oil. Thailand's export price index in that period was dominated by the fluctuations in the world commodity prices. The international prices of primary commodities fluctuate far more than the world prices of industrial goods. In the 1980s, Thailand's exports came to be dominated by industrial goods, so that the pattern of its average export price index became much more stable and also more similar to that of the import price index.

Adding up the three types of current external shocks that are presented in Figure 4.1 gives an impression of the total external shocks to which Thailand had to adjust. These shocks were strongly positive in the years 1972–73, but turned, on average, negative in the period 1974–82. After 1982 external conditions became more friendly.

In the period 1974–82 the capacity to import was negatively affected by the external shocks. Still, in the late 1970s, the volume of imports continued to grow. This was due to two factors. The first was the growth of Thai exports, which exceeded the growth of world trade and added to the import capacity. The second factor was that, precisely when external trade conditions were unfavourable, substantial changes occurred on the international financial markets, making borrowing on international commercial markets easier for countries like Thailand. Therefore, it is not surprising that the adverse trade conditions were partly compensated by an increase in external financing.

The analysis in Chapter 3 strongly suggested that capital inflows from abroad increased by more than necessary to compensate for the external shocks. The total accumulated negative exogenous external shocks since 1974 did not exceed 2 per cent of GDP, but the level of capital inflows increased by substantially more. This shows that capital inflows did more than just accommodate the negative external shocks. The next section will analyse the relationship of Thailand to the international financial markets in more detail.

4.3   Debt-Financed Growth

In Chapter 3 it was shown that the level of capital inflows increased after 1974 and reached a very high level around 1980 (Figure 3.1). Table 3.1 showed that this increase mainly took the form of higher long-term borrowing by the public sector: the government, but particularly the state enterprises. This section will analyse the macroeconomic effects of debt-financed growth, concentrating on the impact of the increase in inflows of external loans in the period 1975–85.

The impact of an increase in capital inflows in a short-term macro-economic context, under a system of fixed exchange rates, is mainly that the external funds help to finance a higher level of expenditure, either directly, when the capital inflows are tied to specific projects, or indirectly, when the capital inflows add to monetary reserves and to the money supply. When domestic supply cannot immediately respond to the higher level of demand, inflationary pressures will emerge. It is to be expected that these inflationary pressures will be particularly expressed in the prices of non-tradeables; the increased domestic demand for traded goods can be satisfied by increased imports.

More interesting may be the medium-term effects of an increase in capital inflows on the levels of investment, savings and debt. To analyse the relationships between the flows of external finance and domestic investment and savings, it is useful to start from the macroeconomic identity equations, derived from the definitions of the national accounting system. The expenditures on Gross Domestic Product, GDP, are defined as

$$GDP = C + I + X - M$$

Adding the net factor payments to abroad, defines Gross National Product, GNP (Y):

$$Y = C + I + X - M + (WR + CT - NFP) \tag{4.4}$$

where:

Y = GNP;
C = consumption expenditure;
I = gross domestic capital formation;
X = exports of goods and non-factor services;
M = imports of goods and non-factor services;

and net income from abroad consists of:

WR = workers' remittances;
CT = current unrequited transfers;
NFP = net other factor payments.

National savings are defined as:

$$S = Y - C \tag{4.5}$$

Inserting equation 4.5 into equation 4.4, and re-arranging to define the investment-savings gap, leads to:

$$I - S = M - X - (WR + CT - NFP) \tag{4.6}$$

The right-hand side of equation 4.6 is equal to the current-account deficit of the balance of payments. This current-account deficit can also be defined by re-arranging the terms of the balance-of-payments equation 4.1 above:

$$M - X - (WR + CT - NFP) = F - RES + E\&O \tag{4.7}$$

For the definition of the variables, see equation 4.1 above. Combining equations 4.6 and 4.7 gives:

$$I - S = M - X - (WR + CT - NFP) = F - RES + E\&O \tag{4.8}$$

According to this identity, *ex post* the net flow of foreign capital is equal to the external gap (the current-account deficit) and equal to the internal gap (i.e. the investment-savings gap). Equation 4.8 is an identity; for instance, if capital inflows *(F)* increase, investment *must* rise or savings *must* fall to maintain the identity. But an identity says nothing about *causality*: it may be a higher investment demand that leads to higher capital inflow, or it may be the higher supply of foreign funds that leads to an increase in investment. However, as argued in Chapter 3, in the mid-1970s the access to commercial foreign borrowing rather suddenly increased for developing countries. Hence, in this chapter the increase in capital inflows *(F)* is interpreted as an exogenous supply shock, to which the other variables in equation 4.8 had to adjust. The analysis in this chapter will concentrate on the main variables in the equation, savings and investment (*S* and *I*, see section 4.3.2), exports (*X*, section 4.3.3), and debt service (*NFP*, section 4.3.4). In section 4.4 the impact on private investment will be analysed. The purpose of the analysis in this chapter is to identify the main channels along which capital inflows affect the economy. Later on, in Chapter 6, these transmission mechanisms will be brought together in the CGE model.

First, to provide the background, the role of the public sector in the Thai economy will be discussed.

4.3.1 The role of the public sector

The capital inflows received since the mid-1970s were particularly directed towards the public sector. This section describes briefly the size and role of the public sector in the Thai economy. Two parts of the public sector are distinguished: government and state enterprises. The increase in the level of capital inflows was associated with an increase in public investment, in particular investment by state enterprises.

The political role of the government in formulating and implementing the development strategy was already discussed in Chapter 2. However, the government also has an important role to play in resource allocation and macroeconomic management. The government budget is a channel through which burdens and resources are allocated over the various institutions and sectors of the economy, and the level of government spending and its financing is an important instrument of macroeconomic stabilization policies.

A first observation is that, compared to other developing countries, the ratio of total government expenditures to GDP is low in Thailand.[2] This confirms the point, made in Chapter 2, that the Thai development strategy is based on the predominance of the private sector. The state is given a relatively modest role.

The trends in the level and composition of the tax ratio are presented in Table 4.1. The income tax on both personal and corporate incomes increased. This increase is due to a number of factors. In the first place, the tax base has grown: the 'modern' corporate sector is rapidly expanding. With this growth is associated the growth of more tractable, and therefore more taxable, profit and labour incomes. Tax administration has also improved over the years. There have been no major tax rate reforms, although with the progressive rate structure and the growth of nominal incomes, more of taxable income is in the higher tax brackets.

Despite the growth of income tax revenues, the Thai tax system is still dominated by indirect taxes. In comparison to the tax structure of other middle-income developing countries or of other Asian countries, the Thai system has a larger share of domestic indirect and a smaller share of direct taxes, while the share of taxes on international trade is comparable to the average for these other countries (see World Bank 1988: 83–84).

Table 4.1   National government actual revenue classified by major sources (% of GDP)

	1970–74	1975–79	1980–82	1983–86	1987–90	1991–94
Taxation	11.6	12.1	13.2	14.1	16.1	16.7
Income taxes	1.6	2.2	2.8	3.2	3.7	5.2
– Personal	0.9	1.0	1.3	1.8	1.6	1.8
– Corporation	0.7	1.2	1.6	1.5	2.0	3.2
Indirect taxes	10.0	9.9	10.3	10.9	12.4	11.5
– Import duties	3.3	2.9	2.8	3.0	3.8	3.3
– Export duties	0.7	0.4	0.4	0.2	0.0	0.0
– Business taxes*	2.5	2.7	2.8	2.9	3.5	3.4
– Selective sales taxes	2.2	2.6	3.3	3.7	3.9	3.8
– Other taxes	1.3	1.2	1.1	1.1	1.2	1.0
Sales and charges	0.3	0.3	0.2	0.2	0.3	0.3
Contrib. from gov't enterp. & dividends	0.4	0.4	0.4	0.5	0.5	0.9
Miscellaneous revenue	0.4	0.4	0.7	0.7	0.5	0.5
Total revenue	12.8	13.3	14.5	15.6	17.3	18.3

* After 1992 value added tax.

Source: Bank of Thailand.

Within the category of indirect taxes there were significant shifts. The import duties/GDP ratio stagnated and the export duties/GDP ratio decreased, while the ratio of domestic indirect taxes increased. In 1992 a value added tax was introduced to replace the business tax. The taxes can also be related to their various tax bases. The ratio of income tax to national income increased steadily. Of the indirect taxes, the ratio of import duties revenue to total merchandise imports fell in the 1970s, but stabilized in the 1980s. The ratio of export duties to merchandise exports, which was dominated by the taxes on rice exports, decreased rapidly and almost disappeared in 1986 when the rice tax was abolished.

The import duties/imports and the export duties/exports ratios also indicate changes in trade policy. The decrease in the import duty ratio may be seen as an import liberalization during the 1970s. Import tariffs are always ambiguous: they are an instrument of revenue collection, but also of market protection. If they fulfill their second purpose well, they lose their first purpose. It could thus be that the decrease of the import duty ratio in the 1970s was the result of increased market protection rather than a reflection of import liberalization. However, as was discussed in Chapter 2 (section 2.6), in the early 1970s the share of final consumer goods in total imports, on which protection tends to concentrate, was already minor. The decrease in the import duty ratio is the result of the decrease in the average import tariff. In the 1980s, however, that process had come to an end and import duties stabilized. This strongly suggests that import tariffs and import liberalization have not played a major role in the adjustment strategy of the 1980s, but this will be further discussed in section 4.5.

The ratio of domestic indirect taxes to total private consumption significantly increased over the years. Particularly the selective sales taxes, a tax on the more luxury consumption items, increased sharply.

The total government expenditure to GDP ratio increased, along with the revenue ratio, from period to period, as Table 4.2 shows. Government investment and government expenditure on 'Economic Services' continuously declined over the periods. In the last period, however, a sharp reversal is observed. Table 4.2 also shows the growing burden of interest payments on government debt.

It is, however, also interesting to study the short-term fluctuations in the government expenditure ratio that are not captured by the period

Table 4.2   National government actual expenditure by economic and functional classification (% of GDP)

	1970–74	1975–79	1980–82	1983–86	1987–90	1991–94
Total expenditures	15.8	16.0	18.4	18.9	15.1	15.6
Economic classification						
Current	11.6	12.1	14.5	15.8	12.9	11.3
Capital	4.2	3.9	3.9	3.1	2.3	4.3
Major functional classification						
Economic services	3.9	3.7	3.4	2.9	2.3	4.0
Social services	4.4	4.9	5.4	5.6	4.6	5.6
Defence	3.0	3.0	3.7	3.8	2.9	2.5
General administration	2.3	2.1	2.5	2.5	2.0	1.8
Other items, of which:	2.3	2.2	3.4	4.0	3.4	1.7
– Interest domestic debt	1.1	1.2	1.4	2.2	—	—
– Interest external debt	0.2	0.2	0.4	0.6	—	—
– Total interest	1.3	1.4	1.8	2.8	2.5	1.0

Source: Bank of Thailand.

Figure 4.2   Government expenditure and revenue ratios (% of GDP)

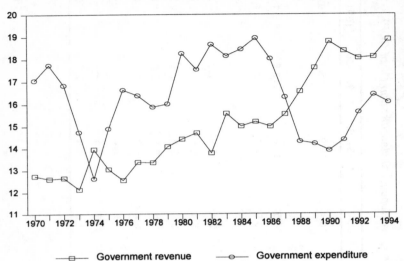

averages of Table 4.2. Figure 4.2 depicts the government expenditure and revenue ratios from year to year. The revenue ratio shows a relatively stable and slowly increasing level, but the expenditure ratio strongly fluctuates from year to year. A further disaggregation (not included in Figure 4.2) would show that these shifts are mainly due to variations in capital expenditures. These fluctuations reflect policy interventions.

The high fiscal deficits of the early 1970s led to a restrictive fiscal policy. This contractionary policy was strengthened when Thailand was hit by the first oil shock in 1974, and led then, in fact, to a budget surplus. Government expenditure recovered up to 1976, after which a consolidation of the expenditure ratio can be observed. In 1980 an expansionary phase in the fiscal policy stance started again, continuing up to 1985. After 1985 the expenditure ratio collapsed.

These trends suggest that fiscal policy is executed through expenditure policies. The revenue ratio is rather stable and gradually increases over time. But substantial short-term variations are effectuated in the government expenditure ratio. The policy background to these changes and their effect on the macroeconomic performance will be discussed in section 4.5.

The state enterprise sector in Thailand is relatively small. A recent study states that Thailand has 62 state enterprises, against 189 in Indonesia, 202 in the Philippines and even 1171 in Malaysia (Fres-Felix 1992: 26). The present number of 62 is down from 102 state enterprises that were in existence in 1960, and the current drive towards privatization is likely to reduce the number further. About one-third of these state enterprises are public utilities (in sectors of Transport & Communications, and Electricity & Water Supply). Other enterprises are in the manufacturing sector, petroleum and natural gas, and in the commercial and financial sectors (the latter including the central bank). The financial relations between state enterprises and government vary among individual state enterprises and over periods, but a recent study concluded that over the 1970s and 1980s state enterprises transferred more money to the government than they received in transfers from the government (Singhaumpai & Sukkankosone 1992: 401). The profitability of state enterprises decreased in the period 1975–81 and recovered again in later years (Singhaumpai & Sukkankosone 1992: 399). This latter point was already established in Chapter 3 (Table 3.3), where it was noted that the savings ratio of state enterprises decreased in the late 1970s, to recover after 1981. In section 4.3.2 below this point will be further analysed.

4.3.2   Foreign capital and investment and savings

This section will focus on the relationship between external capital flows and domestic investment, savings and growth. There has been an extensive debate in the development economics literature on the relationship between external finance and domestic accumulation. This debate concerned the *ex post* accounting identity, derived from equation 4.8 above:

$$I = S + F \qquad\qquad (4.9)$$

according to which investments *(I)* are financed by, and equal to, domestic savings *(S)* and net foreign savings *(F)*, ignoring for the time being the error term *(E&O)* and the changes in foreign assets *(RES)*. This identity can be linked to Harrod-Domar type growth models, in which output growth depends on the level of investments:

$$\Delta Y = \frac{1}{k} I \qquad\qquad\qquad\qquad (4.10)$$

Equation 4.10 is the simplest of growth equations. It relates the increase in production and income (ΔY) to the level of investment. The coefficient 'k' is the 'Incremental Capital Output Ratio' *(ICOR)*. Inserting equation 4.9 into equation 4.10 and dividing by Y gives:

$$\frac{\Delta Y}{Y} = g = \frac{1}{k} \left[\frac{S}{Y} + \frac{F}{Y} \right] \qquad\qquad (4.11)$$

The interpretation of the simple growth model contained in equations 4.10 and 4.11 is that investment and growth in developing countries can be constrained by the availability of savings. Any increase in F would lead to an increase in I, along the lines of equation 4.9, and to an acceleration of growth, along the lines of equation 4.11. (See for example the 'locus classicus' of the two-gap approach, Chenery & Strout 1966.)

Griffin (1970) attacked this position. He suggested that an increase in F would lead to a drop in S, since the capital inflow could also induce increased consumption. In addition, the foreign funds may be used to finance inefficient projects, so that the *ICOR* would rise, and there would be less growth induced by a given level of investment. On the whole, the increase in the inflow of foreign funds could lead to a decrease in the growth rate rather than to an improvement.

Others have criticized Griffin by showing that, even if part of F is used to increase consumption, another part of it finances investment, and this will increase income (e.g. Papanek 1972).

The debate has continued. For recent contributions see for instance Gupta and Islam (1983), Mosley (1980), Bowles (1987), Snyder (1990) and, for a recent survey, White (1992). The recent contributions mainly discuss causality (do F lead to low S or do low S invite more F?), and emphasize the interaction between the variables (simultaneous equation systems to capture the interaction between I, S, and F). It would appear from these studies that the results of empirical studies on the interaction between I, S and F depend largely on method (cross-country or time series), on the composition of the sample of countries, and on the period covered. This would suggest that the relationships are too complex to be captured by the analysis at the level of macroeconomic aggregates.

Yet almost all studies have studied the problem at that level. A few studies disaggregated capital inflows into component parts: direct investment, aid, commercial loans, and so on (e.g. Papanek 1973 and Newlyn 1977). They found that the different components have different impacts on investment levels or growth rates. This is to be expected in developing countries, where capital markets are imperfect and segmented. Such findings would suggest a further disaggregation. Different types of capital inflows are aimed at and received by different agents in the economy, and one would expect that a change in the level of any type of capital inflow would affect, initially, the accumulation behaviour of the sector at which it is aimed. For instance, aid flows *(ODA)* would be particularly related to savings and investment patterns of the government, whereas direct investment would be more related to those of the private sector.

This approach is used in the 'fiscal response' models. In these studies, the fiscal response to aid inflows is the focus of the analysis, but most of the arguments extend to the case of public sector responses to external loans as well. The approach started with Heller (1975) and has been further elaborated by Mosley (1987) and White (1993), who placed the approach in a dynamic context.

To analyse the effects, it will be useful to give three definitions:

$$I_{pu} = I_g + I_{se} \qquad\qquad (4.12)$$

$$S_{pu} = T - C_g + S_{se} \qquad\qquad (4.13)$$

$$I_{pu} - S_{pu} = PSBR = F_{pu} + Z \qquad\qquad (4.14)$$

Public sector investment (I_{pu}) is composed of government investment (I_g) and state enterprise investment (I_{se}). Public sector savings (S_{pu}) is the sum of government savings, defined as the difference between tax revenue *(T)* and current government spending (C_g), plus state enterprise profits or savings (S_{se}). The public sector investment-savings gap, or the public sector borrowing requirement *(PSBR)*, is financed by foreign capital inflows (F_{pu}) and by domestic funds *(Z)*.

The investment, savings and capital flows of equation 4.9 can be split up into public and private sectors:

$$I_{pu} + I_{pr} - S_{pu} - S_{pr} = F_{pu} + F_{pr}$$

This equation can be combined with equations 4.12 to 4.14 to give:

$$I_g + I_{se} + I_{pr} - (T - C_g) - S_{se} - S_{pr} = F_{pu} + F_{pr}$$

or:

$$I_g + I_{se} - (T - C_g) - S_{se} = F_{pu} + F_{pr} + S_{pr} - I_{pr} \qquad (4.15)$$

Comparing equation 4.15 with 4.14 makes clear that

$$Z = F_{pr} + S_{pr} - I_{pr}$$

that is, the financing available for the domestic *PSBR* is equal to the private sector financial surplus. Equation 4.15 can be used to trace the impact of an increase in external funding to the public sector (F_{pu}).

An increase in aid or other foreign funding for the public sector is likely to increase public sector expenditures, in particular investments, and may lead to a relaxing of revenue collection efforts, i.e. a lower tax ratio or lower state enterprise prices. Although most foreign capital inflows may be directly linked to specific investment projects, and will therefore have an immediate impact on investment spending, they are likely to have a broader impact on public sector spending for four reasons:

(a) Public investment may rise by more than the foreign financing when the external funds finance only part of the total investment. In particular, local cost financing will have to be undertaken from domestic resources. This implies that total investment expenditures may rise by more than the capital inflow.

(b) Public investment projects lead, upon completion, to additional re-current expenditures on operation and maintenance. For instance, a new road needs maintenance and a new school requires teachers. These expenditures are generally not financed by the foreign funds, and need to be included in the regular government budget.

(c) To the extent that the foreign funds came in the form of loans, an external debt will have accumulated, requiring future expenditures on debt servicing.

(d) The access to foreign finance may reduce the efforts of the government and the state enterprises to collect revenue. Tax reforms and price increases by state enterprises are difficult political decisions and may be postponed when not urgently required.

It is also possible that the foreign funds finance a project that would have been undertaken anyway, so that the foreign funds simply replace domestic financing, without any expansionary effect on total expenditure. In a strongly resource-constrained public sector such a fungibility may be unlikely, and one would thus expect that public spending increases by at least as much as, and probably by more than, the increase in capital inflows.

An increase in the inflows of foreign funds (F_{pu} in equation 4.15) is thus likely to lead to an increase in public investment. In fact, public investment may well rise by more than the capital inflow itself. Moreover, it is also likely that recurrent spending will increase. If tax efforts and state enterprise pricing reforms are also relaxed, public sector savings will decrease.

The increase in public sector spending will stimulate the economy. When idle capacity is available, output and income will rise in the medium term. The relaxation of revenue collection will furthermore increase private sector disposable incomes and will stimulate private consumption expenditure. The income increases will, in the medium term, increase private savings and will generate more public sector revenue. It is, therefore, unclear what will happen to total savings in the medium term. The initial impact of the public sector responses to the foreign capital inflow will be a reduction of public sector savings, but the subsequent increases in private income will generate new private savings and may even restore some of the public sector savings.

The ultimate impact on total savings is important, because this will be an important determinant of the impact on private investment. Equation 4.15 can be used to show that, if public investment rises and public savings decrease, it is likely that the *PSBR* increases by more than the increase in public sector foreign capital inflows, so that the claims of the public sector on the domestic financial markets increase. If private savings have increased, it is possible that the claims may be satisfied without too much negative effect on the ability of the financial markets to finance private investment. If, on the other hand, private savings have not increased and the private sector's access to additional foreign loans (F_{pr}) is limited, then the increased domestic financing claims of the public sector are likely to crowd out private credit demand on the domestic financial markets.

The impact on medium-term growth is the outcome of these process-es. Total investment is the sum of public and private investment. Public investment has risen and so has income. Normally, this should provide an impulse for private investment demand to rise as well. But it is pos-sible that the availability of credit to finance such an private expansion is inadequate, due to the increase in the *PSBR*. Total investment may thus rise or fall, and so may growth. It has also been argued that growth depends on the composition of investment and that, as the share of public investment rises, the growth efficiency of investment decreas-es (Khan & Reinhart 1990).

The trends in the accumulation balances, described in Chapter 3, can be reconsidered against the background of these theoretical arguments. As Table 3.1 showed, after 1975 and up to the early 1980s, foreign cap-ital flows to the public sector increased. The increase of capital flows to the state enterprise sector was associated with a sharp increase in the state enterprise investment ratio and a decline in the state enterprise savings ratio. International capital flows to the government also in-creased, but the government investment ratio showed a declining trend. The government savings ratio decreased as the modest and gradual increase of the revenue ratio was overwhelmed by the rapid growth of current spending (see Tables 4.1 and 4.2, and Figure 4.2 above). All in all, the increase in international capital flows to the public sector led to an increase in the public sector investment ratio, a decline in the public sector savings ratio, and a sharp increase in the public sector borrowing requirement. In fact, the *PSBR* increased by far more than the capital inflows did, so that public sector claims on the domestic financial mar-kets also increased.

It would thus appear that, in the public sector, the capital inflows did have the expected effects on investment and on savings. The ultimate effects on total investment and growth depend, of course, on the private sector response to the changes in the public sector accumulation balan-ces. These interactions will be analysed in section 4.4 below.

4.3.3 Foreign capital and anti-export bias

Recently, the macroeconomic impact of capital inflows has been ana-lysed in the framework of the dependent economy models (see Van

Wijnbergen 1986, De Melo 1988). In these models an increase in capital inflows will increase domestic demand for both traded goods and non-traded goods. The increased demand for traded goods can be satisfied by domestic production or, if production capacity is inadequate, by imports. If the production capacity in the non-traded goods sectors is inadequate to satisfy the increased demand, prices will rise. It is thus likely that the increase in capital inflows will lead to an increase in the relative price of non-traded versus traded goods. This change in relative prices is equivalent to a cost increase to producers in the traded goods sector, which will undermine the competitiveness of the sector and may reduce exports.[3]

The extent of the relative price change depends on the marginal propensity to spend on non-traded goods, on the price elasticity of demand for non-traded goods, and on the supply responsiveness of the non-traded goods sector. It should be noted that the upsurge in capital inflows in the period 1975–85 was mainly aimed at state enterprises, and helped to finance investments in particularly the public utilities sectors of 'Transport & Communications' and 'Electricity & Water Supply' (see Chapter 3, especially Table 3.2). Thus, the foreign-capital-financed investments concentrated on non-traded activities. To some extent this may help to prevent the 'Dutch disease' effect, as the investments increase the supply of these non-traded goods and services to match the increased demand. On the other hand, shortages may arise in other non-traded sectors, so that relative price changes still would occur.

The model in Van Wijnbergen (1986) is static, i.e. investments do not play a role, but presumably the results would also hold in a more dynamic model. The shift in relative profitability as a result of the relative price change would shift investments towards the non-traded goods sector, and away from traded goods in general and export goods in particular (see also Chhibber et al. 1992). Investments in public utilities may create investment opportunities for, and reduce the production cost of private investments in both the traded and non-traded sectors, but the shift in relative profitability would probably bias such investment towards the non-traded sectors. The result is that, both in the short run and in the medium run, exports may suffer and balance-of-payments problems may emerge.

Foreign capital inflows are thus associated with increases in domestic expenditures, and these demand pressures may lead to domestic price increases that would affect the value of the domestic currency. What, in fact, happened to the exchange rate? The 'Dutch disease' models referred to above focus on the 'internal' real exchange rate, the relative price of traded *versus* non-traded goods. To study the impact on exports and the balance of payments, it is more useful to focus on the external real exchange rate, which is the nominal exchange rate corrected for changes in domestic prices and world prices.[4]

In Figure 4.3 the real exchange rate index is presented. Two indices are presented. The 'real exchange rate' corrects the nominal exchange rate (bahts per US dollar) for changes in world prices and changes in prices in Thailand. This index thus measures the changes in the real exchange rate index that are due to (i) changes in the nominal exchange rates (these took place in 1981 and 1984) and to (ii) changes in relative prices, i.e. increases in the price level in Thailand compared to price increases in other countries. Figure 4.3 shows that, throughout the period 1971–83 the real exchange rate was gradually appreciating, as Thai inflation was higher than world inflation. There was a mild depreciation around 1981–82 as result of the 1981 devaluation. The 1984 devaluation resulted in a more substantial correction, but after 1985 the gradual appreciation continued. By the end of the period under study, the level of the real exchange rate index was lower than it had been in 1970. With the exception of a few years in the entire period, Thai inflation was higher than world inflation, leading to an appreciation of the real exchange rate, which was not sufficiently corrected by devaluations. This appreciation was in favour of importers, and they formed a strong lobby to maintain the increasingly overvalued exchange rate. The nominal exchange rate of the baht to the dollar was made a symbol of economic stability. The ministers of finance who presided over the devaluations of 1981 and 1984 both faced fierce criticisms and had to resign shortly after they had taken the decision to devalue.

The trends in the real exchange rate are mainly determined by Thai inflation. Inflation in Thailand is strongly determined by movements in international prices. Changes in the prices of imported goods affect directly their domestic prices, but prices of export goods also have an impact on domestic prices. The primary commodities that Thailand exports are also consumed domestically (e.g. rice, sugar, fruits, seafood) and, in the absence of local price controls, world market prices are the main determinant of domestic prices. Most industrial exports are simple, stan-

Figure 4.3   Real exchange rate indices

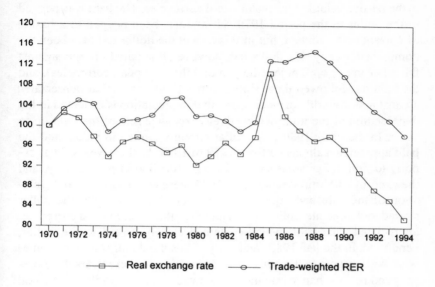

dardized products, which are sold at current world market prices; again domestic prices tend to follow world price trends.

But local price increases tended to exceed world inflation. The extent of the excess is determined by the state of aggregate demand in the economy, which is strongly influenced by the capital inflows from abroad.[5] There is thus reason to conclude that the variations in capital inflows from abroad have been reflected in variations in the rate of inflation, and that capital inflows themselves have thus contributed to an anti-export bias.

However, it would appear that the anti-export bias cannot have been too strong. As established in Chapter 2, export growth has been strong over the last two decades, and the export/GDP ratio has increased sharply. Admittedly, the real exchange rate index gives an inadequate impression of the anti-export bias that may occur. A better view may be obtained using the other index included in Figure 4.3. The trade-weighted real exchange rate measures the exchange rate of the baht *vis-à-vis* the currencies of Thailand's major trading partners, and corrects these for changes in the price levels in the different sets of countries.[6]

Changes in the trade-weighted index are strongly influenced by shifts in the relative values of the major world currencies. The baht was pegged to the dollar in the period 1970–84, and has been pegged to a basket of currencies since then, but in this basket the dollar has also been the dominant currency. The dollar has, however, fluctuated strongly against the other major currencies (the yen and the European currencies), and the baht has followed these shifts. In the 1970s, the dollar depreciated against major world currencies, and that depreciation is reflected in the depreciation of the trade-weighed real exchange rate of the baht up to 1979. In the early 1980s, the dollar strongly gained in value, and the baht appreciated alongside from 1979 to 1983. In these years, Thai exports to non-dollar areas suffered from a decline in profitability, and the export/GDP ratio stagnated. In 1984 there was a substantial devaluation of the baht and, after the Plaza Agreement of 1985, the dollar started to depreciate while the yen and the other major world currencies appreciated. The baht, which remained closely linked to the dollar, benefitted. In the late 1980s and early 1990s the dollar stabilized somewhat with respect to the other main currencies. In these years the trade-weighed real exchange rate index followed a pattern similar to the real exchange rate index, with the baht appreciating due to the impact of relatively high domestic inflation, fuelled by the spending boom initiated by the new upsurge of capital inflows. At the end of the period under study, the trade-weighted real exchange rate index was back to its value at the beginning of the period.

Exports have been very sensitive to the trade-weighted real exchange rate. The gradual, halting, depreciation in the period 1970–79 was associated with an increase in the export/GDP ratio from around 15 per cent in 1970 to around 23 per cent in 1979–80. The period 1979–84, when the real exchange rate appreciated, was characterized by stagnation and even decline of the export ratio. Only after the devaluation of 1984 and the depreciation along with the dollar after 1985, did the export ratio improve, increasing sharply to a level of 35 per cent in 1989.[7] The renewed appreciation of the real exchange rate after 1988 did not result in stagnating exports: the export/GDP ratio continued to increase to over 38 per cent in 1994. In these years export-oriented foreign and local investment compensated for the negative impact of the real exchange rate appreciation (see for further discussion Chapter 5).

4.3.4 Foreign capital and the debt burden

Persistent external borrowing, as occurred after 1974, will result in the accumulation of a stock of external debt, burdening the country with debt-servicing obligations. This section examines the extent of Thailand's external debt in relation to the size of the economy, and its debt servicing capacity.

In Chapter 3 (see Table 3.1) it was shown that the inflow of foreign loans started to increase around the mid-1970s. Table 4.3 presents the total debt, indicating that the size of foreign debt was relatively small and slowly growing until the end of the 1970s. In the late 1970s, however, the substantial increase in foreign borrowing led to a rapid acceleration of the growth of the external debt. The size of foreign loans continued to grow rapidly until 1985. As a result, the external debt outstanding increased from 3 billion US dollars in 1978 to 15 billion in 1985. After 1985 there were a few years with low capital inflows and a consolidation of the stock of outstanding debt, but in 1989 a new period of heavy borrowing started. The total external debt increased to 54 billion dollar in 1994.

In relation to the economy, the ratio of external debt to GDP rose sharply from merely 12 per cent in 1977 to an all-time peak of 39 per cent in 1985. After 1985 and up to 1989, debt accumulation continued, but at a much slower pace, and GDP grew very rapidly, so that the debt/GDP ratio fell substantially to 27 per cent in 1989. After that, the accumulation of debt accelerated again, and the debt/GDP ratio jumped back up, almost reaching its earlier peak in 1994, when the ratio was 38 per cent.

It is also useful to express the external debt as a percentage of exports of goods and services, rather than as a percentage of GDP, because the exports generate the foreign exchange income out of which the debt servicing has to be paid. Over the same period, the ratio of debt to exports also increased sharply, from 59 per cent in 1977 to a peak of 162 per cent in 1985, after which it decreased, due to the rapid growth of exports, to 77 per cent in 1989. The subsequent increase in debt did not increase the debt/export ratio by much, as exports themselves were also growing very rapidly; in 1994 the debt/export ratio was 97 per cent.

The composition of the debt has also changed radically over the years. In 1975 the public and publicly-guaranteed debt accounted for 46 per cent of total debt. Almost all of this outstanding debt was to

Table 4.3   External debt and debt ratios

| Year | Total external debt (million US$) | | | Ratio of debt | |
	Long-term	Short-term	Total	to GDP (%) Total	to exports (%) Total
1970	749	n.a.	n.a.	10.6	70.6
1971	793	n.a.	n.a.	10.8	67.4
1972	913	n.a.	n.a.	11.2	61.5
1973	920	n.a.	n.a.	8.5	45.7
1974	1 176	n.a.	n.a.	8.5	39.5
1975	1 360	n.a.	n.a.	9.1	49.5
1976	1 616	n.a.	n.a.	9.5	46.8
1977	2 031	297	2 328	11.7	58.7
1978	2 719	330	3 049	12.6	63.5
1979	3 957	454	4 410	16.0	71.0
1980	5 704	1 107	6 811	21.1	86.9
1981	7 175	1 626	8 801	25.1	105.4
1982	8 318	1 811	10 129	28.3	120.2
1983	9 528	1 640	11 169	28.1	138.1
1984	10 797	2 042	12 839	31.0	139.7
1985	12 776	1 923	14 698	39.2	162.1
1986	14 071	1 958	16 029	38.3	144.7
1987	15 748	1 773	17 520	35.8	119.6
1988	15 379	2 531	17 910	28.9	87.6
1989	16 300	3 117	19 417	26.8	76.7
1990	18 598	6 467	25 065	29.2	85.7
1991	22 147	11 137	33 284	33.8	95.4
1992	23 976	13 378	37 354	33.7	92.8
1993	26 948	18 761	45 709	36.4	98.1
1994	29 390	24 359	53 749	37.5	96.7

Note: Since 1993, short-term debt includes off-shore credits from the Bangkok International Banking Facilities (BIBF).

Source: Bank of Thailand.

official bilateral and multilateral creditors, i.e. it was debt accumulated from aid flows. By 1985 the share of public and publicly guaranteed debt had further increased to 62 per cent of total debt, but now more than one-third of the outstanding debt was to private creditors. This change is a reflection of the changing conditions on the international financial markets that were described in Chapter 3. The public sector financial reforms that were undertaken after 1985 led to a reduction in public sector foreign borrowing; in the years 1987–90 outstanding public sector debt even decreased. The rapid accumulation of external debt after 1989 is entirely the result of private sector borrowing. The share of public sector debt in total debt decreased from 62 per cent in 1985 to 29 per cent in 1994.

The fast accumulation of external debt has led to a fast increase of interest payments. The interest payments on external debt rose from less than 1 per cent of GDP during the early 1970s to 3.1 per cent in 1986 and then levelled off, but remained close to 2 per cent (see Table 2.6 in Chapter 2). During the 1970s, the majority of the interest payments on external debt were the responsibility of the private sector. However, the picture changed during the 1980s when the public sector accounted for majority of the interest payments on external debt. The share of public sector in external interest payments rose from 34 per cent in 1970 to 47 per cent in 1980 and to 71 per cent in 1989.

The debt service payments (interest charges plus repayments) as a percentage of exports of goods and services, the debt-service ratio, also rose sharply from 11 per cent in 1977 to a peak of 23 per cent in 1985 (see Figure 4.4). This rising debt-service ratio alarmed many economists, since the burden was causing a substantial drain on domestic investable resources. For instance, the 1983 *Annual Economic Report* of the central bank referred to the external debt problems of a number of developing countries, and warned that 'the Government must, therefore, be extremely careful in raising more loans in order to pre-empt the debt problem' (Bank of Thailand 1983: 14).[8] In 1985, interest payments on foreign debt were equivalent to 57 per cent of the current-account deficit. However, from a comparative perspective, Thailand's external debt remained moderate. According to World Bank data, Thailand's total external debt in 1986 was estimated at about 14 billion US dollars, compared to, for instance, 36 billion for Indonesia, 20 billion for Malaysia and 22 billion for the Philippines. Compared to the debt-

Figure 4.4   Debt-service ratio

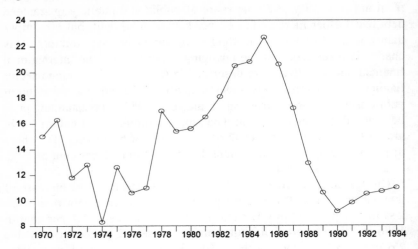

carrying capacity, the Thai debt burden was lower than that of the other countries. The debt/GNP ratio was 35 per cent in 1986, against 77 per cent for Malaysia, 72 per cent for the Philippines and 50 per cent for Indonesia in the same year. In terms of the debt/export ratio, Thailand also scored considerably better than most Asian countries.

It is both the more modest level of the debt burden and the quick recovery of the economy after 1986 that reduced the debt ratios quickly. By 1990, the debt-service ratio had decreased to 9 per cent. This was the result of the government restriction on foreign public borrowing and of the rapid growth of exports, the denominator of the debt-service ratio.

Table 4.2 above showed yet another aspect of the debt problem. The interest payments on the external debt of the government claimed an increasing share of government expenditures. In the period 1970–74 such payments amounted to only 1 per cent of total government expenditures, but in 1983–86 this share had increased to 3 per cent. It should be noted that the Thai government did most of its borrowing on the domestic capital market; the external borrowing in the public sector was mainly done by state enterprises. In the process the domestic government debt increased from a level of 100 billion baht around 1980 to a peak level of 322 billion in 1987, or, as percentage of GDP, from 16 per cent to 27 per cent. After 1987 it declined rapidly, to only 7 per cent of GDP in 1992. If the payments of interest on the domestic government debt are added to the payments on the external debt, total interest payments amounted to about 15 per cent of total government spending in the early 1980s. In this way the outstanding debt can become a major factor in causing fiscal imbalances.

4.4   Foreign Capital, Public Investment and Private Investment: Crowding Out or Crowding In?

As was argued above, a crucial determinant of the sustainability of public sector external borrowing is the impact on private investment and growth. The boom in foreign capital inflows in the period 1975–85 gave rise to an increase in public investment: how did private investment respond?

In Chapter 3 private investment was split up into residential construction by the household sector and investments by private corporations (see Table 3.4 and Appendix Table A.3.1). The relatively strong trend of private investment in the 1980s was due to the increase in residential construction; the investment ratio of the private corporations did far less well.[9] In terms of expansion of production capacity and growth potential, the investments by private corporations are more important than the other elements of private investment, so the analysis will focus on this.

Recently, there has been an increase of interest in the determinants of private investment in developing countries. The background for this is the philosophy that guided the structural adjustment efforts of the 1980s, emphasizing the role of the private sector as the main dynamic agent creating economic growth (see e.g. Mosley et al. 1991, Haggard & Kaufman 1992). Still, in most developing countries, even in those where sustained structural adjustment policies have been implemented, the recovery of private investment has been disappointing (World Bank 1990, Mosley et al. 1991). This has led to a series of studies on the determinants of private investment in developing countries (e.g. World

Bank 1990, Greene & Villanueva 1991, Serven & Solimano 1992, Chhibber et al. 1992, FitzGerald, Jansen & Vos 1994).

The standard approach to the explanation of private investment demand includes three types of variables: (a) variables reflecting (expected) demand conditions, usually in the form of an accelerator mechanism, based on aggregate demand changes; (b) variables reflecting the cost of investment, such as the interest rate or the cost of capital goods; and (c) variables reflecting the availability of investment finance, such as the internal cash flow (i.e. retained profits) or available credit from domestic or foreign capital markets (see e.g. Evans 1969, Fazzari, Hubbard & Petersen 1988). A typical private investment function would then include variables like:

$$I_{pr} = f(\Delta Y; \ i-p; \ \Delta CR) \qquad\qquad (4.16)$$

ΔY is the growth of aggregate demand; $(i-p)$ the real interest rate; and ΔCR the expansion of credit. The special conditions facing developing countries are captured by adding variables to this standard private investment equation in an *ad hoc* manner. Two aspects deserve particular attention:

(a) the interaction between public and private investment;
(b) the role of international variables in modelling private investment.

4.4.1 Public and private investment

The relationship between public and private investment has been extensively discussed in the economic development literature (see e.g. Greene & Villanueva 1991, Blejer & Khan 1984, Taylor 1988). The terms on which this debate has centred are 'crowding in' and 'crowding out'.

Public investment can invite private investment if there is idle capacity and the demand impulse from the public investment leads to a multiplier-accelerator process. Public investment in infrastructure and public utilities can make private investment projects possible that previously could not be undertaken, or it can reduce the cost of such projects. These are the channels for crowding in. In many developing countries there are serious shortages in physical and social infrastructure that undermine the profitability and competitiveness of the private sector, and one would expect, certainly in the longer run, that public investment in infrastructure will induce private sector activities.

Crowding out can occur when public investment projects cover activities that could also be undertaken by the private sector; in that case public investment competes with private projects. Public investment can also pre-empt claims on domestic real resources (e.g. construction capacity, foreign exchange reserves or skilled manpower) or increase their prices, which would reduce the level of investment the private sector could undertake.

The emphasis in the crowding-out debate has been on the channels of financing public investment. Quite often the increase in public investment leads to a greater public sector deficit that needs to be financed. Financing of public sector expansion by domestic capital markets may raise interest rates or lead to rationing of credit to the private sector. Public sector financing by domestic or foreign credit markets will also lead to a growing debt overhang. If the public sector expenditures are financed through money creation, inflation and macroeconomic imbalances will result. These effects would increase the cost of investment, undermine the confidence of private investors, or reduce their access to domestic and foreign credit.

In most empirical studies, the various channels of interaction between public and private investment have been tested by adding the public investment variable in the private investment equation. For instance, Greene and Villanueva (1991) and Serven and Solimano (1992) included the public investment to GDP ratio in the equation that explained the private investment ratio, and found that this variable had a significant though small, positive impact.

Blejer and Khan (1984) argue that public investment creates infrastructure, which would induce private investment, but that public investment will also claim physical and financial resources, or produce output that competes with private sector goods, thus crowding out private investment. Only public infrastructural investment, would crowd in private investment. Of course, it is not easy to separate the part of total public investment devoted to infrastructure from the rest. In their regressions, Blejer and Khan separated the trend value of public investment, which they claim represents the long-run, long gestation period infrastructure investment from the deviations around this trend, which reflect non-infrastructural public investment. They found that the trend value had a significant positive effect, and the deviations a significant negative effect.[10]

There seems to be little reason to assume that the separation between public investment in infrastructure and other public investment would run along the lines suggested by Blejer and Khan. It could be suggested that their outcomes reflect the fact that sudden changes in public investment, away from its more stable trend, will create imbalances on the markets for investment goods and on financial markets, negatively affecting private investment.

Most studies are imprecise in their definition of crowding in and crowding out. When investment is measured as a proportion of GDP, at least two definitions are possible:

(a) When an increase in the public investment ratio is combined with a decrease (increase) in the private sector ratio, there is crowding out (in).

(b) When an increase in the public investment ratio is combined with such a decrease in private investment that the total investment ratio decreases, there is crowding out. When private investment increases, or when the decrease in private investment is less than the increase in public investment, the total investment ratio rises and there is crowding in.

Implicitly, studies that add the public investment ratio to the private investment equation to test for crowding in or out, measure effect (a), but from the perspective of economic growth, effect (b) may be more relevant.

4.4.2 International factors and private investment

There are, however, more reasons to analyse in some more detail the effects of public investment on private investment, particularly during the 1980s, and its fiscal implications. The discussion about crowding in and out, as summarized above, implicitly assumes a closed economy. Public investment crowds out through the domestic financial markets. But a considerable part of public investment in developing countries is financed by external finance, including both aid and commercial loans, and this changes the channels of crowding in and out. Tensions on domestic financial markets are less likely, but the external debt overhang may undermine private investors' confidence.

Private investment is a long-term decision, which presupposes confidence in the growth and stability of the economy. The external debt position is one of the crucial variables influencing domestic and foreign investors' confidence. A high external debt will have direct and indirect effects on private investment (Greene & Villanueva 1991, Borensztein 1990, Serven & Solimano 1992, Savvides 1992). The debt-service burden will reduce the funds available for investment. The external debt overhang will reduce the expected returns to investment and will increase the risks of investment projects. The future conditions of the economy are less certain, and this uncertainty is translated into a greater variance in the expected returns of investment projects. The debt overhang will also affect the creditworthiness of the country and may restrict its access to, or the cost of, future foreign credit to finance investment or trade, i.e. the import capacity of the country becomes less certain. The debt burden will also have indirect fiscal and monetary effects. The debt-service burden on the public external debt may lead to a deterioration of fiscal balances and to an increased crowding out of private investment through credit rationing or taxation or both. The decline in international creditworthiness of the country may result in higher domestic interest rates or less access to international reserves and, therefore, to rationing of domestic credit.

Greene and Villanueva (1991) include two external debt variables in their regression equation. The two debt variables – the debt-service ratio and the ratio of outstanding debt to GDP – have both significant and negative coefficients.[11] Serven and Solimano (1992) also find a significant negative impact of the debt/GDP ratio on private investment.

Another international variable that has received attention in the private investment literature is the exchange rate. As noted above the increase in capital inflows in the period 1975–85 was associated with an appreciation of the real exchange rate. The impact of this on investment demand can be important. An appreciation of the real exchange rate can have a number of different effects on private investment (see e.g. Chhibber et al. 1992). First of all, the cost of imported capital goods decreases, making investments cheaper. The cost of imported raw materials, intermediate and final goods also decreases. This reduces the relative profitability of the import-competing and exporting sectors, while non-traded activities benefit. Investment incentives would thus shift to the non-traded activities and balance-of-payments problems may emerge as imports are encouraged and exports discouraged. The relative cost of debt servicing, measured in local currency, decreases with the appreciation of the real exchange rate, thus encouraging further external borrowing. There may be further indirect effects, but on balance the expectation is that the appreciation will reduce the cost of investment and will shift investment incentives to non-traded activities. More complex, however, is the question of how the appreciation will influence the expectations of investors. Clearly, many of the processes identified will be unsustainable. The anti-export bias will lead to current-account problems, the appreciation will create expectations of future devaluations, and the growing debt overhang will undermine private sector confidence.

The foregoing discussion has shown that private investment demand is determined by many factors, and that the fluctuations in the flows of international finance, and their impact on public investment, have many direct and indirect effects on private sector investment demand. These effects include (a) the supply of infrastructure and (b) the expansionary effect on aggregate demand of the increase in public investment. The financing of the public sector deficit may lead to (c) credit rationing or high domestic interest rates. The demand pressures may also induce instability in the form of (d) inflation and (e) current-account deficits. The acceleration of inflation can result in (f) an appreciation of the real exchange rate, which may further undermine the current-account position. The capital inflows, and the deterioration of the current account lead to (g) an accumulation of external debt and to a growing debt-service burden.

These seven items can be seen as the transmission mechanisms through which capital inflows influence ultimate macroeconomic performance. They will be introduced in the CGE model in Chapter 6 to enable a complete and consistent analysis of their impact. To prepare for that analysis, it may be useful to trace here the main trends of the various variables.

In Table 4.4 information on these variables is brought together. Capital inflows to Thailand started to increase in period II and further increased in period III (see also Chapter 3, Table 3.1 and Figure 3.3). This was associated with a sharp increase in the public sector investment ratio in these periods. Table 4.4 shows that the private investment

Table 4.4 Patterns of adjustment

Period	I 1970–74	II 1975–79	III 1980–82	IV 1983–86
Public investment (% GDP)	5.9	6.9	8.6	8.1
Private investment (% GDP)	17.2	17.6	19.0	19.4
Private corporate inv. (% GDP)	14.0	14.2	13.9	12.6
Total investment (% GDP)	23.1	24.5	27.6	27.5
Growth rate GDP	5.8	7.9	5.5	5.4
ICOR	4.0	3.1	5.1	5.1
Inflation	11.3	7.0	12.5	2.2
Domestic inflation	-0.6	3.7	7.4	2.0
Current account (% GDP)	-1.5	-4.9	-5.5	-3.9
Real exchange rate (1970=100)	99.2	96.4	94.4	101.3
Trade-weighted RER (1970=100)	102.3	103.2	101.8	106.5
Real interest rate	0.5	3.9	1.7	9.6
External debt (% GDP)	10.0	12.0	24.7	33.4
Domestic PSBR (% GDP)	0.8	1.4	2.5	2.8
DCE, public sector (% GDP)	2.6	2.5	4.2	2.9
DCE, private sector (% GDP)	4.8	7.6	6.2	7.9

Note: DCE, or domestic credit expansion, is the domestic liabilities obtained from financial institutions (see Tables 3.3 and 3.4 of Chapter 3).

Figure 4.5   Public and private investment (% of GDP)

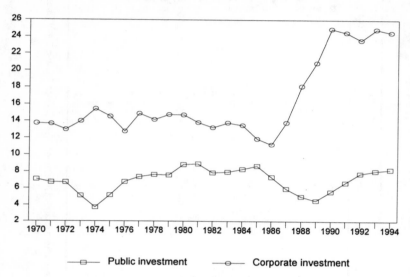

ratio also increased in these periods, but if we concentrate on non-residential private investment the picture is different. The investment ratio of private corporations increased from period I to II, but fell back in period III. Thus, in period II both public and private corporate investment were rising, and total productive investment was increasing. In this period the GDP growth rate also improved. In period III there was crowding out of corporate investment, although the total investment ratio continued to rise. But the growth rate fell. The period 1983–86 is the period of structural adjustment: both the public sector and the private corporate investment ratios decreased, and the growth rate continued to stagnate at its low level.

It is interesting to look behind the medium-term averages of Table 4.4. In Figure 4.5 the trends of the public and private corporate investment ratios are plotted. It is clear that in the early 1970s, the 1980s and the 1990s the change in the two ratios was almost always in opposite directions. Only in the late 1970s was there no trade-off between the two ratios: in this period the increase in public investment was accompanied by first a rise and then stability in the level of the private corporate investment ratio. The continued high level of the public investment ratio in the period 1980–85 was associated with a decrease in the corporate investment ratio to an all-time low in 1986. After 1985 the decrease in the public investment ratio was more than compensated by the rise of the private corporate investment ratio. When public investment recovered after 1988, corporate investment came down somewhat from its extremely high level.

Table 4.4 shows that the increase in public expenditures was associated with an acceleration of domestic inflation, first rather mildly in period II, but then more strongly in period III. Of course, in these years international inflation was also very high. To correct for this, domestic inflation is measured as the increase in consumer prices corrected for the impact of international price changes. The real interest rate (i.e. the nominal interbank rate minus total inflation) remained relatively modest in periods II and III, and increased substantially only in the fourth period.

With the acceleration of inflation, the real exchange rate appreciated (see Figure 4.3). However, the real exchange rate gives an incomplete picture. The trade-weighted real exchange rate in fact depreciated between 1974 and 1979, due to the relative decrease of the US dollar in these years. After 1979, however, the trade-weighted real exchange rate also started to appreciate. In these years the appreciation of the US dollar, together with the increase in the relative price of Thai products, caused a significant decrease in the competitiveness of Thai exporters.

The expansion of public spending was partly financed by external loans, but claims on domestic financial markets also increased: the domestic credit expansion (DCE) to the public sector increased in period III, and the credit growth for the private sector decreased. Whether this is due to credit rationing or to a decline in the private demand for credit is difficult to say. It can be noted that the average real interest rate was quite low in period III, suggesting that there were no great tensions on the financial markets. Table 3.4 of Chapter 3 showed that in these years the private corporate sector obtained more funds from non-financial domestic sources and from abroad. In this way, they could compensate for the decline in the supply of domestic credit.

The predicted balance-of-payments problems did indeed arise: the current-account deficit rose to high levels in periods II and III and, with it, the external debt ratio increased rapidly.

The years up to the early 1980s thus showed a mixed picture: the private investment demand was faced with contradictory factors. The high level of public investment created infrastructure and stimulated domestic demand. The acceleration of inflation and the high current-account deficit are further indications of an excess demand situation. The appreciation of the real exchange rate made (imported) capital goods cheaper. Along with these positive effects, however, a number of negative effects occurred. Domestic credit markets tightened up. The appreciation of the real exchange rate undermined the profitability of the traded goods sector; in the end the export ratio even decreased between 1980 and 1984. Private investors' confidence was undermined by the growing domestic instability – as reflected in inflation, current-account deficits and public sector imbalances – and by the rapidly rising external debt overhang.[12]

In summary, it can be concluded that the interaction between external finance, public sector activity and the private sector is very complex. Firstly, an increase in public investment may affect the *need* for private investment. Investment by government and state enterprises may take over activities that used to be provided for by the private sector. Of course, this process can also be reversed. Particularly in the most recent years, there have been attempts at privatization, with the private sector assuming responsibility for activities previously carried out by the public sector.

Secondly, an increase in public investment may affect the *desire* for private investment when the increasing role of the state dampens or increases private profit expectations. If the growth of public investment is accompanied by a rising domestic and external-debt burden and an appreciation of the real exchange rate, or if financing demands of the state push up interest rates, the private sector's investment demand may weaken. Alternatively, the demand and supply conditions created by public investments may create profitable investment opportunities for the private sector.

And, thirdly, a rise in public investment may affect the *ability* of the private sector to invest. Public investment can forcefully reduce private investment when it exerts priority claims on scarce factors, such as foreign exchange, construction capacity, skilled personnel or domestic financial resources.

It is quite difficult to assess which of these factors hold true for Thailand. The first factor mentioned – the need for private investment – may not be so relevant for the period of the public sector loan boom. Public investments in these years were largely restricted to traditional public sector concerns such as physical and social infrastructure and public utilities, activities that support, rather than compete with, private sector activities. But the reverse case may be more relevant: the retreat of the public sector in recent years has opened many opportunities for the private sector in activities that used to be dominated by the public sector.

In assessing the impact of public sector investment on the private sector's investment demand, one should realize that the level of desired investment is also dependent on other factors. Particularly in period III, when private corporate investment dropped significantly, the external factors were quite ominous. The world economy in those years was shocked by a rise in oil prices and interest rates, and the growth of world trade stagnated (see Figure 4.1). These factors together resulted in a poor growth performance of Thailand in this period. One would expect such events to have a negative impact on private investment demand in an open economy like that of Thailand. In period IV, however, the world economy recovered somewhat: one would expect that this would have stimulated private sector's investment demand. But in fact private corporate investment dropped further in those years. It is quite likely that in this period the great macroeconomic imbalances of the Thai economy negatively affected the expectations of the private sector. Economic growth in this period was relatively slow, and there was a large public sector deficit, a rising external debt burden and an overvalued currency. The real interest rate was high, partly due to the high public sector demand for domestic finance, and partly due to the need to support the overvalued baht.

There is little evidence that the private sector could not realize the desired level of investment. There was no foreign exchange rationing, there were no apparent shortages on the construction or labour markets, nor was there evidence of rationing of private sector credit demand on the financial markets. As Table 3.4 in Chapter 3 has shown, liabilities incurred by private corporations with domestic financial institutions declined as percentages of GDP declined in period III, but recovered in the subsequent period. The private corporations incurred substantial 'other domestic liabilities' as well as foreign liabilities, and acquired substantial 'other financial assets' in periods III and IV, indicating the acquisition of assets outside the private sector. These patterns do suggest that, while credit from financial institutions may have been limited or expensive, private corporations could easily shift to other liabilities.

It can also be observed in Table 3.4 that the household sector reduced its acquisition of 'other financial assets' in period III and increased its deposits with financial institutions. These 'other assets' of the household sector consist largely of share capital provided to private corporations. As the links between the corporate and the household sector are direct and at a personal level, it could be suggested that, had corporations wanted to invest more, they would have been able to obtain more resources from the household sector in the form of direct transfers, e.g. in the form of share capital.

It can be concluded that the crowding-out that occurred in periods III and IV was caused more by the effects on the private sector's desire to invest than by the effects on the sector's ability to invest.

Section 4.3 and this section have analysed the macroeconomic impact of capital inflows as they occurred since 1975. On the basis of theoretical arguments and empirical analysis, the main ways in which the capital inflows affected the economy can now be summarized. The rise in capital flows invited an increase in public investment and a decline in the public savings ratio. In fact, the PSBR increased strongly, and claims by the public sector on domestic financial markets increased as well, leading eventually to tensions on these markets and to high interest rates. The capital inflows and the higher level of public spending created demand pressures which were partly reflected in an acceleration of inflation and in an appreciation of the real exchange rate. The anti-export bias was further strengthened by the fact that investment shifted to the public sector and thus to non-traded activities.

The international loans accumulated in an external debt, and gradually the debt-service burden increased, adding to the balance-of-payments problem. The debt servicing on the growing government debt aggravated the budget problems.

Initially, the positive effects dominated. The expansion of demand induced higher private investment. With the high level of investment, growth also increased, which explains the growth boom of 1976–78. Gradually, however, the negative elements took over. The tight money market with the high interest rate, the appreciating real exchange rate, stagnating exports, the growing debt burden and the large current-account deficits all combined to reduce private corporate investment demand and to slow down economic growth.

However, the poor performance of the Thai economy in the early 1980s cannot be fully attributed to the impact of external finance. Obviously, the external shocks of 1979/80 and the poor condition of the world economy in the early 1980s also contributed, and it is difficult to separate the impact of the systemic effects of international capital inflows from the impact of the external shocks in the historical account. In Chapter 6 the CGE model will be used to investigate this question further. One simulation made with the model analyses the impact of an increase in government spending. Such an increase stimulates the economy, induces higher levels of private investment, and accelerates growth. It also leads to higher inflation, an appreciating real exchange rate and to current-account problems. Towards the end of the simulation period, the balance-of-payments problem becomes very serious, the external debt explodes and the central bank runs out of foreign reserves. These trends make clear that such an expansionary public sector policy is *not* sustainable in the long run, and the simulation confirms the actual trends as they occurred in the early 1980s. From this simulation, it can be concluded that the external shocks of the 1980s have quickened a process that would have occurred anyway.

4.5   Structural Adjustment, Thai Style

The story about the loan boom that unfolded in the previous sections can be summarized briefly. Initially, the loan boom led to an increase in total investment and an acceleration of growth, but this positive picture gradually faded as the macroeconomic performance started to suffer from growing public sector deficits, stagnating and declining private investment, an anti-export bias and stagnating exports, and a growing burden of external and domestic debt. In this experience Thailand was not alone. Similar stories have been told about many developing countries (for an overview, see Vos 1994; examples of other country studies are Vos & Yap 1996 for the Philippines, and Calderón & FitzGerald 1994 for Mexico; for a recent account of the adjustment experience in a number of Southeast Asian countries, see Talib 1993). Many developing countries experienced a loan boom in the late 1970s, and in almost all of them this boom ended in crisis in the early 1980s.

4.5.1 The international context

The crisis of the 1980s had important international causes. In 1979–80 the second oil crisis hiked up import prices for oil-importing countries like Thailand. The rapid rise in world interest rates, that started in 1979, badly hurt developing countries whose external debts consisted largely of variable-interest rate loans. The world recession of the early 1980s was reflected in a slow growth of world trade and decreasing primary commodity prices. Oil-importing and indebted developing countries were thus hit by negative shocks on both the income and the payments side of the current account.

These external shocks hit developing countries that were badly poised to deal with them. The economies were weakened by considerable domestic imbalances. The loan boom had resulted in large current-account deficits, in public sector deficits, in high debt burdens and in inflation. A number of countries with particularly severe imbalances and onerous debt burdens experienced a real 'debt crisis' when they could no longer service current debt obligations. The first of these debt crises occurred in Mexico in August 1982. As a result of the Mexico crisis, international banks rather abruptly turned away from new lending to developing countries. Thus, countries that escaped external insolvency were also affected. Their access to new loans suddenly became much more difficult, so that the current-account deficits could no longer be financed.

The severe crisis and the sudden halt in commercial lending forced developing countries to turn to official financial flows, in particular to the IMF and World Bank. The World Bank responded to that need by creating a new form of lending, Structural Adjustment Loans (SALs), programme loans with policy conditions attached to them. The growing dependence of developing countries on the IMF and World Bank made the policy views of these agencies increasingly dominant.

The two Washington agencies' view on structural adjustment – Lance Taylor calls it, somewhat mischievously, the Washington Consensus, or 'WC' (Taylor 1993) – can be summarized in three steps (see e.g. World Bank 1990, Mosley et al. 1991, Taylor 1993).

Firstly, the diagnosis of the Washington agencies is that the typical developing country in the 1980s was facing unsustainable macroeconomic imbalances, as reflected in large current-account deficits, fiscal deficits and high rates of inflation. Moreover, excessive government intervention created distortions in many markets. For instance, trade barriers and overvalued exchange rates were responsible for anti-export bias, public subsidies resulted in inefficient use of resources and in fiscal deficits, and controlled financial systems failed to ensure an efficient allocation of investment funds. These distortions were considered to undermine the efficiency of resource allocation and resource use, and to keep the level of output below what could have been achieved.

Secondly, from this diagnosis followed the prescribed cure. Structural adjustment has two main tasks: to restore macroeconomic stability and to increase efficiency. Stabilization is seen as an absolute precondition for the recovery of economic growth. The key to stabilization is public sector financial reform. This takes the form of

(a) tight expenditure controls on public investments, but also on current spending (e.g. on subsidies);

(b) tax reforms to effectuate a broadly based tax system, preferably with modest marginal rates to avoid distortions;

(c) privatization of state enterprises;

(d) tight monetary policy: the fight against inflation will be impossible as long as the public sector deficit remains large, but even with public sector financial reform, tight monetary policy remains an essential part of the package.

Thirdly, stabilization constitutes an essential precondition for recovery, but it will not be sufficient. The restoration of sustainable growth requires 'structural adjustment', i.e. the creation of an efficient market economy, in which the private sector can assume its dynamic role of creating income and wealth. Reforms in many areas have been proposed. They may be summarized in three points:

(e) price reforms to eradicate government intervention in the determination of domestic prices for, for instance, agricultural commodities or energy;

(f) trade reform: the removal of trade barriers and the reduction of import tariffs will help to increase the efficiency of domestic markets.

Devaluation and export incentives should remove the anti-export bias. A welcoming attitude towards foreign investment is recommended;

(g) a liberalization of the financial system, consisting of removal of controls on, and an increase in, (real) interest rates. This is expected to improve the allocation of resources and to increase savings.

The policy views of the Washington agencies, as summarized in points (a) to (g) above, were reflected in the policy conditions attached to the Stand-by Agreements of the IMF and the SALs of the World Bank. Thailand was also subjected to these conditions, as it received support from the IMF in the form of Stand-by Agreements in 1981, 1982 and 1985 (Robinson et al. 1991: 9) and from the World Bank through SALs in 1982 and 1983 (Mosley et al. 1991).

4.5.2 The Thai experience

To analyse Thailand's adjustment to the shocks of the 1980s, it is useful to look back at an earlier period. Severe external shocks hit the economy in the period 1970–74 (see section 4.2 above and Figure 4.1). These shocks were severe not only because of their relative size, but also because they followed a period of strong expansion and relative stability of the world economy. The oil price increase did have immediate impact on domestic prices. Inflation went up from 0.3 and 5.1 per cent, in 1971 and 1972 respectively, to 15.4 and 24.4 per cent in 1973 and 1974. This acceleration of inflation invited an immediate and strong policy reaction in the form of a tight fiscal and monetary policy. Real government expenditure declined sharply in 1973 and 1974 (see Table 4.5 below). The government spending ratio was brought down from 17.7 per cent in 1971 to 12.6 per cent in 1974, while the government revenue ratio increased, resulting first in a smaller fiscal deficit and then in a small surplus in 1974. Interest rates were increased in this period, as the domestic loan and deposit ceilings were raised from 14 and 6 per cent in 1972 to 15 and 8 per cent in 1974. The bank rate of the Bank of Thailand was also increased in 1973, and again in 1974. Despite these increases in the nominal rates, given the high inflation rates, the real interest rates in 1973 and 1974 were negative.

The policy reaction to the external shocks of the early 1970s was very much a 'shock' reaction to unanticipated external shocks, and, with the benefit of hindsight, it can be said to have been an over-reaction. The increase in import prices (particularly oil) had been accompanied by an increase in prices of Thai exports, and the international recession that followed the first oil shock was mild and short-lived. Hence, the adverse impact of the external shocks on the Thai economy was probably less than the adverse impact of the contractionary policies.

The policy response to the shocks around 1980 and the structural adjustment efforts of Thailand in subsequent years have been analysed in detail in several studies (see e.g. Bank of Thailand 1992, Leeahtam 1991, Robinson et al. 1991, Sahasakul et al. 1989, Uathavikul et al. 1987).

The initial response to the 1979–80 shocks was half-hearted. Unlike in the first oil crisis, when public expenditure had been sharply curtailed, this time public spending continued to grow, financed by an increasing level of capital inflows from abroad. The capital inflows were dominated by foreign loans, directed mostly towards the public sector, in particular towards the state enterprises.

In response to the worldwide increase in interest rates and the low liquidity on the domestic financial market in 1979 and 1980, the government raised the ceiling of loan and deposit interest rates at commercial banks by 3 percentage points in early 1980, and further by 1 per cent in 1981. Still, due to the high rate of inflation, real interest rates were strongly negative in 1980. They turned positive thereafter, and rose to very high real levels in 1983 and 1984. To stimulate exports, and to compensate for the rising value of the dollar and the poor world market prices for primary commodities, the government decided to devalue the baht against the US dollar by 8.7 per cent in July 1981, following a smaller devaluation of 1.07 per cent in April of the same year. The move was strongly criticized in both Parliament and the mass media, and the uproar did not subside until the departure of the finance minister (see Uathavikul et al. 1987: 42). However, as the baht remained tied to the dollar, the effect of the devaluation was largely offset by the continued appreciation of the US dollar against other major currencies. In fact, the trade-weighted real exchange rate appreciated during the period 1979–83, resulting in a decrease in Thailand's competitiveness in the world market. The export ratio stagnated in these years, also due to the poor growth of world demand.

The main policy problem in these years was the large public sector deficit, as the public sector borrowing requirement hovered around 6 per cent of GDP. Attempts to deal with this problem were largely unsuccessful until the mid-1980s. Government expenditures and state enterprise investment remained at high levels throughout the period 1980–85. The ratio of government revenue to GDP increased, but only very slowly, due to a series of *ad hoc* policy measures (see Leeahtam 1991). The only bright spot was the improvement of the financial performance of the state enterprises. The domestic oil prices were progressively raised to bring them more or less in line with the international prices, the electricity price was increased by 17 per cent in October 1980 and 16 per cent in January 1981, and bus and train fares were increased in January 1981. This was designed to correct serious price distortion and to encourage energy conservation, as well as to increase the state enterprises' income and savings.

The policy mix of lax fiscal and tight monetary policy was successful in some respects. The domestic inflation rate dropped rapidly from 19.8 per cent in 1980 to 5.2 per cent in 1982, and the current-account deficit decreased to merely 2.8 per cent of GDP in 1982. But the public sector imbalances remained high.

It was gradually becoming clear that this adjustment to the second oil shock was leading to an unsustainable situation. The public sector imbalances were huge, the external debt was rapidly rising and the debt-service burden had increased with the hike in world interest rates, export earnings were not growing rapidly enough, and private investment was decreasing, leading to poor growth rates.

Like many other countries, Thailand took recourse to the IMF and the World Bank to agree on a structural adjustment program and obtain a structural adjustment loan (SAL). The 1981 Stand-by Agreement with the IMF aimed to reduce the public sector deficit and to restore international competitiveness. The increase in state enterprise tariffs and the 1981 devaluation were signs of these attempts. But the fiscal reforms proposed were largely unsuccessful.

The policy packages under the 1982 and 1983 SALs contained a long list of measures (for a full list of policy conditions see the relevant tables in Sahasakul et al. 1989). It would seem fair to say that the IMF Stand-by Agreement and the two SALs concentrated on:

(a) public sector financial reform: the main measures were to impose expenditure discipline, to improve tax administration, to increase state enterprise tariffs, and to lower ceilings for public sector external borrowing;

(b) export promotion: measures included the devaluation of 1981, the removal of export quota for cassava, maize and sugar, the reduction of export taxes on rice and rubber, tax incentives for industrial exports, improved operation of the customs department and import duty reform.

Not all of these measures were effectively implemented.[13] Public sector financial reform, in particular, turned out to be a difficult and slow process. The tax ratio started to increase somewhat after 1982, but government savings remained negative or negligible up to 1986, as current spending continued to increase.

Table 4.5 presents the level of government expenditures in constant prices. It shows that government investment stabilized after 1980 in real terms, and declined as a percentage of GDP. But control over current spending was less effective. Real current expenditure continued to increase up until 1985–86. The ratio of total government expenditures to GDP also continued to increase, reaching its peak at 18.9 per cent of GDP in 1985 (see Figure 4.2), despite stated aims to reduce the ratio.[14] State enterprise investment also continued to expand up to 1985, so that total public sector expenditure increased significantly. Public utilities price reforms led to higher state enterprise savings. The growth of government revenue and of state enterprise savings was not so strong as to compensate for the increase in spending. As a result, the public sector investment-savings gap, as a percentage of GDP, remained high up to 1985.

Fiscal performance in these years suffered from two weaknesses (see Leeahtam 1991). The first was that budgets were based on ambitious revenue estimates based on overly optimistic economic growth targets. As a result, expenditure continued to grow, but in all years between 1980 and 1986 actual revenue fell short of budget estimates.

The second hindrance to fiscal reform was the lack of effective expenditure control. There were several reasons for this. Government

Table 4.5   *Government spending (billion bahts, at constant 1970 prices)*

	Total expend-iture	Current expenditure		Capital expend-iture	Revenue
		Total	excl. interest payment		
1970	25.1	17.2	15.6	7.9	18.8
1971	27.5	19.0	17.0	8.5	19.5
1972	27.1	19.8	17.5	7.4	20.4
1973	26.1	19.8	17.1	6.2	21.5
1974	23.3	19.1	16.3	4.2	25.8
1975	28.8	22.4	19.0	6.5	25.2
1976	35.2	25.8	22.5	9.4	26.6
1977	38.1	28.3	24.6	9.8	31.1
1978	40.8	30.8	26.1	10.6	34.3
1979	43.3	34.0	28.8	9.4	38.1
1980	51.9	40.5	34.6	11.4	41.0
1981	52.8	41.7	34.1	11.2	44.3
1982	59.2	47.4	39.4	11.7	43.7
1983	60.7	50.0	41.0	10.8	52.1
1984	65.3	55.4	45.1	9.9	53.1
1985	70.1	58.5	46.8	11.6	56.3
1986	70.5	59.9	45.9	10.6	58.6
1987	69.8	59.5	47.4	10.3	66.6
1988	69.4	60.2	47.7	9.2	80.3
1989	77.3	66.3	53.4	11.0	95.9
1990	84.4	69.1	58.0	15.3	114.1
1991	94.9	73.1	65.1	20.6	121.2
1992	111.4	83.5	74.9	29.1	128.7
1993	126.9	88.6	82.5	38.3	140.0
1994	135.0	92.2	87.1	42.8	158.4

Note: Government expenditure and revenue, deflated by the GDP deflator.

investment was already low, and current spending consisted mainly of salaries, which are difficult to cut. Moreover, in these years interest payments on the government debt increased sharply. Altogether, the government had to use more than 21 per cent of its current expenditure for interest payments in 1986. This share had doubled since the latter part of the 1970s. But the budget bureau also lacked effective control over cash expenditure. Budget allocations were made to government departments and agencies, and these spending units could carry unspent monies over to next years. The result was an absence of central control over actual cash expenditures during any one year.

As a result of these two weaknesses, the budget deficit remained high. Each year from 1981 to 1986, when the budget deficit appeared to exceed the target, discretionary measures were introduced to contain the deficit. Such packages typically concentrated on revenue measures, including *ad hoc* increases in import duties. The expenditure cuts included in these packages were rarely successful (see Leeahtam 1991 for the measures included in each of these packages).

Around 1985 the government shifted to another, more effective way of controlling the public sector budget. Strict total expenditure ceilings were included in the formulation of the budget, and the use of carried-over funds was limited. These policies started to have an effect on total government spending in 1986 and 1987.

To deal with the emerging external debt problem and to control public investment, the government tried to limit public sector external borrowing. After its peak in 1981, the net inflows of foreign funds to the public sector (as a percentage of GDP) declined. The government had adjusted its ceiling on annual public sector external borrowing in 1983 (from 2.6 to 2 billion dollars per year) (see Sahasakul et al. 1989), and reduced the ceiling more decisively in 1985 (to 1 billion dollars per year). This was an effective measure to control state enterprises' foreign borrowing as well as the foreign loans for military procurement. Consequently, the ratio of foreign debt to GDP and to exports, and the debt-service ratio reached their peaks in 1985 and thereafter gradually declined. The loan ceiling was effective in bringing down the investment by state enterprises, which decreased sharply after its peak in 1985.

The result of these measures was that total real government spending stagnated between 1986 and 1988 (Table 4.5). Moreover, the state en-

terprise investment ratio fell sharply after 1985 (see Appendix Table
A3.1). The state enterprise savings ratio had continuously improved
since 1981. With the recovery of economic growth in 1987 government
revenue and government savings also improved.[15] The budget deficit
decreased from 3 per cent of GDP in 1986 to 0.8 per cent in 1987 and
a surplus in 1988. The total public sector borrowing requirement (of
government and state enterprises) had been around 6 per cent of GDP
in the years 1980–82 and close to 5 per cent during 1983–86. The
PSBR fell to about zero in 1987, just in time so that the private investment boom, which started in 1987, was not hampered by public sector
claims on domestic financial resources.

As the decline in foreign borrowing by the public sector, which started in 1982, was initially not accompanied by a decrease in the public
sector borrowing requirement, domestic financing had to increase
sharply to fill the gap. The increase in domestic borrowing by the public sector resulted in a tight situation at the domestic financial markets.
The monetary policy was, on the whole, contractionary. Despite the
lower interest rate in the international financial market after 1982, the
authorities still maintained the high interest-rate policy, hoping that it
would stimulate savings and attract foreign capital inflows. The real
deposit rate of interest on savings deposits was around 12 per cent in
1984! As a consequence, the domestic interest rate was significantly
higher than the international rate, stimulating the private sector to
borrow abroad.

The temporary recovery of private business in 1983 led commercial
banks to increase credit to the private sector at an extremely high
growth rate of 36 per cent. As a result of this private spending boom,
together with the large public sector deficit, the current-account deficit
increased sharply, reaching 7.2 per cent of GDP. In order to reduce the
increasing current-account deficit, the Bank of Thailand imposed a
credit expansion ceiling of 18 per cent for commercial banks in 1984.

Monetary policy in this period faced several difficulties. Given the
high level of the current-account deficit, a tight monetary policy to control aggregate expenditure was desirable. But the implementation of this
policy met with a number of difficulties.

The first of these was the weak state of the financial system. Excessive speculation on the stock market in the late 1970s had resulted in
the SET crash of 1979, and the collapse of one finance company and

severe problems for many others. The recession and the devaluation of 1981 further affected the health of financial institutions and led to a further crisis in 1983, which affected a large number of finance companies and a few commercial banks. The central bank was forced to come to the rescue and had to pump liquidity into the system to keep it afloat (see Bank of Thailand 1992).

Secondly, with the appreciation of the real exchange rate, the baht was increasingly overvalued. Export growth slowed down, but pressures to devalue were resisted. A high interest rate was necessary to support the currency and to attract capital from abroad to finance the current-account deficit.

The high interest-rate policy induced private companies to borrow abroad, where funds were cheaper. Table 3.1 of Chapter 3 has shown that in the period 1983–86 private short-term borrowing abroad was relatively high. More detailed data show that this foreign borrowing was particularly high in 1984, when domestic real interest rates were very high and the credit ceiling controlled domestic credit growth. The escape valve to abroad meant, however, that domestic monetary policy was not so effective in controlling the economy.

With the low level of private spending in 1985 and 1986, and the declining PSBR in these years, the financial markets became more liquid. In 1986, the private corporate investment ratio reached its lowest level since 1970. Private investment demand suffered from the poor external conditions and from the poor growth record in these years. Confidence was further undermined by the public sector imbalances, the high interest rates, the overvalued exchange rate and the external debt overhang. The fiscal contraction that started in 1985–86 may have further discouraged private investment. Monetary policy did not do much to counterbalance these negative factors. Only in 1986 did the Bank of Thailand decrease the interest ceilings for commercial banks' deposits and loans as well as its own bank rate. It could do so since global interest rates had decreased, and the low level of economic activity had reduced credit demand and had thus led to considerable liquidity on financial markets. However, in the face of the contractionary fiscal policy, the lower interest rates could do little to stimulate the economy. In the end the central bank had to issue bonds to soak up the excess liquidity.

A major obstacle to the economic recovery was the overvalued exchange rate. The baht was tied to the dollar, which was steeply appreciating *vis-à-vis* the other major currencies. As a result, the trade-weighted real exchange rate appreciated, undermining export competitiveness. The growing current-account deficit and the sharp decline in international reserves, to less than 2 months of imports in 1984, eventually led to the devaluation of the baht by 14.8 per cent against the US dollar in November 1984. The IMF encouraged the devaluation (see Sahasakul et al. 1989: 6). The international encouragement and commitment helped the government to overcome political obstacles and to have the policy implemented.

In 1985 the 'Plaza Agreement' between the world's main economies followed, leading to a depreciation of the dollar. The 1984 baht devaluation had been used to switch Thailand's exchange rate system from being pegged to the US dollar only to being pegged to a basket of currencies. Under this new system, the weighting scheme was based on the relative importance of the countries as Thailand's trade partners. In this scheme the dollar accounted for about 50 per cent. The weighting scheme was adjusted after the Plaza Agreement, when the dollar was given more weight in the basket, around 80–85 per cent. Thus, while the 1984 baht devaluation against the dollar had been only 14.8 per cent, the dollar depreciation *vis-à-vis* other major currencies meant that the baht was eventually depreciated by about 30 per cent with respect to the currencies of other major trading partners. The substantial depreciation of the trade-weighted real exchange rate between 1984 and 1988 put an end to an era of overvaluation, and contributed to the export boom in the following period.

The implementation of the structural adjustment package was, on the whole, mixed and confused. The two main problems – the public sector financial imbalance and the overvalued exchange rate – were dealt with hesitantly and with delays. The slow response of public sector financial policies is surprising, considering the experience of the sharp and quick reaction to the first oil shock, which suggested that drastic fiscal policy action is possible. A possible explanation for the slow response is that in the early 1980s the political climate was less stable and less supportive of drastic action (see Leeahtam 1991).

As the public sector did not 'adjust' in the early 1980s, and maintained substantial deficits, the 'adjustment' was enforced in the form of declining and low private investment. This reduction was not so much enforced through credit or foreign exchange rationing, but more through variables like external and internal debt overhang, high interest rates, and declining confidence, which reduced private sector investment demand.

With regard to the exchange rate policy, a similar story emerges. Here, there had been some early action with the devaluation of 1981. But the effects of this devaluation were short-lived, as they were wiped out by the appreciation of the dollar to which the baht was tied. Further devaluation was resisted in 1983 and throughout most of 1984 (Leeahtam 1991). The overvalued baht was defended by high domestic interest rates and, in 1984, by ceilings on domestic credit growth. Not until November 1984 was the baht devalued, and even then the devalulation met with substantial political protests. This resistance came from those who feared that a devaluation would increase import prices (for example of military hardware) and thus lead to inflation, and from those who argued that volatility of the exchange rate would deter domestic and foreign investors. Clearly, a devaluation also increased the domestic currency cost of external-debt servicing. Subsequent events did not prove the opponents of the devaluation right. Inflation in 1984 and 1985 remained very low, and, helped by the subsequent further depreciation of the real exchange rate, the devaluation contributed to the growth of exports after the very poor export level of 1983.

Monetary policy was more consistently contractionary, with the exception of 1983, but its effectiveness was undermined by the fact that domestic loan rates far exceeded international rates, inviting the private sector to borrow abroad.

In conclusion, important policy changes were set in motion: public sector financial reform was initiated, and a much more active and supportive exchange rate policy was developed. It is remarkable that, when decisive action was undertaken, its effects were almost immediate. By the end of 1986 the Thai economy was more or less approaching balance in the following aspects.

(a) The government budget deficit was reduced from 4.9 per cent of GDP in 1982 to 3.0 per cent in 1986 and 0.8 per cent in 1987. The total public sector borrowing requirement had decreased, from its peak of 6.3 per cent of GDP in 1981, to 3.2 per cent in 1986 and to a very small surplus in 1987.

(b) The current-account deficit was substantially reduced from about 7 per cent in 1983 to a small surplus of 0.6 per cent of GDP in 1986, and to a very small deficit in 1987.

(c) The external debt-GDP ratio reached a peak of 39.2 per cent in 1985, and declined thereafter. The debt-service ratio declined as well after 1985 (see Figure 4.4).

(d) The cautious monetary policies helped to keep inflation low: the inflation rate in 1986 was only 1.8 per cent. The low domestic inflation implied that the nominal devaluation of the baht and the fluctuations of the nominal exchange rates of trading partners were translated into a depreciation of the real exchange rate. This was reflected in an improvement of the export ratio. The surplus on the current account of 1986, however, should be mainly ascribed to the poor state of the economy, particularly to the very low level of private investment, which reduced the demand for imports.

It is interesting to note that the Thai structural adjustment programme contained elements of the IMF/World Bank package – summarized in seven points in section 4.5.1 above – but also had some surprising variations.

The focus has been on public sector financial reforms. Action to control expenditures was slow in coming. Not until 1985 could political resistance be overcome and stricter expenditure controls on government and state enterprises be effectuated. On the revenue side, earlier action can be noted. From 1981 onwards, the rates and tariffs of state enterprises (including oil, telephone, water, transport) were adjusted. Government revenues were increased by a number of *ad hoc* tax measures. Ironically, these included surcharges on import duties, contrary to the trade liberalization drift of the World Bank views. Furthermore, in 1985 and 1986 some small state enterprises were privatized (Leeahtam 1991: 110).

A number of specific export-promoting measures were included in the two SALs, but their impact was not strong enough to neutralize the dampening effect of the overvalued exchange rate. Exports could recover only after the 1984 devaluation.

In general, monetary policy was tight, but its effectiveness became increasingly questionable. The high domestic interest rates, combined with the growing integration with international financial markets, invited capital inflows from abroad (see Robinson et al. 1991), thus reducing the effectiveness of monetary policies.

It would thus appear that, with regard to stabilization policies, Thailand followed the general lines of the IMF/World Bank approach (i.e. points (a) to (d) of the IMF/World Bank package described in of section 4.5.1). Though there were some delays, by 1985–86 significant and drastic policy action was underway. However, there is little evidence that Thailand really engaged in 'structural adjustment'.

Section 4.5.1 summarized adjustment measures under three headings: price, trade and financial reforms. Price reforms included the removal of subsidies implied in the low state enterprise tariffs of around 1980, and the reduction and removal, in 1986, of the export tax on rice. The two SALs contained policy conditions to simplify and lower the import duty structure, but throughout the entire period no progress was made in implementing these (Robinson et al. 1991). In fact, some import duties were increased for revenue purposes. Some specific tax incentives were introduced to compensate for the anti-export bias of the protection structure.

Reforms of the financial system were not even mentioned in the two SALs and none were undertaken by the government. It is surprising that no policy conditions in this area were included in the SALs, for the World Bank had clear proposals on this topic. In 1983, it had issued a report, *Thailand, Perspectives for Financial Reform*, which proposed, for instance, to remove interest rate ceilings, to remove the subsidies implied in the selective credit schemes or, better still, to abolish such schemes, and to facilitate the entry of new (also foreign) financial institutions to increase competition and enforce efficiency (World Bank 1983). It is possible that such proposals were not implemented because of the resistance of the powerful Thai banking lobby. It is also possible that the authorities found that the time was not ripe. As noted above, the Thai financial system had been hit by a number of crises. All in all, the financial system of the early 1980s hardly looked like a system that could cope with an increase in competition.

It may thus be concluded that the adjustment efforts of the 1980s were dominated by conventional stabilization measures, rather than by

structural reforms. The liberalization of trade and finance that characterized structural adjustment in many other developing countries, was
absent in Thailand. It could, of course, be argued that there was less
need for such reforms, as the distortions were much less serious than
they were in other countries. But it should be noted that the attempts
of the IMF and the World Bank to effectuate such reforms were resisted. It was only much later, after the years of double-digit growth in the
late 1980s, that Thailand engaged in structural reforms. This suggests
that the influence of the IMF and the World Bank on Thai structural
adjustment policies has been more limited than it has been in many
other developing countries. The original timetable agreed upon by
Thailand and the World Bank had involved a series of five SALs, but
after two SALs Thailand decided to stop.[16] The 1985 Stand-by Facility
with the IMF was interrupted by Thailand half-way. The reason for this
self-confident behaviour was that Thailand was never so financially
dependent on the Fund and the Bank as to have to accept unpalatable
policy conditions or embarrassments. Moreover, Thailand was increasingly determined not to increase its public sector external debt, including its debt with the Washington agencies.

It may also be concluded that the adjustment policies of the early
1980s were typically 'Thai'. Traditionally, Thai economic policies were
conservative. The primary concern is the stability of prices and the
exchange rate. Cautious fiscal and, particularly, monetary policies are
used to ensure stability. If possible, structural reforms are implemented
gradually, not only because of the resistance of vested interests, but
also because of the cautious nature of economic technocrats.

After the years of double-digit growth had strengthened the economy
and the position of economic technocrats, significant reforms were undertaken. Tax reforms included the reduction, in 1991, of the personal
and corporate income tax rates, and in January 1992, after years of hes-
itation and resistance, the introduction of a value added tax. The central
bank prepared a 'Three-year Financial Reform Plan' to be implemented
in 1990–92. In 1990 Thailand accepted the obligations of Article VIII
of the IMF Articles of Agreement. In 1991 international capital transactions were liberalized. In 1992 ceilings on interest rates were fully
abolished. And at the end of 1992 the Bangkok International Banking
Facility was opened, allowing domestic and foreign financial institutions to engage in off-shore international borrowing and lending (see

Robinson et al. 1991 and Bank of Thailand 1992). As a result, in the years following 1990 there was a significant liberalization of the financial markets.

Trade liberalization also started in 1990, with the reduction of the import tariffs on capital goods. In 1991 and 1994 import duties on numerous other goods were reduced or removed. The total import duties, which had increased from 10.3 per cent of total merchandise imports in 1980 to 12.2 per cent in 1985, had dropped to 8.7 per cent in 1994.

The 'benefits' and 'costs' of the period of loan boom and structural adjustment are difficult to assess. Comparison of the economic growth over the ten-year period from 1976 to 1985 to the long-term average (see Figure 1.1 in Chapter 1) shows that there are three years of above average growth (1976–78) and seven years of below average growth (1979–85). The average growth rate for the entire ten-year period is lower than the longer-run average, but not much. Of course, the external shocks of 1979–80 and the world recession of 1980–82 are, to a considerable extent, responsible for the poor growth record in these years. However, since 1983 the external conditions improved. Could Thailand have recovered sooner? It could be argued that in 1983 and 1984 recovery was held back by the imbalances in the economy and by the overvalued exchange rate, and that in 1985 and 1986 the contractionary public sector policies were responsible for the poor growth rates. It should always be remembered that even during the years of recession (1979–86), Thailand experienced an average growth rate of 5.4 per cent per year, poor by Thai standards but well above the best performance of many developing countries and better than the growth performance of most other ASEAN countries.

It should also be mentioned that the public sector investment boom of this period helped to create an infrastructure of public utilities that helped Thailand to absorb the enormous levels of private investment in the subsequent period without much difficulty, and helped to reduce Thailand's dependency on imported energy.[17]

Almost inevitably, the recession and the adjustment policies involved a social cost. Poverty, which had been decreasing from the early 1960s until 1980, increased again. In 1975, 32 per cent of the population lived below the poverty line. By 1981 that proportion had dropped to 24 per cent, but in 1986 it had again increased to 30 per cent (Krongkaew 1993). In the early 1980s income inequality also increased significantly. To a considerable extent, the deterioration of the income position of the poor should be attributed to the poor performance of the agricultural sector in these years. This poor performance is generally ascribed to the poor world market prices in 1984–85. But government policies, in particular the overvalued exchange rate, will also have contributed. After the devaluation of 1984 and the recovery of the world market prices, the incidence of poverty decreased, and by 1988, it had decreased to a level below that of 1981.

Although stabilization in Thailand was delayed, it did come in time. As noted above, by 1987 stabilization had been completed, just in time for Thailand to be ready for the upsurge in foreign investment, which is the subject of the next chapter.

5 The Foreign Investment Boom, 1987–94

5.1 Introduction

The second boom in foreign capital flows to the Thai economy started in 1987. Its nature was totally different from the 'loan boom' analysed in the previous chapter. A first difference was that the level of the capital inflows (as a percentage of GDP) exceeded that of the loan boom (see Figure 3.3 of Chapter 3). A more important difference was that the composition of the capital flows changed radically. Table 3.1 of Chapter 3 showed that in recent years capital flows to the public sector became negligible, so that the entire inflow of funds was directed towards the private sector. In particular, flows of direct and portfolio foreign investment surged to levels never before experienced, and there was also a sharp increase in private sector foreign borrowing. Another difference can be observed in the impact of the capital inflows on the economy. The upsurge in capital inflows was associated with a spurt of economic growth not unlike that experienced during the initial loan boom of 1976–78. But this time the growth spurt was stronger: the years 1987–90 were years of double-digit growth. And, unlike in the earlier period, they were not followed by a growth recession. After the years of double-digit growth, the growth rate decreased in the early 1990s to just over 8 per cent per year.

This second boom was initiated by, and dominated by, flows of direct foreign investment (DFI). Within one or two years, DFI flows increased to an unprecedented level. The causes for this sudden and sharp increase are found, to a large extent, in the trends of the global economy. These trends are briefly described in section 5.2.

. Section 5.3 analyses the new patterns of DFI in Thailand, emphasizing shifts in level, origin and sectoral distribution of the DFI flows.

The impact of the DFI boom on Thailand is far-reaching. The transmission channels are similar to those analysed in the previous chapter, but a number of aspects deserve special attention. Four aspects are particularly striking: the DFI boom has been associated with sharp increases in private investment and growth, in exports, in imports and in other foreign capital inflows. This chapter will analyse each of these aspects.

The first is the impact on private investment and growth. As section 5.4 shows, up to 1986 the private investment ratio remained at a level at or below 20 per cent of GDP. It now increased to a level around 30 per cent, with a peak of 34 per cent in 1990–91. With this increase, growth jumped to double-digit levels.

A second radical impact is on exports. As a substantial part of the DFI projects is in export-oriented activities, the export ratio, which had stagnated in the early 1980s, shot up from 25 per cent in 1986 to 38 per cent in 1994 (section 5.5). The increase in the import ratio was even more dramatic. In section 5.6 it is argued that the pattern of DFI-led development substantially increased the import propensity of the Thai economy.

A final aspect that needs attention is the sharp increase in foreign capital flows other than DFI. The title of this chapter characterizes the second foreign capital boom as a 'DFI boom' because the upsurge in DFI initiated the boom. When DFI inflows subsided after 1990, capital inflows continued to be very high; in these years, most of the foreign capital inflows came in other forms. In particular, long-term and short-term foreign borrowing by the private sector increased sharply, and in some years there were substantial inflows of portfolio investment funds (see section 5.7).

The final section of this chapter looks into the economic policy problems of handling such a large capital inflow and into some more structural policy problems facing the Thai economy in the 1990s.

5.2   The Global Background

After the debt crisis hit the developing world in the early 1980s, conventional wisdom was quick to consider it to have been unwise for countries to borrow so heavily from international banks or on international bond markets. Rather, countries should try to attract non-debt creating private capital inflows. Such inflows consist mainly of direct foreign investment (DFI), and to some extent of foreign portfolio investment (PFI). The perceived financial advantage of DFI is that such investments would only lead to an outflow of funds (remittances of profits) when the economy is performing well. Balance-of-payments crises due to financial obligations are thus less likely.[1]

It was also observed that, so far, the structural adjustment efforts of the 1980s had failed to lead to new patterns of sustained growth in most developing countries. In particular, it was observed that structural adjustment programmes failed to restore private investment to desirable levels (see World Bank 1990, Mosley et al. 1991, Serven & Solimano 1992). Again, it is hoped that DFI will play a useful role: the World Bank observes that 'direct foreign investment can be an important complement to the adjustment effort, especially in countries having difficulty increasing domestic savings' (World Bank 1990: 91).

Against this background of balance-of-payments problems and low levels of private investment, it is probably not surprising that in the developing countries attitudes towards DFI have shifted. Research on the impact of DFI on the host country has suggested a wide range of possible beneficial and detrimental effects. In the 1960s and 1970s, these findings led many countries to adopt a rather cautious, and sometimes an outright negative, position with respect to foreign investment. In the 1980s, however, the attitudes shifted radically towards a more welcoming policy stance. This change was due not so much to new research findings on the impact of DFI as to the economic problems facing the developing world.[2]

At the global level the flows of DFI and PFI to developing countries have indeed increased. The average annual net inflow of DFI in developing countries was around 11 billion US dollars in the period 1980–86, but in 1987 it started to increase, and by 1992 the annual net flow had risen to 43 billion dollars.

Figure 5.1 traces the flows of DFI to developing countries since 1975. It shows (i) that the level of net DFI flows to developing countries has increased since the 1970s, particularly after 1986; and (ii) that the share of Asian developing countries in total DFI flows to developing countries has increased. There was an earlier peak in DFI

Figure 5.1   Net DFI flows to developing countries (billion US dollars)

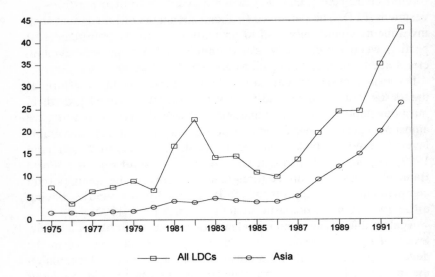

flows to developing countries in 1981–82, in which Asia did not strongly participate. After the debt crisis of 1982 there was a sharp decrease in DFI flows, but after 1986 a strong recovery set in.

The upsurge in the flows to the developing world was part of a more general increase in DFI flows worldwide in the second half of the 1980s. Although the volume of DFI flows to developing countries strongly increased, the share of developing countries in global DFI flows actually decreased from around 30 per cent in the early 1980s to around 15 per cent in the late 1980s.

The increase in the worldwide volume of direct investment flows, particularly among rich countries, reflects a global restructuring of production, captured by the term 'globalization'. Two main explanations for this process are possible (see Dunning 1995). Firstly, the growing pressures on producers to continuously introduce new products and to improve the quality of existing products requires high expenditures on research and development (R&D), which can only be recovered on wide, global, markets. Secondly, the shift in many countries to more market-oriented and outward-oriented policies has made such globalization strategies more feasible.

The flows to the Asian countries have been more stable than the overall flows and have shown a gradual increase over the years, with a significant acceleration since 1986. The share of Asian countries in total DFI flows to the developing countries increased from around 28 per cent in the period 1975–84 to around 45 per cent in the period 1985–91.[3]

It should be noted that the recent upsurge in DFI flows to developing countries is highly concentrated, among a small number of receiving countries. A few countries in Latin America (Brazil and Mexico) and Asia (Indonesia and Malaysia) together received close to 40 per cent of all flows. In the 1980s China joined this select group, so that these four countries and China received more than 50 per cent of all DFI flows to developing countries.[4] The extent of this concentration should not be exaggerated, however: all developing countries in the list of main recipients are large economies. When the DFI flows are expressed in relative terms, e.g. as percentages of GDP or the levels of their investment, the ratios of these countries are not dissimilar to those of other, smaller, developing countries (World Bank 1993).

This concentration is also characteristic of the source side of the DFI flows. Five main countries (United States, Japan, the United Kingdom, Germany and France) accounted for 79 per cent of all outflows to developing countries in the period 1970–72, for 86 per cent around 1979–81, and for 89 per cent around 1986–87 (see Kitchen 1986: 220, Brewer 1991: 9). Particularly striking is the increasing share of Japan in total DFI flows to developing countries, from only 6 per cent in 1970–72, to 11 per cent in 1979–81 and 33 per cent in 1986–87. This shift towards Japan, which further increased in subsequent years, is partly due to the appreciation of the yen, which increased the dollar value of Japanese capital outflows, but this relative price change explains only a small part of the increase in the Japanese share: even when measured in yen, the DFI outflows from Japan increased fourfold between 1985 and 1990–91.

The rapidly increasing share of Japan in global DFI flows in particular has drawn attention (see e.g. Das 1993, Tejima 1993, World Bank 1993). The large and growing current-account surpluses of Japan in the 1980s were reflected in an increase in capital outflows from Japan.

Initially, these outflows mainly took the form of short-term and long-term loans and portfolio investments, but since 1986 there has also been a sharp rise in direct investment outflows (see Healey 1991). The shift to DFI was made easier by liberalization of capital account transactions in Japan (World Bank 1993).

Two further explanations may be offered for these shifts. The first relates to the re-alignments among the major currencies that occurred after the Plaza Agreement of 1985. The Japanese yen started to appreciate in relation to the US dollar and the European currencies. Exporters thus found it increasingly difficult to compete on international markets for price-elastic commodities. A second explanation is that in Japan labour cost was rising, so that it lost some of its competitive edge, particularly in labour-intensive manufacturing. These two factors made export-oriented firms in Japan look for low-cost production opportunities elsewhere (Pongphaichit 1990, Healey 1991).

The appreciation of the yen also made foreign assets relatively cheaper and thus more attractive (Das 1993). And the good performance of the Japanese stock market (until recently) made capital relatively cheap for Japanese firms. Japanese DFI in the USA and in the European Union was furthermore motivated by the desire to service the (protected) local markets and to avoid the trade frictions that had emerged among these major trade partners.

This shift in the world's outflows of DFI in favour of Japan had a positive effect on Asia, because historically Asia had held a higher share in DFI outflows from Japan than in the outflows from other major source countries. The increase of Japanese DFI in Asian countries directly reflected the restructuring of Japanese industry after the appreciation of the yen. Within Japan there was a shift in investment towards domestic-demand based industries and to high-tech, R&D-intensive industries, and away from the low-tech and labour-intensive industries that could no longer compete internationally under the appreciated yen and the rising labour cost (Das 1993). The latter type of activities were moved to other Asian countries.

Similar processes of appreciation of the currency and rising labour cost occurred in the Asian NICs, in particular in Korea and Taiwan, and gave rise to an outflow of DFI from these countries to other Asian countries, particularly to the ASEAN countries Indonesia, Malaysia, Thailand and, to a lesser extent, the Philippines. This explains why so many of the recent DFI projects have been export-oriented. Production activities that used to take place in Japan or in the NICs for their domestic markets or for exports, have now been moved to ASEAN countries, from where the products are exported to Japan, the NICs or to third countries.

However, there are many reasons for DFI in ASEAN countries. Jha (1994) mentions the export-oriented policies, adequate infrastructure and the quality of labour as factors attracting DFI. Annual surveys conducted by the Japanese EXIM bank (in 1990, 1991 and 1992) revealed that Japanese firms invested in the ASEAN countries

(a) to enter, or increase their share in, the dynamic markets of the host countries (60 per cent of the firms);

(b) to take advantage of the low labour cost (30 per cent);

(c) to establish export platforms from where to export to Japan or to third countries (25 per cent);

(d) to establish regional networks of specialized production facilities (35 per cent) (Tejima 1993).

Of course, firms have many reasons for investing abroad, and give multiple answers to the survey questions. A typical DFI project may simultaneously try to enter the domestic market and to establish a low-cost export base. The answers in the surveys are dominated by arguments of domestic market access and the establishment of regional production networks. In these networks, each type of product can be produced, or each stage of the production process established where the conditions are most suitable, so that the firm can take full advantage of economies of specialization and of scale. This type of foreign investment is new, and distinguishes the current boom from earlier foreign investment; it could be taken to suggest that the boom in DFI may be more structural and permanent than it would have been if the sole argument for DFI were the low labour cost, which tends to be associated with the more footloose type of export processing.

A relatively new phenomenon in the financial flows to LDCs is the portfolio investments in the stock markets of developing countries. The World Bank has identified a number of developing countries as countries with an 'emerging stock market'. The largest markets among these include: Argentina, Brazil, Chile, India, Indonesia, Korea, Malaysia,

Mexico, the Philippines, Thailand, Turkey and Venezuela. The dynamism of these markets is generated by both foreign and domestic investors.

It is striking that these countries are also among the main recipients of DFI. The reasons behind the formation of this select group of developing countries are quite complex. It is often suggested that DFI is attracted to countries with relatively large domestic markets. The list of 12 LDCs given above indeed contains mainly large countries. Measured by the size of their (1992) GDP, the list includes the eight largest developing countries. All 12 countries listed are among the 20 largest LDCs.[5] It is thus clear that DFI and PFI flows are primarily directed towards large economies.

It has been argued that, in addition to large countries, countries with an adequate infrastructure and with rapid rates of growth also attract such flows (see e.g. Cable & Persaud 1987). However, it is somewhat difficult to accept that it is the excellent economic performance of the host countries that invited the foreign attention. In the case of the Latin American countries, the growth performance in the 1980s had been modest, and macroeconomic instability, as measured by the inflation rates, has been high.[6] Painful adjustment programmes have been implemented after the debt crisis, but recovery is still hesitant. The capital flows to these countries and the upsurge of their stock markets may be more related to factors like debt restructuring, debt equity swaps and the repatriation of flight capital. In the case of the Asian countries, there does seem to be a closer relationship between economic performance and the attractiveness to foreign investors.[7]

It could be suggested that, with the shift of DFI from import-substituting to export-oriented industries, the size of the domestic market may become less important and the level of local production cost (including wage cost) more important. However, recent data on DFI and PFI flows do not show a trend away from the large economies, and the survey among Japanese firms quoted above also indicated the continuing importance of the domestic market as an incentive for investment.

The change in attitude of governments in many developing countries towards DFI was already noted above. In their attempts at structural adjustment many countries have effectuated measures to facilitate the inflows of DFI and PFI, such as investment incentives schemes and the liberalization of international capital transactions.

5.3   Foreign Investment in Thailand

Thailand was among the more favoured nations of international investors because of its low labour cost, the linkage of the baht to the US dollar, and because of the fact that many firms from Asian countries already had investment and trade links with Thailand.

Figure 5.1 showed the upsurge in DFI flows to the developing world after 1986. As Figure 5.2 shows, Thailand fully participated in that upsurge (see also Table 3.1 of Chapter 3). DFI inflows had been relatively high in the period 1981–84, compared to the 1970s. After a dip in 1985, DFI inflows started to increase in 1986.[8] The inflows in 1987 were double those of 1986, but that was only a first sign of the much higher levels which were to follow, from 1988 onwards.

At the same time the net inflows of foreign portfolio investment (PFI in Figure 5.2), which had been at insignificant levels up to 1986, started to increase.

With the increase in DFI flows, the share of DFI in private corporate investment increased. In the years 1988–90 DFI funds financed nearly 12 per cent of all private corporate investment in Thailand.

The share of non-debt-creating funds (DFI and PFI) in total capital inflows also increased substantially. This share had dropped to a very low level (between 10 and 20 per cent) in the period between 1975 and 1985, when bank loans dominated the capital inflows. But in 1986 and 1987, non-debt-creating inflows accounted for more than 80 per cent of all capital inflows; in 1988 and 1989 this share dropped back down to about 50 per cent, and in the period 1990–94 it further decreased to around 28 per cent. This decrease was partly the result of decreasing levels of net DFI inflows and of net PFI inflows (in some years), but the main reason is the rapid increase in other capital inflows (mainly long-term and short-term private loans).

The recent trend in DFI differs in at least three respects from the patterns of the past: in scale, in sectoral destination and in country of origin.

5.3.1   The level of DFI

Figure 5.2 showed that the level of DFI inflows before 1986 was relatively modest. The average annual DFI inflow in the period 1970–85 in Thailand was only 0.6 per cent of GDP, a level much lower than

Figure 5.2   Foreign investment in Thailand (billion baht)

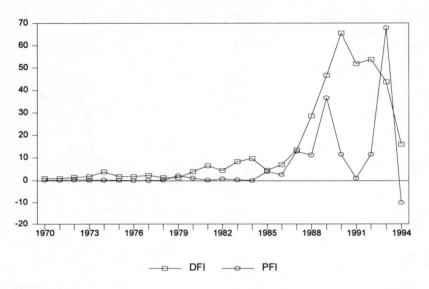

—□— DFI   —○— PFI

that in most other ASEAN countries. The stock of DFI in Thailand was valued in 1985 at about 2 billion US dollars, compared to 8.5 billion in Malaysia, 12.7 billion in Singapore and 25 billion in Indonesia (United Nations 1992). But after 1986, DFI flows to Thailand jumped to levels comparable to those of its ASEAN partners.

Table 5.1 shows that the accumulated net inflows of DFI in the nine years since 1985 are already a multiple of the total accumulated flows in the preceding 16 years since 1970. The average amount coming in per year was around 150 million US dollars in the period 1970–85. For the years 1980–85, this average amounted to 267 million dollars per year, but these figures are dwarfed by the inflows after 1986.

Figure 5.2 shows that after 1992 DFI inflows drop. The decline in 1993 and 1994 can be ascribed to three factors (see Bank of Thailand *Annual Economic Report 1994*). The first is the poor economic conditions in some of the source countries; in 1994 particularly DFI from Japan was decreasing. Second, it appears that DFI is shifting to other countries with lower wage levels, such as China and Indonesia. Moreover, the financing of foreign investment has shifted from equity flows

Table 5.1   Net flows of direct foreign investment to Thailand

	Accumulated net flows, in mln US$		Percentage distribution		Ave. amount per year, in mln US$	
	1970-85	1986-94	1970-85	1986-94	1970-85	1986-94
1 Financial institutions	120	800	5.0	6.2	7	89
2 Trade	454	2 080	18.9	16.1	28	231
3 Construction	356	815	14.9	6.3	22	91
4 Mining	432	349	18.0	2.7	27	39
5 Agriculture	20	142	0.8 .	1.0	1	16
6 Industry	777	6 908	32.4	53.4	49	768
– food	57	509	2.4	3.9	4	57
– textiles	138	353	5.8	2.7	9	39
– metal & non–metal	70	711	2.9	5.5	4	79
– electrical appliances	207	1 969	8.6	15.2	13	219
– mach. & transp. eqpt	61	376	2.5	2.9	4	42
– chemicals	100	898	4.2	6.9	6	100
– petroleum products	102	867	4.2	6.7	6	96
– construction materials	0	291	0.0	2.3	0	32
– others	43	934	1.8	7.2	3	104
7 Services	238	1 627	9.9	12.6	15	181
– transport. & travel	103	—	4.3	—	6	—
– housing & real estate	34	877	1.4	6.8	2	97
– hotels & restaurants	33	—	1.4	—	2	—
– others	68	—	2.8	—	4	—
8 Others	0	208	0.0	1.6	0	23
Total	2 396	12 928	100.0	100.0	150	1 436

Source: Bank of Thailand.

to the cheaper financing on the BIBF.[9]

The increase in the DFI flows cannot be related to any change in policy with respect to DFI. Thailand's policy with respect to foreign investment has always been relatively open and welcoming. Foreign investors face few restrictions and have access to investment incentives (GATT 1991, Pongpisanupichit et al. 1989). There have been no significant changes in these regulations and incentives in the 1980s that could explain the increase in DFI inflows. There were relevant policy changes, but they came *after* the DFI boom. For instance, in 1990 the import duties on machines were reduced and in 1991 the rates of the corporate income tax were reduced. In 1990, 1991 and 1994 significant liberalizations of international capital transactions took place, making operations for foreign affiliates easier. Such changes may have made foreign investment in Thailand still more attractive, but it should also be noted that these general measures reduce the extent of privileges that the Board of Investment can give and thus may reduce the relative advantage that foreign investors could have (Sibunruang 1992).

Earlier studies on the determinants of foreign investment in Thailand had found the usual factors, such as

- the domestic market which foreign firms wanted to serve, in some cases by jumping tariff walls and import restrictions;
- the availability of raw materials for exploration and processing;
- the low production cost, due to low labour cost, adequate infrastructure and attractive investment incentives;
- the generally stable political environment and sound macroeconomic policies (see e.g. Sibunruang 1984, Tambunlertchai 1980).

Can such factors explain the increase in DFI in 1986–87? Around the mid-1980s the domestic market did not look very attractive, with the deep recession of 1985–86. The recession and the adjustment policies may have meant that real labour cost had stagnated or declined. The infrastructure supply had benefitted from the public sector investment boom. As noted, there were no significant changes in investment incentives. In the early 1980s, the traditionally sound and conservative macroeconomic policies made way for unsustainable imbalances, particularly in public sector finance, but, as was shown in Chapter 4, by 1987 macroeconomic balance had been restored. Moreover, the devaluation of 1984 made Thailand more attractive for export-oriented foreign investment.

It is thus possible to identify some factors which had made Thailand a more attractive destination for foreign investors by 1986–87. One study which analysed projects receiving Board of Investment support in the period 1986–88 found that

(a) about 15 per cent of the invested capital came to Thailand to exploit natural resources (e.g. canning of fruits and seafood, rubber products);

(b) about 60 per cent came to regain or maintain cost advantages in production, i.e. to find a cheap location to produce for exports (e.g. electrical appliances, computer parts, automobile parts);

(c) and about 20 per cent aimed at the local market (Pongpisanupichit et al. 1989).

It would thus appear that most of the investments were motivated by cost considerations: Thailand would have looked attractive from that perspective. These factors may explain why the foreign investment boom started earlier in Thailand than in, for instance, Malaysia or Indonesia.[10] But, on the other hand, it does not seem that the factors had shifted so radically that they can explain why foreign investment boomed the way it did.

Lucas analyses the determinants of DFI flows to seven Southeast Asian countries, including Thailand, for the period 1960–87. He finds that, for Thailand, the level of domestic production cost (wage cost and capital cost) and political conditions (reflected in dummy variables for specific periods) provide a significant explanation for variations in DFI flows (Lucas 1993). These findings are interesting, but it is doubtful that they can explain the enormous increase in DFI flows just after the period covered in Lucas' study. The average level of DFI flows throughout the period 1970–87 was 4 billion baht per year. In 1987 itself the inflow was 13 billion baht. But in the period 1988–94 the average inflow increased to 44 billion baht per year. Such a sharp rise cannot be explained by changes in the cost of production in Thailand, nor by political events.

It may thus be concluded that the upsurge in the DFI flows to Thailand was, to a considerable extent, determined by events in the countries of origin of the DFI. It was Thailand's good fortune that, at the time that the supply of DFI increased, Thailand was just completing its successful stabilization, having restored macroeconomic stability and improved export competitiveness. This made Thailand an obvious destination for the DFI flows.

*Table 5.2   Net inflows of direct foreign investment in Thailand by
investing country (% distribution)*

Country/Region	1970–85	1986–94
USA	32.2	14.7
Japan	27.8	34.0
Asian NICs[a]	15.5	35.0
ASEAN[b]	1.2	0.5
EC	15.9	10.2
Others	7.4	5.6
Total	100.0	100.0

a   NICs include: Hong Kong, South Korea, Singapore, Taiwan.
b   ASEAN include: Brunei, Indonesia, Malaysia, Philippines.
Source: Bank of Thailand.

5.3.2   The origin of DFI

In Table 5.2 the DFI inflows are traced back to the countries of origin.
The shifts between the period 1970–85 and 1986–94 are substantial and
sudden. There is a very sharp increase in the share of Japan and of the
Asian NICs (Hong Kong, Korea, Singapore and Taiwan). The conclusion
is that, in the period after 1985, almost three-quarters of total DFI orig-
inates in the East Asian region. The shares of the USA and the EC
have been drastically reduced.

The percentage distribution can be deceiving. Although the share of
the USA in DFI in Thailand decreased from 32 to 15 per cent, in the
most recent period, the average annual amount invested was more than
three times as high as it had been in the first period.

5.3.3   The sectoral allocation of DFI

Table 5.1 shows the sectoral distribution of DFI in Thailand. A comparison of the period 1970–85 with 1986–94 reveals some significant
changes. The shares of DFI going to construction and mining decreased, whereas the shares of industry (particularly electrical appliances) and of services (among which real estate is the major activity)

increased. It was observed that in industry there was a shift from the light consumer goods to electrical and electronic products, chemicals, metal-based and non-metallic products, as firms are seeking a cheap and reliable location to produce for export (GATT 1991).

These shifts are, to some extent, part of a global pattern. The outflows of DFI from major source countries (such as the USA, Japan, the UK, Germany, the Netherlands) are also increasingly focusing on the service sector (including banking, insurance, trading companies, real estate). Dunning (1995) reports that in 1992, 50 to 55 per cent of all DFI went to the services sector. In 1975, Japan's stock of foreign investments in developing countries had been more or less equally distributed over the primary (extractive) sector (32 per cent), the manufacturing sector (44 per cent) and the services sector (24 per cent). By 1986, these shares had changed to 19, 30 and 51 per cent respectively (Healey 1991).

But these sectoral shares can be deceiving, given the sharp increases in absolute values. The last two columns of Table 5.1 give the average annual amount of the inflows. These columns show that, in many cases, sectors which experienced a decrease in their share in total DFI, still received substantially increased absolute amounts of DFI. For instance, the textile sector's share in total DFI declined from 5.8 to 2.7 per cent, but the average annual amount invested in the sector increased from 9 million to 39 million US dollars.

In a recent study, Pongphaichit (1990) refers to a 'new wave' of Japanese investment to indicate both the change in level and the change in composition of the DFI from Japan. She notes that within Japan, networks of subcontracting firms are important: large corporations are surrounded by small and medium-sized companies that supply machines, parts and components and services. This pattern of industrial organization is different from that in the USA or Europe, where firms are more often vertically integrated. The Japanese structure is mainly advantageous for the large corporations, that benefit from the flexibility in times of recession, and from the low cost of inputs, due to the economies of specialization within small firms and due to the lower wage levels of the small firms. This loose organization also made it easier to move the subcontracting abroad when Japan's competitiveness was decreasing due to the appreciation of the yen and the increase in production cost due to wage increases after 1985. Indeed, in this period many smaller Japanese firms (subcontractors) started to invest abroad. In the emerging pattern of foreign investment, the more sophisticated activities were moved to the Asian NICs and the simpler activities to the ASEAN countries. A noticeable feature of the recent inflows of DFI to Thailand is the growing role of small and medium-sized firms, particularly from Japan (Pongpisanupichit et al. 1989).

Some of the subcontracting may have gone to local firms, supported by technology contracts. Official DFI statistics may thus capture only part of this process of restructuring, as international co-operation among firms increasingly takes the form of cross-border alliances and networks (through licensing or technology contracts rather than through joint ventures or take-overs), and this trend appears to be particularly strong in East Asia (Dunning 1995).

The outcome of this process is that Asian networks are emerging, particularly in sectors like electronics and automobiles, with various parts and components being produced in various countries, brought together in one country for assembly, and then exported from that country to Asian countries, including Japan, and to the USA and the EC (see also Borrmann & Jungnickel 1992). Machado (1995) gives an example of networking in the automobile industry: Toyota concentrates the production of diesel engines in Thailand, of gasoline engines in Indonesia, of transmissions in the Philippines and of steering gears in Malaysia. The outcome of this is a high level of intra-firm trade. For Japanese overseas manufacturing firms in Asia in 1989, intra-firm trade accounted for 63 per cent of all purchases (Machado 1995). Another indicator of growing regional networking is that the exports to Japan, as a percentage of total exports by Japanese affiliates in Thailand's manufacturing sector, increased from 31 per cent in 1985 to 45 per cent in 1989 (Ichikawa 1990).

Thus, the regional networks cover investment and trade, and are also reflected in the trade statistics. Table 2.8 of Chapter 2 showed that, since 1985, the share of Japan and the Asian NICs – the major sources of DFI in Thailand – in Thailand's imports has increased. The share of exports to these countries had also increased. Previously, in the period before 1985, foreign investors from Japan set up businesses in Thailand to produce for the American and European market. The result then was an increase in the share of imports from Japan and of exports to first

Europe and then to the USA. But in the more recent period, the emphasis has been on the extension of the intra-regional trade links.

The growing importance of regional production networks is also reflected in the sharp increase in Thailand's imports of intermediate goods. Wiboonchutikula established in a recent study that before 1985, Thailand's exports were dominated by natural-resource based goods and labour-intensive goods. After 1985 the emphasis shifted sharply to technology-intensive and human-capital intensive goods, like electronics, electric machinery and equipment, and automobile parts. Interestingly, he shows that these are also the sectors on which DFI concentrates, and the sectors in which the extent of intra-industry trade is high and rapidly increasing (Wiboonchutikula 1993).

5.4   The Impact of DFI on Private Investment and Growth

Chapter 4 discussed the macroeconomic impact of capital inflows. The analysis focused on the main variables included in equations 4.8 and 4.15. The main transmission mechanisms identified were:

(a) the impact of capital flows on investment and savings of the receiving sector;

(b) the indirect impact on investment and savings of other sectors;

(c) the effect on inflation and, through this, on the real exchange rate and exports;

(d) the impact of the growing debt burden; and

(e) the effect, resulting from the factors listed, on economic growth.

The theoretical arguments listed in Chapter 4 need not be repeated here, though many of them are relevant for the analysis in this chapter as well. However, there is a need to extend the argument to take into account some special aspects of the capital inflows in recent years.

Since 1986, capital inflows have been dominated by DFI and other flows to the private sector. The analysis of the impact of DFI inflows on the host economy has received ample attention in the development literature. A wide array of economic and non-economic effects have been analysed (for surveys, see Grieco 1986 and Helleiner 1989). The studies on the impact of DFI on the host economy have tended to concentrate on (i) its impact on investment and growth, (ii) the employment it generates, (iii) its impact on the current account of the balance of payments, and (iv) the technological knowledge that is transferred through the DFI projects. This chapter focuses on the macroeconomic impact, in particular on the impact on investment and growth (this section) and on the balance of payments (sections 5.5 and 5.6). With regard to the impact on the balance of payments, it is not sufficient to study the impact on the current-account items (exports, imports, investment income payments). It is also necessary to study the effects of DFI flows on other items in the capital account (section 5.7).

The inflow of DFI provided an impulse for private investment. In 1987, real private investment increased by 31 per cent, and this increase was at least partially caused by the rise in DFI inflows.[11] As was noted in the previous chapter, Thailand was in a deep recession in the years 1985–86, but by 1986–87 the success of its structural adjustment programme was becoming evident, so that the country was 'ready' for the impulse provided by the capital inflows. In the DFI literature some specific attention was given to the relationship between DFI and local investment. The arguments are not unlike those encountered in the discussion of crowding in or crowding out in Chapter 4.

For a number of reasons, one would expect that DFI would have an impact on the level of private investment.

(a) DFI is part of private investment, so that any increase in DFI will, by definition, contribute to an increase in private investment. In addition, DFI and local private investment are likely to be determined, to a considerable extent, by similar variables reflecting the investment climate of the country. An increase in DFI is therefore likely to be accompanied by an increase in local investment. This increase in investment results in a demand impulse with further multiplier and accelerator effects on income and investment.

(b) New DFI projects may invite complementary local private investments that provide inputs to, or use outputs of, the foreign firm.

(c) It is likely that private investment will increase by more than the DFI flows because foreign equity capital finances only part of the total investment project. A substantial part of foreign investment projects is usually financed through local financial markets. This is clearly the case if the project is a joint venture, but even in cases of full foreign ownership local financing is quite prevalent. Statistical information is difficult to obtain. Helleiner (1987) refers to a survey of DFI projects in the 1960s which concluded that about half of the investment funds were locally raised. Local financing provides the foreign investor with the opportunity to reduce the investment risk and to obtain cheap finance (particularly when local financial markets are 'repressed'). It could be assumed that foreign transnational corporations (TNCs) will have privileged access to domestic credit. Local financial institutions will see them as first-class borrowers, and TNCs may have bargained for some credit facilities as part of the investment incentive package.

It has been emphasized that these interaction on the domestic financial markets may also lead to crowding-out of domestic investment (see e.g. Bos et al. 1974, Lall & Streeten 1977, Hughes & Dorrance 1987). The extent to which claims by foreign investors will crowd out local borrowers depends on the conditions of the financial markets. If markets are tight – due, for example, to large claims by the public sector to finance its deficit, or because of low deposit supply due to unattractive interest rates – crowding out is more likely. On the other hand, the presence of TNCs may ease the country's access to international financial markets, so that tension on domestic financial markets can be resolved by foreign borrowing. It should also be noted that the foreign capital inflows can themselves lead to an increase in domestic credit supply. Inflows of foreign funds – DFI, PFI or other capital inflows – may increase the level of foreign reserves, and thus the monetary base of the monetary system, and will thus initially increase the credit supply capacity.

(d) Crowding out may also occur on commodity and factor markets. This may be the case when foreign investors claim scarce resources (such as import licences, skilled manpower, credit facilities, etc.) or when foreign investors foreclose investment opportunities for local investors.

In a recent article, Buffie presents an analytical model which shows, under rather restrictive assumptions, that DFI in a protected, domestic-market oriented manufacturing sector is likely to crowd out domestic investment, while DFI in an export-oriented primary sector or in a manufacturing export-processing zone will crowd in domestic investment and will lead to higher income and employment (Buffie 1993).[12]

To the extent that an increase in DFI inflows has a positive effect on total investment, DFI inflows are also likely to have a positive effect on growth. Capital inflows may not only affect the level of investment, but also the growth efficiency of investment (i.e. the incremental output capital ratio may change). One difference between DFI and other capital flows is that DFI is not just a transfer of funds, but consists of a collection of elements, including capital, new technologies, management skills, marketing channels, etc. DFI can thus contribute to the transfer of technologies and to an increase in productivity, although these effects may be difficult to measure (Helleiner 1989).

In this context, it is relevant to note that two characteristics set DFI apart from most other types of capital flows to developing countries. The first of these is that DFI flows to the private sector of the host country and increases private investment. Other capital flows, such as aid or loans, are often received by the public sector (government and state enterprises). It has been suggested that the impact of private investment on growth is stronger than that of public investment (Khan & Reinhart 1990).[13] The second aspect is that DFI generally consists of investments in the traded goods sector. Other capital flows, such as aid or loans to the public sector, tend to predominantly finance investments in the non-traded sectors of physical and social infrastructure. The assumption is often made that technical progress in traded activities is faster than that in non-traded activities (see e.g. De Melo 1988 or Van Wijnbergen 1986). Due to these two characteristics, DFI could exert a stronger impact on growth than other capital inflows from abroad.

In recent years there has been a renewed interest in growth theory. In the new brand of 'endogenous growth' models, differential growth among countries is explained not so much by the differences in the level of investments, but by differences in the efficiency of these investments. These differences are related to differences in 'knowledge' and 'human capital' (see e.g. Barro 1991). DFI projects could be interpreted as a channel by which knowledge is transferred to developing countries and by which human capital is formed in developing countries. If this interpretation is correct, one would expect a positive relationship between the level of DFI inflow and the rate of growth.

Empirical studies on the link between DFI and growth use two approaches. The relationship between DFI and growth has been analysed in cross-country comparative analysis, linking the rate of growth to both the level of DFI inflows and to the value of the accumulated stocks of foreign investment. These studies failed to lead to systematic results, and have been criticized on conceptual grounds (see Grieco 1986 and Helleiner 1989).

Other studies analyse the link between capital inflows and growth using a growth equation derived from the production function, which is then tested on (pooled) time-series data for a group of countries. The studies start from the general form of the production function

$$Y = f(A, K, L) \qquad (5.1)$$

In this general form the level of production depends on available capital (K) and labour (L) and on a factor (A) that represents the level of technical knowledge. When expressed in growth rates this leads to

$$g = \frac{\Delta Y}{Y} = f\left[a, \frac{I}{Y}, g_L\right] \qquad (5.2)$$

where g_L is the growth rate of the labour force and a some appropriate indicator of technical progress. In comparative analysis of growth in developing countries, the tendency has been to use the export/GDP ratio (X/GDP and sometimes $\Delta X/GDP$, or the growth rate of exports) as a proxy for a, based on the assumption that export markets require and impose a higher efficiency.

The identity $I = S + F$ can be substituted into this equation to shift the attention from the level of investment to its financing. This leads to the general form:

$$g = f\left[\frac{X}{Y}, \frac{S}{Y}, \frac{\Sigma F_i}{Y}, g_L\right] \qquad (5.3)$$

The F_i are the different types of capital inflow: DFI, aid, private loans, etc. This is the basic form of the equations that are tested in, for instance, Gupta and Islam (1983) and Husain and Jun (1992).

In most of these studies, total capital inflows are split up into component parts, one of which is DFI. If DFI inflows increase the competition and efficiency on domestic markets, and if they introduce superior technologies and management and marketing methods, an improvement of investment efficiency is to be expected.

Gupta and Islam (1983) ran a regression with a set of pooled cross-country and time-series data for a large group of developing countries in various periods between 1950 and 1973. They distinguished three types of capital flows: aid inflows, DFI inflows, and other capital inflows. For almost all periods and all groups of countries, and in all types of regression equations tested, the coefficient of the DFI variable was insignificant. More recently, Husain and Jun (1992) applied a similar method to pooled data for the ASEAN countries over the period 1970–88. They found a significant positive effect for the DFI variable.

The contrast between the findings of Gupta and Islam and those of Husain and Jun raises the question whether the nature and impact of DFI changed between the period covered in the former study (the 1950s and 1960s) and that covered in the latter study (1970–88). The contrast may also be explained by differences in the country sample.[14]

Fry (1993) goes a step further. He does not restrict himself to single equation testing, but uses a simple simultaneous equation model, in which capital flows, investment, saving and growth interact. Estimating the model on pooled data for a sample of 16 developing countries, he finds that DFI does not increase the level of investment, but has a negative effect on savings. However, here again there are regional variations. The sample of 16 includes five Asian countries (Indonesia, South Korea, Malaysia, the Philippines and Thailand). For this group of five countries Fry established a positive relationship between DFI and investment and growth, although the negative impact on savings remains. He suggests that this may be because there is less financial repression and trade distortions in the Asian countries than elsewhere (Fry 1993). There is thus reason to suggest that the link between DFI and growth is dependent on characteristics of the country and may differ from period to period. The analysis by Buffie, referred to above, suggests that it may also depend on differences in the type of DFI.

Kwan (1994) takes quite a different approach in analysing the growth impact of DFI flows. He concentrates on Japanese investment in the ASEAN countries and argues that if the yen appreciates, growth in Japan slows down and demand for imported primary commodities, from ASEAN countries, among others, decreases. This reduces the export price and quantities of ASEAN countries, while the appreciation

Table 5.3 Adjustment patterns

	1980	1985	1986	1987	1988	1989	1990	1991	1992	1993	1994
Percentage of GDP											
DFI	0.6	0.4	0.6	1.0	1.8	2.5	3.0	2.1	1.9	1.4	0.4
PFI	0.2	0.4	0.2	1.0	0.7	2.0	0.5	0.0	0.4	2.1	-0.3
Corporate investments	14.8	11.9	11.3	13.9	18.2	20.9	24.9	24.5	23.6	24.9	24.5
Private investments	18.9	18.5	18.4	21.7	25.6	29.6	34.1	34.2	31.2	32.2	31.9
Total investments	27.8	27.2	25.8	27.6	30.7	34.6	40.2	41.2	38.8	40.4	39.0
Corporate savings	7.8	8.1	8.4	9.1	9.2	9.9	11.3	11.8	13.6	13.5	13.8
Household savings	11.4	11.8	11.9	12.4	13.5	14.4	10.5	10.5	9.8	8.9	7.6
Private savings	19.1	20.0	20.3	21.5	22.8	24.3	21.8	22.3	23.4	22.4	21.4
Total savings	22.2	23.1	24.4	27.5	32.0	34.1	33.7	34.7	34.3	34.3	34.7
Private borrowing abroad	3.1	1.1	0.3	0.0	2.2	4.2	7.6	8.8	4.9	—	—
Private domestic credit expansion	4.9	5.2	2.5	9.9	14.5	18.1	22.1	16.4	19.2	36.7	18.7
Exports	24.1	23.2	25.6	28.9	33.0	34.9	34.0	35.2	36.3	37.1	38.7
Imports	30.4	25.9	23.6	28.3	34.4	37.5	41.5	42.3	40.5	41.3	43.4
Growth rates and indices											
Trade-weighted real exchange rate	102	113	113	114	115	113	110	106	103	101	98
Growth rate	5.1	4.6	5.5	9.5	13.3	12.2	11.6	8.1	7.9	8.4	8.6
Inflation	19.7	2.4	1.8	2.5	3.9	5.4	5.9	5.7	4.0	3.4	5.1

of the yen makes their imports from Japan more expensive. This deterioration in terms of trade would reduce growth. Kwan runs regressions linking the growth rate to the yen exchange rate. The results support the hypothesis for Indonesia, Malaysia and the Philippines, but *not* for Thailand (Kwan 1994). The exception in the case of Thailand is not explained by Kwan. Two possible reasons may be suggested. The first is that the share of primary commodities in the exports of Thailand is lower than for the other ASEAN countries. The second is that, while the appreciating yen may have negative effects on trade, it has positive effects on DFI flows to Thailand.

Tables 3.1 and 3.4 of Chapter 3 showed that when DFI increased in Thailand after 1986, private investment also increased sharply. More detailed information can be gained by analysing annual data. In Table 5.3, the ratios of (i) private investment, (ii) gross DFI inflows, (iii) expansion of domestic credit for the private sector, and (iv) net inflows of other foreign capital flows to the private sector are presented, together with some other macroeconomic indicators.

Table 5.3 shows that the DFI inflows started to increase in 1986 and 1987. However, investment by private corporations was very poor in 1986, and even in 1987 the private corporate investment ratio had just started to recover to the levels of before the recession. From 1988 onwards the private corporate investment ratio jumped to unprecedented levels. Domestic credit also expanded sharply in 1987, and other foreign capital inflows started to increase only in 1988. Thus, these patterns suggest that the DFI boom preceded, and probably initiated, the private investment boom.

This private investment boom was initially financed from own funds and domestic credit, but subsequently, foreign borrowing became more important. The shift to foreign borrowing in 1988 does not reflect any crowding out by the public sector on domestic capital markets. In fact, after 1987 the public sector had a savings surplus. Foreign borrowing was required because domestic savings were inadequate to finance the enormous increase in private investment.

In an earlier study it was established that capital inflows have a positive effect on both households and corporate savings (see Akrasanee et al. 1993). But, as the evidence of the last few years has shown, this pattern seems to be breaking down. Along with the sharp rise in the investment ratio and in the growth rate after 1986, there has been an increase in the private sector savings ratio from its average of 18.3 per cent of GDP in the period 1970–86 to an average of 22.5 per cent in the years thereafter. As the analysis in Chapter 3 had shown, the boom stimulated corporate profits and savings, but the increase in income and wealth also led to a consumption spree, and the household savings ratio decreased from a peak of 14.4 per cent in 1989 to 7.6 per cent in 1994. The private sector investment-savings gap used to be small, with the household sector's savings surplus more or less matching the corporate sector's gap, resulting in a small private sector savings surplus in many years. In recent years the corporate savings gap widened, while the household savings surplus almost disappeared. Since 1987 the private sector's savings gap has risen to high levels, equivalent to 10 per cent of GDP in the early 1990s. The private sector savings gap could be financed by foreign capital inflows and on domestic financial markets, also because the public sector borrowing requirement had disappeared.

These patterns confirm that the increase in DFI affects virtually all the variables included in the macroeconomic balance equation: private investment increases, private savings increase a little, domestic credit increase sharply and so do other capital inflows from abroad.

Did the DFI flows cause the high growth rates? There are at least three explanations possible for Thailand's double-digit growth.

A first explanation would arise from the normal cyclical nature of the economy. Over the years, the Thai economy has known booms and busts (see Figure 1.1 of Chapter 1). After the prolonged and deep growth recession of the first half of the 1980s, one would expect a vigourous recovery, also because in the late 1980s most of the external conditions were relatively favourable (see the external shock indicators in Figure 4.1). Yet this argument cannot explain why private investment increased so strongly, far beyond levels experienced before, and why private investment continued to remain at that high level, also in the early 1990s.

In a second explanation, the upsurge in foreign investment is seen as the 'key' to double-digit growth. The inflows of DFI increased the level and the efficiency of investment, thus accelerating growth significantly. Figure 5.2 showed that DFI rose sharply between 1987 and 1990: these were the years of double-digit growth. After 1990 DFI flows gradually declined, and the growth rate also fell. However, this explanation is not fully convincing. The level of DFI inflows increased from below 1 per cent of GDP before 1987 to a peak of almost 3 per cent of GDP in 1990, after which it dropped again. The private corporate investment ratio increased by much more, from around 13 per cent before 1987 to around 24 per cent in recent years. This investment ratio also remained high when DFI flows slowed down. The Incremental Capital Output Ratio (ICOR) measures the growth efficiency of investment. The average ICOR over the entire period 1970–94 was 4.2. In the years 1987–90 it dropped to only 2.9, but after 1990 it increased again to an average value of 4.8. This pattern would suggest that the growth efficiency of DFI is a relatively short-term effect. The double-digit growth may thus reflect the catching-up after the long recession, more than a fundamental change in the investment efficiency. The ICORs of the most recent years suggest that the growth efficiency is decreasing. It could be suggested that Thailand is entering the next stage of development, in which the capital requirements are increased by the greater share of the industrial sector and, in particular, of capital-intensive industrial activities, and by the increasing expenditure on infrastructure. The direction of the DFI flows certainly contributed to this shift in the pattern of growth. Other studies established that foreign firms tend to be more capital-intensive than local firms (e.g. Kantachai et al. 1987).

The third explanation for the double-digit growth looks at exports. In a country like Thailand, export growth is one of the main determinants of overall growth. As noted above, export growth has been quite sensitive to movements in the (trade-weighted) real exchange rate. The years 1979–83 were characterized by an appreciating real exchange rate and a stagnating export ratio. The growth rate of the volume of exports had been 10.2 per cent per year in the period 1970–78 and dropped to 8.9 per cent per year in the years 1979–84 (the poor primary commodity prices of these years further helped to keep the growth of export values low).

After the devaluation of 1984 and the further depreciation following the Plaza Agreement, exports recovered quickly. The average growth rate of export volumes in the period 1985–89 was 19 per cent per year, with three years (1987, 1988 and 1989) having growth rates well over 20 per cent. Since 1988 the real exchange rate has been appreciating again, and the growth rate of the volume of exports dropped down to

15 per cent in the years 1990–94. The close correspondence between the ups and downs of the growth rates of exports and those of GDP is striking. However, it should be noted that the high growth rates of exports after 1984 need not be attributed exclusively to the changes in the real exchange rate. There may also be an indirect effect of DFI flows. As will be argued in the next section, the DFI boom concentrated strongly on export-oriented manufacturing, thus creating a rapidly expanding production capacity for export.

A tentative conclusion from the above discussion of the explanations of growth boom is that Thailand's double-digit growth was the result of the strong recovery, after 1986, from the prolonged recession of the early 1980s. It would appear that DFI flows helped to ignite that recovery, and also helped to set Thailand on the road to growth based on industrial exports. The main impulse for the boom was the strong export performance, supported by a depreciating exchange rate and by export-oriented DFI. Local private corporations quickly joined this process and increased their investments considerably, thus increasing the pressure for export-oriented industrialization. The conclusion is that, although it cannot be claimed that DFI in itself caused double-digit growth, DFI did make significant contributions which made the growth boom possible. The model simulation which will be conducted in Chapter 6 will confirm that DFI inflows make a direct, significant though quantitatively relatively modest contribution to economic growth.[15]

5.5   Foreign Investment and Exports

One of the motives for foreign investors to invest in Thailand is to establish an export base, using cheap local labour. To the extent that DFI flows are thus motivated, one would expect that an increase in DFI would stimulate an increase in exports.

Foreign firms were already more export-oriented than local firms prior to the period of double-digit growth. In the early 1980s it was estimated that foreign subsidiaries exported 28 per cent of their output, compared to 14 per cent for Thai firms (Wonghanchao & Pongpisanupichit 1987). The DFI inflows in recent years have been strongly biased towards export production. In 1991 the Board of Investment (BoI) in Thailand issued promotion certificates for 534 investment projects; 304 of these projects planned to export between 80 and 100 per cent of their output and a further 30 projects planned to export between 30 and 79 per cent. These projects include investment by Thai and foreign firms, but it should be noted that the foreign investment projects in particular are export-oriented. The share of export-oriented projects in BoI approvals increased from 10 per cent in 1984 to 75 per cent in 1988 (GATT 1991: 68).

Sibunruang (1992) quotes studies which estimated that foreign firms accounted for at least 25 per cent of manufactured exports at the end of the 1970s, that share having increased to between 30 and 40 per cent by 1990. Another study even attributed 39 per cent of the 1980 manufactured exports to foreign subsidiaries (Pongpisanupichit et al. 1989). However, it should also be remembered that, as was noted above, one characteristic of the recent DFI boom was that a greater share of DFI was directed towards non-traded activities, such as the services sector. Particularly the shares of sectors like 'finance' and 'real estate' in DFI flows increased significantly (see Table 5.1).

But capital inflows at the levels recently achieved can also have a negative effect. In Chapter 4 (section 4.3.3) reference was already made to the dependent economy models (Van Wijnbergen 1986, De Melo 1988). In these models an increase in capital inflows increases domestic demand, and leads to an increase in the relative price of non-traded (NT) goods (in other words, an appreciation of the real exchange rate) and to an anti-export bias.

The concern about the anti-export bias may be less acute when capital inflows are not dominated by aid or public sector loans (as was the case in Chapter 4), but by export-oriented DFI. In such a case, the increase in the profitability of NT goods may even be useful by stimulating an increase in the supply of NT goods and services which are complementary to and supportive of the export drive. On the other hand, export-oriented industries operate on highly competitive markets, where even small changes in relative cost levels can have significant impacts.

As was argued in Chapter 4 (section 4.3.3 and Figure 4.3), the inflows of capital did indeed have an appreciating impact on the real exchange rate. Until 1988 this effect was compensated by the changes of the major world currencies to Thailand's advantage, so that the trade-weighted real exchange rate continued to depreciate, but after 1988 there has been an appreciation of the real exchange rate, as Thai inflation has exceeded global inflation. This effect will cause the competitiveness of export producers to decline.

The impact of DFI on exports appears to be quite strong. In Table 5.3 the ratio of exports of goods and services to GDP was presented. Since 1984, there has been a continuous increase in the export ratio, leading to a very high ratio in 1994.

The sharp increase in the export ratio started in 1984, and it is therefore likely that the increase is related to the effective depreciation of the baht that started in the same year, putting an end to a number of years of increasing overvaluation and anti-export bias. But it is also likely that the sustained growth of the export ratio in subsequent years is related to the sharp rise in DFI inflows. Some indirect confirmation of this can be found. In Table 5.1 it was noted that, in recent years, DFI concentrated on manufacturing sectors like electrical appliances and chemical products. These are also sectors with a relatively strong export performance. Between 1985 and 1994 the exports of electrical appliances increased by 40 per cent per year, and those of chemical products by 27 per cent per year, whereas the annual growth rate of total merchandise exports was 22 per cent per year.

Over the last two decades the composition of exports fundamentally changed (Table 2.3 in Chapter 2). In 1970 Thailand was still an exporter of primary commodities. By 1980, manufactured goods already constituted about 25 per cent of total exports of goods and services. This share increased further to 39 per cent in 1985, and to 64 per cent in 1994. The increase in the total export ratio (at current prices) from 25 per cent in 1985 to 38 per cent in 1994 is entirely due to the increase in the export of manufactured goods, the sector on which DFI flows and domestic private investment concentrated. This strong export orientation of private investment in the manufacturing sector has, in recent years, neutralized the negative impact of the appreciating real exchange rate on exports.

5.6   Foreign Investment and Imports

It has been argued that capital inflows would increase the import intensity. Practices like the tying of aid and intra-firm trade of multinationals will result in investment projects financed with foreign capital having a higher than average import propensity.

The import ratios of goods and services were given in Table 5.3. The table shows that the ratio stagnated and decreased in the early 1980s as a result of unfavourable international and domestic conditions. But after 1986 a rapid increase occurred. It seems therefore that the last few years present a significant departure from the longer-term trend.[16] It is often argued in Thailand that this change is caused mainly by the high level of investment, and thus of imports of capital goods, in the recent period.

A disaggregation of the changes in the import ratio will facilitate analysis of this aspect. Total merchandise imports consist of:

$$p_m M = p_m M_c + p_m M_i + p_m M_k \tag{5.4}$$

where:

p_m = import price;
M = total volume of imports of goods;
M_c = volume imports of final consumption goods;
M_i = volume imports of intermediate goods; and
M_k = volume imports of capital goods.

There is only one import price index available in Thailand, and this is applied to all categories. In the case of imports of intermediate goods, the published world market price for oil was used to deflate the value of oil imports.

Some simple linear relationships may be assumed to determine the volumes of the various import categories:

$$M_c = m_c C$$
$$M_i = m_i Y_{ind}$$
$$M_k = m_k I$$

where:

C = total consumption expenditures;
Y_{ind} = value added in the industrial sector (this includes the sectors manufacturing, construction, electricity & water, transport & communications);
I = gross fixed capital formation

all measured at constant prices. Equation 5.4 then becomes:

$$p_m M = p_m m_c C + p_m m_i Y_{ind} + p_m m_k I \qquad (5.5)$$

or, as shares of GDP $(p_y Y)$, the import ratio can be written as:

$$\frac{p_m M}{p_y Y} = \frac{p_m m_c C}{p_y Y} + \frac{p_m m_i Y_{ind}}{p_y Y} + \frac{p_m m_k I}{p_y Y} \qquad (5.6)$$

Each of the three terms on the right-hand side of equation 5.6 contains three elements:

(a) the relative price (p_m/p_y),
(b) the structural relationship $(C/Y, Y_{ind}/Y$ or $I/Y)$, and
(c) the import propensity $(m_c, m_i,$ and $m_k)$.

With these three elements, the change in the current-prices/import ratio can be broken down into a relative price and a volume effect. The volume effect can be further broken down into a structural change and an import propensity effect. This gives:

$$\Delta \left[\frac{p_m M}{p_y Y} \right] = \qquad (5.7)$$

$$\left[\frac{p_{m,1}}{p_{y,1}} - \frac{p_{m,0}}{p_{y,0}} \right] m_{c,1} \frac{C_1}{Y_1} + \frac{p_{m,0}}{p_{y,0}} \left[m_{c,0} \left[\frac{C_1}{Y_1} - \frac{C_0}{Y_0} \right] + (m_{c,1} - m_{c,0}) \frac{C_1}{Y_1} \right] +$$

$$\left[\frac{p_{m,1}}{p_{y,1}} - \frac{p_{m,0}}{p_{y,0}} \right] m_{i,1} \frac{Y_{ind,1}}{Y_1} + \frac{p_{m,0}}{p_{y,0}} \left[m_{i,0} \left[\frac{Y_{ind,1}}{Y_1} - \frac{Y_{ind,0}}{Y_0} \right] + (m_{i,1} - m_{i,0}) \frac{Y_{ind,1}}{Y_1} \right] +$$

$$\left[\frac{p_{m,1}}{p_{y,1}} - \frac{p_{m,0}}{p_{y,0}} \right] m_{k,1} \frac{I_1}{Y_1} + \frac{p_{m,0}}{p_{y,0}} \left[m_{k,0} \left[\frac{I_1}{Y_1} - \frac{I_0}{Y_0} \right] + (m_{k,1} - m_{k,0}) \frac{I_1}{Y_1} \right]$$

The three lines of equation 5.7 give the contribution to the change in the overall import/GDP ratio by the import of consumer goods, of intermediate goods and of capital goods. Each of these lines contains three terms. The first term presents the change in the price of imports relative to the general price level. The second term presents the change in the import base (e.g. the change in the consumption/GDP or the investment/GDP ratio). The third term presents the change in the import propensities.

Table 5.4 shows the total decomposition of the actual change in the import/GDP ratio. The change in the import/GDP ratio in current prices is composed of three effects:

(a) The relative price effect (i.e. changes in p_m/p_y): if import prices rise faster than domestic prices, the import/GDP ratio will rise;

(b) The structural change effect (i.e. changes in C/Y, Y_{ind}/Y or I/Y): if sectors or final demand categories with a relatively high import demand increase their share in GDP, the import/GDP ratio will rise;

(c) The import propensity effect (i.e. changes in m_c, m_i or m_k): if the propensity to import for a particular import category rises, the total import/GDP ratio will rise.

The table presents these three effects for three categories of imports and for total imports of goods for the observed changes in the import/ GDP ratio between 1970 and 1980, 1980 and 1985, and 1985 and 1994. In the 1970s the import ratio increased sharply, mainly due to the relative price effect in intermediate imports; this is the impact of the oil shocks. Structural change and import propensity effects were relatively small in this period.

Between 1980 and 1985, the overall import ratio decreased despite the positive relative price effect, mainly due to a decrease in the import propensity for intermediate goods. This is not surprising. In these years the Thai economy was adjusting to the jump in oil prices that had occurred in 1979–80. The estimated structural change effects and the import propensity effects of the other import categories in this period were all relatively small. The early 1980s was a period of stagnation in the Thai economy, with relatively slow economic growth and structural change. The investment/GDP ratio declined in these years (see the negative structural change effect of investment goods imports).

The decomposition of the increase in the import/GDP ratio in the period 1985–94 reveals a completely different situation. The impact of structural change is considerable: the rapid growth of industrial production and the jump in the investment rate both lead to an increase in the overall import ratio. But the most striking effect in this period is the rapid rise in the import propensities. For all categories of imports, increases in the respective import propensities can be observed, the in-

Table 5.4   Decomposition of changes in the import/GDP ratio

	Actual change import ratio	Relative price effect	Structural change effect	Import propensity effect
1970–80 Imports				
Consumer goods	0.55	1.09	-0.07	-0.47
Intermediate	9.66	6.95	1.30	1.41
Capital goods	0.19	1.83	-0.72	-0.93
Total imports	10.40	9.87	0.52	0.01
1980–85 Imports				
Consumer goods	-1.59	0.60	-0.20	-1.99
Intermediate	-3.26	0.28	-0.14	-3.40
Capital goods	-0.03	1.49	-0.54	-0.98
Total imports	-4.88	2.37	-0.87	-6.38
1985–94 Imports				
Consumer goods	1.40	-0.10	-0.45	1.95
Intermediate	1.01	-2.88	3.28	0.61
Capital goods	11.74	-0.41	2.87	9.27
Total imports	14.15	-3.39	5.70	11.84

Note: For the calculation of import prices, the general import price index published by the Bank of Thailand has been used for imports of consumer and capital goods and services. The imports of intermediate goods was split up into oil imports, for which the international oil price index was used, and other intermediate imports, for which the general import index was used. Thus, little information on relative changes in import prices is included, but available data did not allow a different approach. The GDP deflator was used for p_y.

crease being the strongest in the import intensity of investment. This seems to confirm the conventional explanation that the increase in the import ratio is due to the high level of investment. But the table enables a more precise interpretation of this statement. The shift in final demand toward investment spending implies a shift to a demand category with a relatively high import propensity. This structural change in final demand is responsible for an increase in the overall import/GDP ratio between 1985 and 1994 of 2.87 percentage points. The main factor behind the growth in the overall import figure is, however, the increase in the import intensity of investment demand. This change in the import intensity of investment is responsible for a 9.27 percentage points in the overall import/GDP ratio. It is suggested here that this radical change in the import intensity of investment is related to the fact that a greater share of total investment is financed by direct foreign investment. It is also relevant that during the loan boom period (1975–85), the dependence on foreign finance had not been related to an increase in the import propensity. The growing import intensity is thus not generally related to foreign financing, but more specifically linked to DFI financing and, in particular, to the type of DFI projects that came to Thailand in recent years.

It is sometimes suggested that the present large current-account deficit is a temporary affair. As foreign and local investment increases, the imports of capital goods rise to high levels, but once newly invested projects gain momentum, imports will drop back and the outflow of export goods will start, turning the current-account balance around (see e.g. Kwan 1994). Table 5.4, however, raises some doubts about this hypothesis. Firstly, investments have increased the share of the industrial sector in total production, and this sector tends to have a higher import propensity. Secondly, the increased role of foreign investors and of regional networks implies that the import intensity of investment has increased substantially. These are two structural changes that will persist even if the level of investment should decline in the future.

There is some evidence that foreign investment is particularly import-intensive. It has been established that for foreign investment projects which received promotional privileges from the Board of Investment, 90 per cent of all machinery and equipment was imported, and over 50 per cent of raw materials (Pongpisanupichit et al. 1989). Another survey found that foreign firms have a much higher proportion of imported capital and intermediate goods than local firms do (Wonghanchao & Pongpisanupichit 1987). The recent trend towards intra-regional networks of foreign investments and trade, noted in section 5.3 above, may have further strengthened this import dependency.

Others have also analysed the growing import intensity. Brummitt and Flatters use the 1985 Input-Output Table to calculate net exports – i.e. the exports minus the value of imported inputs used in production

– for major sectors of the Thai economy. They conclude that in the period 1980–90 the average import content of Thai exports rose by 27 per cent just because of the shift of exports towards more import-intensive sectors. Their analysis assumed that (a) the import content of each sector, as measured by the 1985 Input-Output Table, remained unchanged since then, and (b) the import intensity of export production in each sector is the same as that for production for the local market (Brummitt & Flatters 1992). Neither assumption is true. There are indications that, with the growing role of DFI, the import intensity of sectors to which DFI flowed has increased, and also that, within sectors, export production often uses more imported inputs than production for the local market does, in order to meet international quality standards.

There is another effect of DFI on the current account that needs to be noted. DFI does not create a fixed-term debt obligation, but foreign investors do engage in projects in order to make profits, and generally they wish to repatriate at least part of these profits.

One of the advantages often ascribed to DFI is that it has a less pro-cyclical relationship with the current-account deficit than foreign loans do. When the economy is in trouble, the debt service on loans with fixed interest rates continues, while the investment-income payments on DFI are likely to decrease as the poor state of the economy reduces the level of profits and dividends that can be repatriated.

This is, however, only partially true. There are at least two complications. Firstly, not all DFI comes as equity funds. In the balance-of-payments statistics of the Bank of Thailand the item 'direct foreign investment' is split up into two sub-items, 'equity' and 'investment loans'. The latter are intra-firm loans. On average, in the period 1970–90, investment loans accounted for 17 per cent of all DFI inflows. Payments of interest and capital are made on these loans, presumably disregarding the performance of the firm.

Secondly, payments of technical fees and of copyrights and patent royalties will also be related to DFI. The outflow of such payments has increased very rapidly in recent years.[17] Of course, not all of these payments are made by foreign or joint enterprises; Thai-owned firms also make such payments. It has been noted that in many developing countries 'new forms' of foreign investment have become more important in recent years (see Oman 1984 and Dunning 1995). These new forms include licensing, franchising, management contracts, and so on. These activities will lead to payments of fees and royalties.

The outward remittances of profits and dividends were recorded in Table 2.6 of Chapter 2. In 1994 such payments were equivalent to about 1 per cent of GDP. This proportion had not increased compared to 1986, which may reflect the fact that a considerable part of profits are reinvested in Thailand.

It is clear that foreign capital does not come cheaply. It has been suggested that DFI is a relatively expensive form of international finance. The rate of profit remittances and other transfers can easily exceed the international interest rate (Lall & Streeten 1977). The average rate of repatriated profits in the period 1970–92 was 8.7 per cent of the stock of outstanding DFI, comparable to the average international interest rate (LIBOR) in the same period. Adding technical fees and royalty payments would make foreign investment more expensive than international commercial loans. This comparison is partly unfair, however, as DFI does not provide only financing but also a transfer of technology, and so on.

The impact of the DFI inflows can now be summarized. The impact on the receiving sector was strong: inflows led to a strong expansion of private investment and a more modest increase in private sector savings. The growth rate temporarily jumped to double-digit levels, but this exceptional performance should not be fully ascribed to the DFI flows. The successful stabilization policies of the mid-1980s, particularly the exchange rate depreciation since 1984, also contributed. The impact on the accumulation balances of the other sectors of the economy was also strong. With growth, household income and savings and investment increased, although household savings later started to decrease. Public sector savings increased as the growth boom increased revenue and savings, while cautious policies kept investment low.

Inflation accelerated with the high growth, and after 1988 there was an appreciation of the trade-weighted real exchange rate. Still, export growth continued, as the capacity effects of export-oriented DFI and local investment, and the dynamic process of regional networking dominated the negative exchange rate effect. Imports increased even more strongly as DFI-led growth proved to be very import intensive.

The sharp increase in investment outpaced the growth in domestic savings and the jump in DFI flows. Additional foreign borrowing was necessary to fill the gap, as will be discussed in the following section.

5.7   Other Capital Inflows

The capital inflows in recent years have far exceeded the inflows of DFI, to such an extent that one could even question whether the title of this chapter, 'the foreign investment boom', provides a correct interpretation of the events. As Table 3.1 of Chapter 3 showed, inflows of short-term and long-term loans for the private sector accounted for most of capital inflows in the period 1987–94.

The sharp increase in the other capital inflows must be related to the growing integration of the Thai financial system with international financial markets and the liberalization of capital-account transactions since 1990. As already briefly mentioned in Chapter 4, since 1990 there has been a considerable liberalization of the domestic and international financial markets of Thailand.

(a) Ceilings imposed by the central bank on deposit and lending rates of financial institutions have been lifted. First, in 1989 the ceiling on interest on long-term deposits was lifted, and by January 1992 ceilings for all types of deposits had been removed. Later in 1992 the ceiling on lending rates was also lifted, so that financial institutions were now totally free in determining the interest rates offered to their customers.

(b) In 1993 the requirement that banks hold a certain level of government bonds as a precondition for permission to open new bank branches was abolished. This measure was, to some extent, the result of the decrease in the supply of government bonds, with the government running budget surpluses, but it also made it easier for banks to decide on the expansion of their branch network.

(c) In 1993 the range of activities that could qualify as the mandatory 'rural credit' of commercial banks was also broadened, so that this regulation became less restrictive.

These measures were intended to increase competition among domestic financial institutions, and to enhance their efficiency. At the international level several measures were also taken (see Nijathaworn & Dejthamrong 1994):

(d) In 1990 all foreign exchange transactions related to trade were liberalized. In 1991 measures were taken to lift foreign exchange controls on capital-account transactions. And in 1994 foreign exchange transactions, including transactions on travel abroad, were further liberalized.

(e) The Bangkok International Banking Facilities (BIBF) began operations in early 1993. The financial institutions involved with the BIBF draw capital from international markets for lending inside and outside Thailand. The BIBF provides a ready link between the domestic and the international financial markets. To some extent, the BIBF funds replace direct foreign borrowing by Thai companies, but the ease of the transactions and the low cost may also have stimulated additional borrowing.

(f) The Export-Import Bank started operations in 1994. This new bank took over the export re-financing activities of the central bank, but also engages in other activities to provide credit, guarantees and insurance to exporters.

The combination of the growing efficiency of the domestic financial system, its integration with the international markets, the liberalization of foreign exchange transactions, and the stable baht/dollar exchange rate have made it easier to move funds into and out of the country. Even before the liberalization, the Thai financial markets had been relatively open: existing controls were for monitoring and control more than they were for prohibiting the movement of capital.

The open nature of the financial markets forces the domestic interest rate to stay close to the world's interest rate. On a perfectly open capital market, one would expect the domestic interest rate to be equal to the international rate plus the cost of forward cover of the foreign exchange risk. Figure 5.3 compares the Thai real interbank rate, as the closest proxy for the money market rate, to the real international interest rate (real 3-month LIBOR). The similarity in the underlying medium-term trends of the two rates supports the hypothesis of the openness of the Thai financial markets. The short-term differences between the two rates can be explained by instabilities on the foreign exchange markets and by monetary policy interventions. Prior to the devaluations of the

Figure 5.3   Interest rate gap

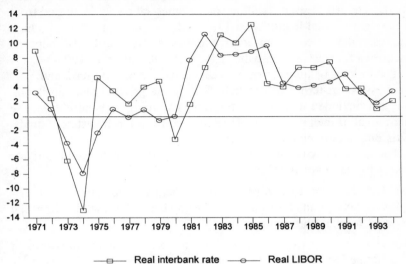

—□— Real interbank rate   —○— Real LIBOR

baht in 1984, expectations of the coming devaluation pushed up the domestic rate significantly higher than international interest rates. The relatively low domestic interest rates in 1980–82 and 1986, and the relatively high rates in 1975–79, 1983–85 and 1988–90 were due to respectively easy and tight monetary policies in those years. It is clear from Figure 5.3 that the liberalizations since 1991 have brought the two real interest rates closer together.[18]

The domestic loan and deposit rates of interest have been higher than the interbank rate shown in Figure 5.3. The relatively high domestic lending and deposit rates in the 1990s encouraged domestic firms to borrow abroad, and invited foreigners to deposit funds in baht deposits. Table 3.1 showed that long-term and short-term borrowing abroad increased strongly. In 1990–91 the interest-rate differential between domestic and foreign rates was substantial, and private sector foreign borrowing was very high. In 1992–93, when the differential was somewhat smaller, foreign borrowing also declined somewhat, and when, in 1994, the differential increased again, so did the capital inflows.

Thai banks also increased their borrowing abroad to source cheaper funds. The net foreign liabilities of commercial banks increased from 1 per cent of total liabilities in 1988 to 17 per cent in 1994. The high interest rates also invited foreign deposits. Non-residents' deposits increased from 21 billion baht in 1988 to 100 billion in 1993–94.

The inflows of funds in recent years consisted of long-term and, particularly, short-term loans to help finance the private spending boom, but also included deposits by foreigners wanting to benefit from the high level of interest rates in Thailand and portfolio investment funds. This dual nature complicates the analysis.

There are at least three reasons for the sharp increase in private sector foreign capital inflows.

(a) The sharp increase in private investment exceeded the rise in private savings and DFI inflows. The gap had to be filled by domestic and foreign borrowing.

(b) The central bank tried to contain the excess demand pressures in this period through a high interest rate policy. High domestic interest rates made borrowing abroad more attractive, and also invited foreigners to bring in money.

(c) The liberalization of capital transactions and the growing integration with global capital markets reduced the transaction cost related to foreign capital flows.

The borrowing abroad did result in an increase in the external debt. Table 4.3 of Chapter 4 showed that total external debt increased from around 17 billion US dollars in 1987–88 to 54 billion in 1994, 70 per cent of which is now private sector debt. However, the moderate level of the international interest rate and the rapid growth of exports have kept the debt-service ratio relatively low, at around 10 per cent.

A new phenomenon in this last period was the sharp increase in portfolio investment. The purpose of PFI inflows is to buy securities of Thai enterprises on the stock market of Thailand in Bangkok.

Figure 5.2 showed the main trends of PFI flows to Thailand. The Security Exchange of Thailand (SET) was established in 1975. The level of net PFI inflows remained very low until 1984. Figure 5.2 shows that after that year, there was a rapid rise until 1989, after which there was a slowdown in 1990 and 1991, and a recovery in 1992, which continued in 1993 and was followed by a drop in 1994.

Just as in the case of DFI flows, the increase in PFI inflows cannot be explained by any policy change in Thailand. The full liberalization of foreign exchange transactions was implemented only in 1991 and 1992. As in the case of direct investment, it appears that policy adjustments follow, rather than precede, the increases in capital inflows.

The level of PFI inflows has been explained by (i) the rate of growth of GDP and (ii) the rate of return on the SET (see Pongpisanupichit et al. 1989). Kangwanpornsiri (1993) performed an econometric analysis on more recent data: his findings confirm these explanations, and also indicate that the liberalization of capital-account transactions since 1990 has encouraged PFI flows, but that the political unrest in 1991–92 discouraged PFI.

The main source of these funds is formed by international institutional investors who look to stock markets like those of Thailand to increase their returns or to spread their risks. The increase in PFI inflows meant a substantial injection of demand on the limited stock market. The supply of securities is relatively fixed in the short run, and thus the main effect of the PFI inflows is to push up the price of the securities.[19]

The increase in the level of the net inflows of PFI in recent years has, of course, increased the demand for securities. This may have invited the issuing of new shares. Pongpisanupichit et al. (1989) could not establish any econometric link between PFI flows and primary market activity, but their analysis concentrated on short-term fluctuations. If one adopts a longer-term perspective, it appears that the value of new capital mobilized on the SET has increased since the early 1980s to a level equivalent to about 5 per cent of total private corporate investment (with perhaps a slight tendency to increase further in recent years). The privatization of some state enterprises has also benefitted from the active stock market. But is difficult to establish a statistical relationship between the short-term ups and downs of PFI flows and the new capital issues. It could be suggested that the increase in the mobilization of equity capital is a more structural process, unaffected by the short-term fluctuations in PFI, but certainly encouraged by the strong performance of the SET, which helped to make new equity capital a cheaper source of finance.

The possibility of financing new investments by issuing new shares may affect the composition of the liability structure of the firm more than the level of investment. When new capital becomes relatively cheaper, it may replace debt financing. Research on the emerging stock markets, however, found no such substitution between own capital and debt. Rather, the leverage ratio of corporations was found to increase with higher stock market activity (Demirguc-Kunt 1992), suggesting that an active stock market increases the debt-carrying capacity of corporations.[20] The data analysed above seem to support this finding: the increased inflows of DFI and PFI have been accompanied by even sharper increases in domestic and foreign borrowing by private corporations.

It would thus appear that the increased inflows of PFI have stimulated activity at the SET and helped to make it more attractive for corporations to issue new shares. It is also likely that the increased access to equity capital has not substituted for debt financing. Rather, the stronger equity base has been used to expand borrowing, pushing up leverage ratios to still higher levels. In all this it is difficult to establish a significant statistical correlation between the net inflows of PFI and the level of private investment over the period 1970–94. The amounts of PFI involved are small, relative to private investment, and PFI flows are highly volatile, thus preventing a good statistical fit.[21] Still, it could be argued that in an indirect way PFI flows have also helped to finance the high levels of private investment.

Figure 5.2 illustrates the short-term and speculative nature of PFI flows. Single events can have large effects on the flow of PFI. For instance, the decrease in 1990 is generally ascribed to the impact of the Gulf War. The further decrease in 1991 may be attributed to the political instability in Thailand. The recovery in 1992 took place in the second half of the year, after the domestic political unrest had settled down. The subsequent rise (in 1993) and fall (in 1994) appear to follow global trends in PFI flows to emerging markets. It would appear that Thailand has become one of the popular destinations for the large flows of capital moving around the world as a result of attempts to spread risks and attempts to find quick profits. Most of the PFI inflows into Thailand come from international institutional investors who carefully manage their investment portfolios, calculating on an almost daily basis the differences in returns and risks among different countries. In the portfolios of these large investors, Thailand has only a small share, but small adjustments in their portfolios are major shifts of funds on relatively small markets like the SET, and have significant effects which go beyond the stock market.

With the changing nature of capital inflows in recent years, the channels along which they influence the economy have also changed. Earlier capital flows, like public sector loans or DFI, were linked to expenditure on specific public or private investment projects. The foreign funds often did not even enter the economy: they were immediately used to pay for capital goods purchased for the project. This has now changed. A part of the foreign borrowing by the private sector may finance local expenditure. PFI funds are initially deposited with domestic banks and non-resident deposits also add to the inflow of foreign exchange. This means that the inflow of funds now has a direct impact on the monetary base and thus an indirect impact on the monetary aggregates of Thailand. The inflows of funds are reflected in the high level of net foreign reserves of the Bank of Thailand (equivalent to 6.5 months of imports in 1994) and in the high growth rate of domestic credit. The monetary expansion contributes to inflation: it is remarkable that in recent years the pattern of inflation has followed the trends in capital inflows quite closely.[22] Under these conditions, the central bank is confronted by numerous difficulties in its attempt to 'cool down' the economy.

5.8 Managing the Investment Boom

5.8.1 Containing inflationary pressures

After the successful structural adjustment, the challenge of economic policy shifted to the economic management of the investment boom. The task was quite different from that of the loan boom period in two respects. Firstly, the level of capital inflows was significantly higher; secondly, all of it was directed towards the private sector.

The *World Economic Outlook* (October 1992) of the IMF identifies 'dealing with capital inflows' as a significant economic policy problem for countries faced with sudden upturns in inflows. The report states that the inflows are largely caused by domestic factors, such as substantial increases in the returns on capital and high rates of interest. It is noted that the inflows may increase domestic investment, but may also lead to inflationary pressures and to an appreciation of the real exchange rate. Monetary policy measures are suggested, as the best way of dealing with these problems (see IMF 1992: 29–40).

Certainly, Thailand was one of the countries confronted by this policy challenge. The large capital inflows and the very high level of investment created significant demand pressures, and indeed, the rate of inflation increased, albeit modestly. To fight inflation, both fiscal and monetary policies were implemented.

Fiscal policy or, more generally, public sector financial policies helped to combat overheating and inflation. Total government expenditure, at constant prices, stagnated between 1985 and 1988, while real government investment actually decreased (see Table 4.5 of Chapter 4). After 1988 real government expenditures started to rise again, but until 1990 the rate of increase was lower than the growth of GDP, so that the ratio of government expenditure to GDP continued to decrease. After 1990 the government expenditure ratio increased again, but it remains considerably lower than the levels of the late 1970s and early 1980s (see Figure 4.2 of Chapter 4). The state enterprise investment ratio fell as well. The reduction in the public sector investment ratio partly reflected the attempt to stabilize the economy in the face of large capital inflows, and partly reflected government policy to allow the private sector more initiative in the economic development process. With the rapid economic growth, tax revenue and state enterprise savings increased. The strong private sector performance implied that actual revenue collection far exceeded budget estimates in all years after 1987. The fiscal deficit and public sector savings gap turned into a surplus from 1988 onwards. These public sector financial policies met the need for short-term stabilization admirably, but at the same time questions arose whether in the longer run public expenditure would be sufficient to support the further growth of the private sector. One could raise the question whether the policies implemented to accommodate the private investment boom may have 'crowded out' necessary public investment.

Monetary policy was also implemented to cope with the excess demand situation. Still, money growth throughout most of this period was strong: credit to the private sector increased very rapidly. Attempts to curb credit expansion were hampered by the large capital inflows, which created high liquidity on the domestic money market. In order to fight the creeping inflation and the rapidly widening current-account deficit, the authorities raised the ceiling on savings deposits at commercial banks twice in 1990, from 7.25 to 9 and 12 per cent in March and November respectively. The ceilings on time deposits were abolished. When the money market became tight in 1988, there was at first no increase in the loan interest-rate ceiling, for fear that higher rates would feed inflation and would hurt smaller borrowers who are not able to borrow abroad. In 1990, however, maximum loan rates were raised, from 15 to 16.5 per cent and later to 19 per cent. Still later, these ceilings were also abolished. The interest rates of finance companies were adjusted along the lines of commercial banks. In addition to adjusting the interest rate structure, the Bank of Thailand also sold central bank bonds to financial institutions to absorb excess liquidity, and reduced the maximum amount of overdrafts in order to combat inflation.

The task of monetary policy has become much more complex in recent years. The main task of monetary policy is to defend the internal (inflation) and external (exchange rate) value of the currency. To do so, the Bank of Thailand sets targets for monetary aggregates (such as M2 and domestic credit) and tries to attain these targets through its transactions with the financial institutions. Such transactions include (i) loans to banks, (ii) refinancing of financial institutions' lending to priority sectors, and (iii) transactions on the repurchase market (see Supapongae & Hataiseree 1993). These transactions enable the central bank to influence the access of financial institutions to reserve monies by varying the availability of such funds or by varying their cost (the interest rate).

Monetary policy used to rely on the control of monetary aggregates through variations in the refinancing facilities of the Bank of Thailand and through open market operations (including operations on the foreign exchange market). Over the years there has been a shift to a more active use of the interest rate instrument, and the Bank of Thailand has started to use variations in its interest rates to indicate its view on monetary policy (see Robinson et al. 1991 and Tseng & Corker 1991).

A high interest-rate policy, such as that of the early 1980s, was expected to (i) induce savings, (ii) slow down credit demand, and (iii) align with international interest rates to prevent capital outflows. The high interest rates in the years 1982–85 did not have any noticeable effect on savings, but private credit growth and private investment were relatively low in these years, possibly due partly to the high interest cost. These policies contributed to the sharp decline in the rate of inflation from its high 1981 level, but they did not help to reduce the large current-account deficits. Hence, the recourse to explicit credit ceilings in January 1984.

By the late 1980s, inflationary pressures emerged again as the economy was becoming overheated by double-digit growth. And again high interest-rate policy was used to fight inflation, but to no avail. The high domestic interest rate, that previously controlled credit growth and prevented capital outflows, now actively attracted capital inflows. Thus, rather than reducing monetary reserves, the high interest rates increased them. This was the result of the integration of Thailand's financial system into the international financial markets. This integration has certainly been enhanced by the growing importance of DFI and PFI flows, and has become more firmly entrenched with the financial liberalizations of recent years.

The free movement of international capital, together with the adherence to a more or less fixed exchange rate, links capital inflows to the foreign reserves of the monetary system. Capital flows thus directly influence the amount of reserve money, and so reduce the control of the monetary authorities over this central operational target of monetary policy.

The large current-account deficit of recent years, like that of the early 1980s, has not been cured by the high interest-rate policy. But the comparison to the early 1980s is not complete. At that time, the current-account deficit was associated with large public sector deficits. Now, the public sector has a surplus, and the current-account gap reflects the large gap between private investment and savings. The high interest rate does nothing to increase private savings, and does little to discourage private investment. Its influence on domestic credit growth is very limited. Variations in the central bank rate for loans to financial institutions only influences the extent to which financial institutions borrow from the central bank or from abroad (Nidhiprabha 1987). More direct interventions, for instance through the repurchase market, are difficult in a market that is very liquid with the government repaying its debt and with large capital inflows, and such interventions can easily be evaded by banks and firms that can borrow directly off-shore. In recent years, the Bank of Thailand has regularly (e.g. in 1988, 1990, 1991 and 1995) sold central bank bonds to financial institutions to absorb some liquidity from the markets. The Bank has also curbed the foreign borrowing by commercial banks by reducing the limits on the banks' foreign exchange exposure, and has increased the cost of non-resident deposits by increasing the reserve requirements for such deposits.

However, the effect of such measures remains limited in an open financial system. The Bank of Thailand can thus do nothing but vary its interest rates to influence international financial flows and foreign reserve holdings. Variations in such flows can help to defend the exchange rate. The high interest rates of recent years have led to very high levels of foreign reserves, and to a very stable exchange rate (with respect to the US dollar). Obviously, the stability of the exchange rate is important as it inspires confidence among domestic and foreign investors who aim mainly at export production. In itself, a stable exchange rate also helps to contain domestic inflation.

The combination of the private spending boom, the cautious public sector policy and the unwillingly accommodating monetary policy resulted in a relatively mild acceleration of inflation. However, the domestic excess demand situation was not so much reflected in the inflation rate as in the current-account deficit. The current-account deficit had widened with the increase in exogenous capital inflows (direct and portfolio investment), but in recent years short-term lending on foreign markets has increased to finance the spending boom.

The high level of investment and the rapid growth of income have led to a very sharp rise in import demand. The depreciation of the real exchange rate came to an end around 1988, when the dollar depreciation stopped. Since then the real exchange rate has appreciated slightly, as the nominal exchange rate was more or less maintained and Thai inflation increased. The depreciation of the real exchange rate, which made imports more expensive, did little to discourage import demand. The appreciation after 1988 made imports relatively cheaper; this effect was enhanced by the tariff reductions in 1990 and 1994. As noted before, the appreciation did not seriously hurt exports.

5.8.2 Structural policy issues

It is clear that, by the early 1990s, the foreign investment boom had helped to strengthen the Thai economy in many ways: incomes increased and the production and exports further diversified. But it is also clear that a number of problems remain. Some studies refer to these as 'emerging issues' (World Bank 1991a) or as 'strains of success' (UNIDO 1992), but in fact they are long-standing structural problems that, in some ways, have even been intensified by the foreign investment boom. The main problems are:

- the large current-account deficit,
- the supply of infrastructure and the proper role of the public sector,
- the income inequality, and
- the environmental degradation.

Some brief comments on each of these will conclude this chapter.

The current-account deficit

After being at a modest level in the 1960s and early 1970s, the current-account deficit has stayed at a high level almost continuously since the mid-1970s. In Chapter 3 the basic accounting identities were set out, according to which:

current-account balance = savings-investment balance = net capital flows.

This identity shows that it is possible to interpret the current-account deficit as reflecting (i) an external finance problem, (ii) a trade problem, or (iii) an investment-savings problem.

If one considers external capital flows as being exogenously determined, and if capital flows are free, the economy has to accommodate high inflows of capital through a large current-account deficit. Above, it was argued that flows of DFI and PFI are indeed largely exogenous, i.e. determined on the supply side of funds. The investment-savings balance and the current account have to adjust to absorb the inflow of these funds. If the inflows are considered undesirable, capital controls are needed. However, it was also shown above that the recent increase in external borrowing was not exogenous, but largely a reflection of the high level of domestic expenditure (i.e. high investment and/or low savings). As shown in Chapter 4, the debt that has accumulated as result of this borrowing is, in relative terms, still modest (see Table 4.3 for debt/GDP and debt/export ratios, and Figure 4.4 for the debt-service ratio). At this point in time there is no reason to worry about Thailand's ability to carry this debt, and no doubt about Thailand's external creditworthiness. Still, many feel that in the medium term Thailand's dependence on external finance should be reduced.

The current-account deficit could also be considered as primarily a trade problem. Export growth has been very fast, but import growth even faster. As it is difficult to imagine an export performance scenario better than what actually occurred, it seems more obvious to look for ways to reduce the import propensity. As was established above, the DFI-induced investment boom strongly increased the import dependence, also because the technological capability of Thailand to produce its own intermediate and capital goods is still limited. The structural shortages in post-primary education, in technical education and in research and development, that were identified in Chapter 1, limit the local technical capacity and help maintain a high level of import dependence.

Most of all, however, it seems that the current-account deficit reflects the investment-savings imbalance. The identity above states that the current-account deficit reflects the high level of investment and the low level of savings. Can Thailand increase its savings ratio? At present the public sector already runs a savings surplus, with the public sector savings ratio at a high level. It is unlikely that the surplus will persist. First of all, there is a strong demand for more public spending, for instance on infrastructure (see below) or on education. Secondly, the public sector surpluses are likely to give rise to pressures for tax reductions.

It would thus appear that if Thailand wants to maintain the high level of investment, but reduce its current-account deficit, it should increase private savings. Compared to the NICs with rapidly expanding economies, or to neighbouring Malaysia, Thailand's private savings ratio is low. Is it possible to raise the private savings ratio? The analysis in section 3.4 of Chapter 3 did not provide reason for much optimism in that respect.

Infrastructure

The rapid growth of the late 1980s quickly outpaced the available infrastructure of roads, electricity, telecommunications, and so on. The costs of these shortages are substantial. A recent study among manufacturing firms in Bangkok and Chiengmai found that losses due to power failures, transport delays and inefficient communication facilities added up to 8.9 per cent of the total output of the firms, thus adding significantly to their production cost (Chalamwong 1993).

The fiscal austerity of the late 1980s prevented early and decisive action to tackle the problem. There were also optimistic expectations – perhaps overly optimistic – about what the private sector could provide in this field. Many of the proposed private sector infrastructure projects have involved prolonged haggling with the authorities, which caused substantial delays, but also gave rise to doubts as to whether private sector initiatives can really effectively implement such huge projects.

A tendency to increasingly rely on private sector initiatives can also be seen in the field of education, another area where public sector spending is under pressure despite widely observed shortages.

As noted in Chapter 1, Thailand's development strategy has always left the initiative in economic matters to the private sector. In recent years there have been attempts to privatize activities previously performed by the public sector, including infrastructure and education. This has reduced the government expenditure ratio to a low level, even from a comparative perspective (see section 4.3.1 of Chapter 4). The question could be raised whether the government is not shedding too many of its responsibilities.

Income inequality

A long-standing problem of Thai economic development is its uneven pattern. Table 2.4 of Chapter 2 showed the growing discrepancies among sectoral labour productivities and the associated growing inequalities of income. Since the first household survey of 1962–63, income inequality has continuously increased. With the rapid growth of the last few years, the incidence of poverty has decreased again, but the income inequality has risen to very high levels.

Another way of looking at this problem is to emphasize the geographical imbalances: too much of economic activity is centred around Bangkok. The greater Bangkok area accounts for close to 50 per cent of GDP and over 80 per cent of manufacturing value added. While the rich concentrate in and around Bangkok, the poor are mainly found in rural areas. It is estimated that 80 per cent of the poor are found in the agricultural sector; 90 per cent of them live in rural areas (Siamwalla 1991). But as the agricultural terms of trade deteriorate, pressure on agricultural incomes increases, and landlessness is increasing, the rural poor drift in greater numbers to the cities. A cynical outcome of this concentration of activities is that the wealth of Bangkok is translated into urban congestion and ever greater traffic jams.

Foreign investment has certainly intensified this pattern, with most of the foreign investment projects being centred on manufacturing and services activities around Bangkok. A more even development would require government intervention to stimulate more rural-based development projects. However, Thai newspapers (and politicians?) are more concerned with the daily traffic jams of the city than with the plight of the rural poor. It is often asserted that an export-oriented development strategy would also help to improve the income distribution. However, when Wattananukit and Bhongmakapat ran a model simulation of an increase in exports, they found that the income distribution became more *inequal*, particularly when the exports come from the manufacturing sector. With the increase in exports, production and income rise, but wage income rises far less than profit income (see Wattananukit & Bhongmakapat 1989).

Environmental degradation

The urban congestion and pollution is one example of the environmental implications of the unplanned and uncontrolled growth that occurred in Thailand. Another example can be found in the excessive deforestation that was slowed down only a few years ago. The waste of the growing industrial sector also contributes to the environmental degradation in Thailand, as is amply shown in the studies prepared for the 1990 Year-End Conference of the TDRI (TDRI 1990). Unfortunately, some foreign investors may be attracted to Thailand by production cost that are low, compared to those in their home country, because environmental controls in Thailand are either absent or easily evaded. Certainly, the rapid growth of industrial production and the geographical concentration of economic activities have put a heavy burden on the ecological balance of Thailand.

The problems briefly noted above are not *caused* by foreign investment; they were there before the foreign investment boom started. But the recent growth boom has certainly increased their urgency. And the foreign investment has, in itself, done nothing to resolve the issues, and may, in fact, have intensified them. Of course, it is not the task of foreign investors to resolve the longer-term structural problems of Thai economic development. That is up to the Thai politicians and economic bureaucrats. As argued in the previous chapter and in this one, their track record is not bad. They successfully stabilized the economy in the mid-1980s and managed to defend stability during the investment boom of the late 1980s. As Chapter 4 showed, structural adjustment 'Thai style' consisted of macroeconomic stabilization without much real structural adjustment. Some of these adjustments were implemented later, in the early 1990s, and took the form of liberalizations of trade and finance.

One could argue that the longer-term structural problems that emerged from the growth boom require structural adjustment once again. Maybe these adjustments need to be more fundamental than those implemented before now. An enormous effort will be required of planners and politicians if Thailand is to embark on a course of development which aims for more balance among the various productive sectors, a greater technological capacity and less dependence on the technology embedded in imported intermediate and capital goods, a better planned and more evenly distributed supply of infrastructure and social services, greater equality of incomes, and adequate environmental regulation.

6 The Macroeconomic Impact of External Finance: Summary of Findings and Model Simulations

6.1 A Summary of Findings

In Chapters 4 and 5, two booms in foreign capital inflows were analysed: the public sector lending boom of the late 1970s/early 1980s, and the private foreign investment boom which started in the late 1980s. Various effects related to the inflows of external capital were identified and explored, and it can be concluded that the two booms had some similar impacts, but that there were also major differences between the two periods. This confirmed the hypothesis that it is not only the *level* of the capital inflows that matters, but also, and maybe more importantly, the *type* of capital that is received.

The conclusions of the analysis so far may be summarized in nine points listing the similarities and the differences between the two foreign capital booms.

(1) Both booms were initiated by and made possible by international events. In the 1970s the liquidity of international financial markets after the first oil shock, and the institutional developments at these markets, increased the access of developing countries to commercial loans rather suddenly and sharply. The increase in DFI flows after 1986 was due to large shifts in the exchange rates of the major world currencies, and to the worldwide restructuring, or globalization, of production that took place in major economies.

During the first period, international loans were available almost exclusively to public sector borrowers, since the international creditors demanded government guarantees. The second boom was, by its nature, directed towards the private sector.

(2) The first period was characterized by large external shocks (see Figure 4.1). Around 1979 there were the increases in oil prices and in global interest rates. In the early 1980s there were the recession in world trade and the debt crisis. Compared to these periods, the late 1980s and early 1990s were periods of tranquillity. In this light, it was perhaps inevitable that in the first period the increased access to international credit market was used to some extent to compensate for the negative external shocks that occurred. In the interpretation of the differential impact of the two foreign capital booms it is important to recognize this sharp difference in external conditions.

(3) In both periods the inflow of international finance had a sharp expansionary impact on the investment ratio of the receiving sector. In the late 1970s the public sector investment ratio rose to high levels, and in the late 1980s the private sector investment ratio increased sharply. There was a contrast in the impact on the savings ratio of the receiving sector. During the loan boom, the public sector savings ratio decreased, whereas during the DFI boom the private sector savings ratio marginally increased. The difference may be due to inherent behavioural differences between the two sectors, but may also be related to the less favourable external conditions during the first period. However, in the second period the increase in the private investment ratio also far exceeded the increase in the savings ratio, so that in both periods the sectoral investment-savings gap widened substantially. In fact, the investment-savings gap widened by more than the increase in external capital inflows, so that the claims of the receiving sector on the domestic financial markets also increased.

(4) It is not sufficient to analyse the impact on the receiving sector; the other sectors in the economy are also affected. There are differences in the impact on the accumulation patterns of the other sectors. During the public sector loan boom, the private investment ratio initially increased alongside the public investment ratio. But then the

private investment ratio, and in particular private corporate investment, stagnated and decreased. Chapter 4 concluded that this was due to the increasingly negative investment climate. The private sector's investment demand was undermined by the appreciating real exchange rate and stagnating exports, widening public sector deficits, a growing external debt burden, and a high real domestic interest rate. All these negative factors were direct results of the loan boom. Of course, in addition to these factors the external shocks of the period, noted above, made the private sector reluctant to invest.

The DFI boom had a direct effect on the investments of private corporations. But the residential investments by households also started to increase rapidly once the boom was on its way. The impact of public investment was delayed. Initially, government policy kept the public investment down, to restore public sector financial balance. The public sector investment ratio started to increase again in 1990, when the public finances were sound and the private sector boom had resulted in urgent demand for infrastructure and public utilities.

(5) The upsurge in capital inflows resulted in an appreciation of the real exchange rate in both periods. The years 1977–80 showed a gradual appreciation, and the years 1988–94 a more rapid appreciation of the real exchange rate (see Figure 4.3). In the first period, this appreciation was reinforced by the appreciation of the US dollar, to which the baht was pegged. This led to an appreciation of the trade-weighted real exchange rate between 1979 and 1984. The question can be raised whether in this period the easy access to international financing allowed an overvalued exchange rate to be maintained. This was done at the expense of stagnating exports.

In the period 1985–88 the appreciation of the real exchange rate caused by domestic inflation was more than compensated by the changes in the international currencies. The dollar depreciated, and the baht, although formally no longer linked to the dollar, followed the dollar's movements closely. The trade-weighted real exchange rate depreciated sharply. After 1988, when the dollar stabilized, the trade-weighted real exchange rate of the baht also started to appreciate.

Exports have proved to be very sensitive to the movements of the trade-weighted real exchange rate, and the trends of the exchange rate largely explain the stagnation of exports during the early 1980s and the export boom of the late 1980s. But the capital flows also played a direct role. In the 1970s the capital inflows led to an increase in investment, mainly in the public sector (public utilities). The DFI boom concentrated investment in export-oriented manufacturing activities.

(6) The debt situations in the two periods differ sharply. The loan boom led to a rapid accumulation of external debt. The ratio of external debt to exports increased from 59 per cent in 1977 to 162 per cent in 1985, as the debt was growing and exports were stagnating. The debt-service ratio was 23 per cent in 1985. After these peaks, the public sector reforms and the rapid growth of exports resulted in a rapid decrease of the debt-export and the debt-service ratios.

Direct foreign investments themselves do not create debt. The debt/export ratio dropped to 77 per cent in 1989. But the DFI boom was accompanied by an unprecedented rise in the private investment ratio and a sharp increase in the private sector investment-savings gap. Section 5.6 showed how import-intensive the pattern of growth set in motion by the DFI boom is. The import/GDP ratio increased by more than the export/GDP ratio. To finance these gaps, which were far in excess of the DFI inflows, considerable foreign borrowing was needed. The total external debt tripled, from 18 billion US dollars in 1988 to 54 billion in 1994. The debt/export ratio also started to rise again after 1989.

The debt-service ratio remains moderate, as the international interest rates are relatively low and the exports are increasing rapidly. In 1994 the debt-service ratio was around 11 per cent.

(7) By the 1990s the relationship of Thailand to the international financial markets had fundamentally changed. Thailand remains sensitive to the strong fluctuations on the supply side of international finance. The recent decrease in DFI flows is at least partly due to poor economic conditions in some of the source countries. The ups and downs of PFI flows follow trends on world financial markets determined by events like interest rate policies in the United States or currency crises in Mexico.

But the supply side no longer dominates as it did in the past. The demand side has become much more important. The Thai financial system has become fully integrated with international markets. Domestic excess demand pressures are no longer constrained by the availability of domestic credit: borrowing abroad has become easy and cheap. Short-term capital inflows and outflows have become very sensitive to interest-rate differences between Thai and international financial markets.

(8) The policy responses to the two foreign capital booms were quite different. In the first period, public sector policies were, by necessity, expansionary. The increase in foreign borrowing was accompanied by an increase in public sector investment spending. The negative external shocks of 1979–80 were also largely accommodated by external borrowing, which softened the impact of the shocks on the growth record, but may also have initiated the negative interaction between external finance and the domestic macroeconomic (im)balances. When adjustment became unavoidable, in the mid-1980s, Thailand fell back on the traditional policy regime of conservative fiscal and monetary policies, with the substantial devaluation of 1984 as the only unusual element.

Cautious and conservative policy also characterized the initial reaction to the DFI boom. Public expenditure remained under tight control, and, as revenue increased with the rapid economic growth, the public sector generated a surplus. Monetary policy was cautious, with very high real interest rates and a stable exchange rate.

Only after the success period of double-digit growth did policy become more adventurous. Public spending increased (although the public sector continued to run a surplus) and structural reforms were implemented in the form of import liberalization, financial liberalization, liberalization of international capital transactions, and the introduction of the value added tax.

In recent years, the liberalization of the financial markets and of international financial flows has posed new policy challenges. Traditional cautious economic policies' effectiveness in controlling the economy has weakened. Even the large fiscal surplus and the high domestic interest rates of the last few years could do little to 'cool down' the economy. These policies could contain inflation but could not reduce it, and they had no effect on the large current-account deficit.

(9) The ultimate question is whether foreign capital helps to accelerate economic growth in a way that is economically sustainable in the longer run. For growth to be sustainable in the longer run, own savings and exports must grow rapidly enough to maintain the required levels of investment and to meet the external obligations on debt and investment income. This requirement is very obvious in the case of loan-finance, which leads to a stock of accumulated external debt. To prevent the external debt from rising too high and to ensure a current-debt servicing that does not reduce the capacity to import, net exports must grow fast enough to generate the foreign exchange required to finance (i) the increased import demand that accompanies faster growth, and (ii) the debt-servicing obligations. This is only possible if own savings rise enough to finance an increasing share of the investments.

In the case of foreign investment, financing these requirements may seem to be less urgent. The foreign investments do not generate a debt, and in principle there is no limit to the stock of foreign-owned capital or to the share of foreign-owned capital in the total capital stock of the country. However, although it does not create a debt, foreign investment does lead to substantial 'investment income' payments, which have to be financed from export earnings. Moreover, DFI-led growth tends to be associated with a rising import intensity.

It is clear, in retrospect, that the pattern of growth of the first period was not sustainable. The foreign loan boom first led to a few years of high investment and rapid growth, but these levels could not be maintained, and gave way to a prolonged recession and to a painful process of stabilization and adjustment. It is difficult to determine to what extent this recession was due to the inconsistencies inherent in loan-financed development, and to what extent the severe external shocks that rocked the Thai economy in this period were responsible. In reality these two aspects interacted. It can be concluded, however, that a situation in which external loans finance investments largely in non-traded sectors, combined with a passive exchange rate policy, is not viable in the longer run because of the anti-export bias.

The second foreign finance boom also led almost immediately to high levels of investment and growth. This time these levels were maintained in the longer run. The growth rate fell from its double-digit levels of the late 1980s, but stayed at very stable and high levels in the early 1990s. There is no indication at the time of writing that these high growth rates cannot be maintained in the medium run. There is a large current-account deficit, but this can be easily financed without leading to excessive debt levels.

It would be dangerous, however, to conclude on the basis of this evidence that the private sector flows of the recent period generate more and longer-lasting growth than the public sector flows of the first period did. The recession of the early 1980s, and the absence of such economic decline in the early 1990s, must be evaluated within the context of the rather different external conditions. Still, it would appear that the second foreign finance boom, with its emphasis on export-oriented activities, provides more guarantees for a sustainable pattern of growth.

6.2 The General Equilibrium Model

6.2.1 Economic model-building in Thailand

Economic model-building in Thailand began in the 1970s.[1] The early models were all econometric models. One of the biggest among these is the Bank of Thailand model (see Chaipravat et al. 1979), which contains a substantial financial block and is used by the central bank in monetary policy analysis.

Nijathaworn and Arya (1987) conclude that the macroeconometric models of the 1970s were ill-equipped to deal with the policy problems of the 1980s. Specifically, it was noted that the models, often designed to study processes related to output growth, could not adequately explain the economy's adjustments to external shocks. Most models also failed to reflect financial interactions, particularly interactions among government deficit financing, domestic finance and foreign borrowing.

Nijathaworn and Arya proceeded to construct an econometric model of 133 equations that would suffer less from these shortcomings and would trace more convincingly the interactions between the real and the financial sectors. Their model includes a rather detailed analysis of the demand for financial assets and liabilities by the private sector and the government, and of the portfolio behaviour of financial institutions. Unfortunately, the financial block of the model is not very convincing.

It is not unlikely that due to the rather rigid assumptions with respect to the role of international finance (assumed to be exogenous), the model fails to capture some of the interactions between international and domestic finance.

Another recent, smaller, macroeconomic model has been constructed with the explicit purpose of modelling external influences on the Thai economy (see Nidhiprabha et al. 1989, Sawamiphakdi & Kamheangpatiyooth 1991, Ramangkura & Nidhiprabha 1991, who all use versions of the same basic model). This model has equations to explain the exports and imports of various commodities, and a few equations that determine the financial portfolio behaviour of the private sector and of the main financial institutions. However, the model is too small to capture the full interaction between external trade and finance and the domestic economy.[2]

In Jansen (1995) a similarly small econometric model is introduced that is specifically designed to trace the macroeconomic impact of foreign investment on the Thai economy. This model enables detailed analysis of the interactions between DFI and private investment, imports and exports, but is rather simplistic in its modelling of fiscal and monetary aspects.

In the 1980s another line of modelling gradually emerged: the general equilibrium models, based on a social accounting matrix (SAM). The advantage of these models is that they more explicitly and consistently include the interdependencies among the main sectors and institutions in the economy. The first computable general equilibrium model (CGE model), by Amranand and Grais (1984) was based on a 1980 SAM with 22 production activities (sectors) and a great variety of domestic institutions (seven groups of households, public and private corporations, government). However, the model has no financial sector: savings from the various institutions are grouped together in a 'savings pool', from which funds are then allocated to the various investing agencies according to certain rules, to finance investments.

In sharp contrast to this first CGE model is the subsequent model of Taylor and Rosensweig (1990),[3] which is specifically designed to introduce financial markets and portfolio behaviour into the CGE model. In this model the real sector is much more simple: it includes only three commodities (traded goods, non-traded goods and goods from state enterprises), produced with CES production functions, and only one type of household.

The financial sector is modelled in some detail. The flow-of-funds block of the SAM defines the financial flows, i.e. the changes in the stocks of assets and liabilities that influence the portfolio decisions of the institutions and the banks. To link the portfolios of (stocks of) assets and liabilities to the financial flows that appear in the SAM, the stocks of assets and liabilities at the beginning of the period are taken as the starting point. The flow of savings throughout the year, and the adjustment in portfolios in response to changes in relative prices then determine the end-of-period stocks.

The accumulation behaviour is captured in explicit investment and savings functions for households, corporations and government. The model contains equations that describe how the households and firms decide on portfolios of financial assets and liabilities. The model explains only 'net' positions: the net holdings of financial assets by households and the funding of the net financing gap of corporations. CES-type functions are used to formulate the portfolio choice that maximizes the utility of returns on assets or minimizes the cost of liabilities. The supply of loans by banks depends on the level of deposits received (at the fixed deposit rate) plus the advances obtained from the central bank and foreign lending. The interest rate fluctuates to clear the market for credit. The central bank can decide on credit to banks, and holds the foreign reserves that arise from the current- and capital-account transactions on the balance of payments.

The model is used in some comparative static simulations of monetary policies. The conclusion is that the effectiveness of monetary policy interventions can be seriously undermined by the openness of the country to international financial markets.

Vongpradhip (1987, 1988) constructs a model that is quite similar to that of Taylor and Rosensweig. Her data base is a 1984 SAM, and the way in which the real sector is broken down is slightly different (into an agriculture and a non-agriculture sector). The financial block of the model adds to the Taylor and Rosensweig model a rather simple informal financial market, where the household sector can borrow. This model is also used in a number of comparative static simulations.

A number of other CGE models are available for Thailand, but they do not include substantial financial blocks.[4]

The model presented here has a number of improvements over those described above.

(a) The model is dynamic: in the simulations over a number of years, the full impact of portfolio behaviour will become evident. In the simulations the portfolio adjustments in one year provide the beginning-of-period stocks for the next year.

(b) The SAM on which the model is built is more recent (1989) and more elaborate than the data used in the other CGE models with financial blocks. The real sector block of the SAM and the model will distinguish between six activities (sectors) or commodities. For each of these sectors, production conditions will be specified, trade patterns will be determined and final demand will be generated. In that way, the model will provide a more detailed representation of the structural features of the Thai economy.

(c) The financial portfolios are modelled in more detail. For each agent, and for financial institutions as well, a detailed analysis of assets and liabilities will be made, so that the full portfolio decision becomes visible, rather than only its net outcome. Financial institutions are modelled, like households and corporations, along a portfolio approach, in which they make marginal decisions based on changes in relative returns or costs. The role of international finance is made more explicit by the inclusion of the main types of international finance (DFI, PFI, loans) and by the definition of the main channels along which these different types of finance flow into and out of the economy. In view of the recent growth of the Stock Exchange of Thailand, the model has created a special account for the stock exchange, which is a destination for investments by domestic agents and by foreigners (portfolio investment).

(d) The model includes a detailed analysis of savings patterns and investment behaviour of each of the main economic agents and of the financial intermediation between them. The financial intermediation is modelled along the lines of the portfolio approach as also found in Taylor and Rosensweig (1990) and Vongpradhip (1987, 1988), but in contrast to these earlier models, the dynamic nature of the present model emphasizes more the role of asset and liability stocks in the adjustment process.

6.2.2 Introduction to the model

The analysis in Chapters 4 and 5 compared economic performance during two periods of high capital inflows. The comparison failed to lead to clear conclusions, not only because there were differences in the level and the type of capital inflows in the two periods, but also because there were differences in accompanying external conditions and in policy responses. This made it difficult to assess the extent to which the different outcomes may be ascribed to the nature of the capital flows and to what extent the differences in conditions and policies are responsible.

This chapter presents another way of analysing the same questions, an approach which can avoid some of these problems. An elaborate model has been constructed for the Thai economy, and this model will be used for simulations to study the effects of assumed shifts in three sets of variables: capital flows, external shocks and policy interventions. In this way the effects of these exogenous variables can be separated.

The present CGE model was developed in an earlier study (see Jemio & Jansen 1993). An outline of the model is presented in the appendix to this chapter. A full description of the functional forms and equations of the model can be found in Jemio and Jansen (1993).

The CGE model is built around the social accounting matrix of Thailand for 1989 that was introduced in Chapter 2. The SAM captures the basic structural features and sectoral and institutional balances of the economy. The CGE model adds the behavioural equations and parameters. The modelling approach fits into the 'structuralist' CGE tradition.[5] This tradition fully recognizes structural characteristics of the economy by allowing different closure rules for distinct commodity and asset markets (flex-fix price rules) and for the savings-investment balances of the different institutional agents (prior savings or investment-led) depending on market conditions. The Thailand SAM includes a fully specified inter-institutional flow-of-funds block. This makes it possible to link sub-matrices for the (stocks of) assets and liabilities to the SAM. The financial part of the SAM distinguishes the Thailand SAM from many other SAMs that have been constructed for developing countries, in which this part is often omitted.[6] The inclusion of the financial block and the satellite assets/liabilities stock sub-matrices in the SAM also allows a full specification in the CGE model of portfolio behaviour, financial market intermediation and savings-investment balance adjustment for each of the institutional agents in the system.

The SAM for 1989 (see Table 2.9 of Chapter 2) recognized four domestic institutions (households, corporations, state enterprises, government) engaged in six production activities (agriculture, etc.). For each of the institutions the SAM gave a current account, with income generation and current expenditure, and a capital account, with savings, investment and financial intermediation, including foreign finance. The financial intermediation occurred through banks, other financial institutions, the stock market and international financial markets. The SAM describes the patterns of all these flows as well as the stocks of assets and liabilities for the year 1989. The CGE model adds behavioural dynamics to these static patterns. For instance, income generation is modelled by production functions and factor markets, and consumption expenditure and saving are modelled using consumption functions. The accumulation behaviour is captured in investment demand functions and in equations describing the formation of optimal portfolios of assets and liabilities.

The dynamic nature of the model is reflected in, among other things, the lag structures incorporated in some of the functions, including investment and export functions, and in portfolio adjustments over the year. These lag structures and adjustments through stock variables make it possible to distinguish between short-term and medium-term adjustments.

The CGE model has been constructed to assess the impact of external factors, and in particular of external finance, on the economy. Chapters 4 and 5 identified the main channels along which external finance affects the economic performance. These findings may be summarized in five points.

(a) Capital inflows have an expansionary effect on the investment of the receiving sector. The model captures this in the investment demand equations of the private corporate and state enterprise sectors. Private corporate investment demand is made a function of an accelerator variable and of the interest rate, but also of the level of DFI inflows. The accelerator and the interest rate will reflect the crowding-in or -out that was discussed in Chapter 4. Other elements that were discussed in Chapter 4, such as the infrastructure effect of public investment or the external debt overhang, are not directly included in the private investment demand function, but are, of course, captured in the overall model structure. The investment demand of state enterprises is also driven by an accelerator term and by the level of capital inflows.

(b) The effect of capital inflows on savings is mixed, but never strongly positive. The result is that investment increases far more than savings do, and that the sectoral investment-savings gap increases. The increase in the gap exceeds the initial capital inflows, so that the borrowing requirement of the sector grows. This effect is captured in the model by the investment and saving functions and by the modelling of the financial markets. The increased demand for domestic credit pushes up the domestic interest rate. However, this effect is rather small, since the model also reflects the fact that in recent years the financial markets have become very open. Any increase in credit demand can thus be satisfied at either domestic or foreign markets, depending on relative cost.

(c) The effect of capital inflows on the trade balance is complex: three channels were identified.

(1) The real exchange rate appreciates. This would encourage imports and discourage exports.

(2) The allocation of the increased investment. Investment in the public sector is allocated to non-traded activities. Imports will increase with the higher level of investment and output, but export supply will not increase. Investment in the private sector is mainly in traded activities, so that both imports and exports can increase.

(3) The DFI-led boom of the last few years was strongly export-oriented but also had a very high import intensity.

The capital inflows in the 1970s were used mainly to finance higher investment by state enterprises. According to the 1989 SAM, state enterprises are almost exclusively engaged in non-traded activities. The capital inflows in recent years are directed towards the private sector which, according to the SAM, is predominantly engaged in traded activities.

In the model, imports are not very sensitive to relative prices. The imports of intermediate goods and capital goods are fixed by the coefficients and shares of the base year SAM. An increase in production or in investment thus causes a proportional increase in imports of intermediate goods or investment goods, independent of price changes. Only the level of imports of consumer goods is somewhat sensitive to relative price changes, but of course consumer goods imports are only a small part of total imports. The low price elasticity of import demand in developing countries is often justified by the fact that these countries lack industries producing intermediate and capital goods, and thus have no substitution possibilities in the face of rising prices. The growing import intensity that came with the DFI boom is already reflected in the 1989 SAM.

The level of exports of manufactured goods is determined by (i) the production capacity of the sector, which can be expanded by investment; (ii) relative prices, reflecting the real exchange rate; and (iii) to capture the impact of the strongly export-oriented foreign investment, the level of DFI was modelled to have an additional impact on exports of manufactured goods, i.e. an impact in addition the capacity effect under (i). The exports from other sectors are determined by relative prices.

(d) The impact of capital inflows on the stock of external debt and on debt service payments is fully reflected in the model. The external debts of the various institutions constitute part of their beginning-of-period stocks of assets and liabilities. The end-of-period stocks are the result of new borrowing and of repayment of outstanding debt. Interest payments on debt are part of the transfer payments made by the institutions. For instance, government current expenditure rises with the increase in government debt or with the rise in the interest rate. The more psychological effect of the debt overhang on the confidence of investors is not included in the model.

(e) The ultimate effect of capital inflows on growth is the outcome of all adjustment processes listed above. The CGE model is dynamic and can thus capture shifting impacts as they occur throughout the years. For instance, the initial impact of an increase in capital flows may be an acceleration of growth, but after some years rising interest rates and debt service burdens may start to slow down growth.

The main purpose of the model is to perform simulations of fluctuations in external variables (terms of trade, access to international finance) and of economic policy measures, to study their impact and effectiveness. The impacts of these shocks will be determined by the structure of the economy, as reflected in the base year SAM, and by the model's behavioural characteristics, as reflected in its elasticities and behavioural equations. It is expected that these simulations will provide useful insights into the working of the economy and will increase the understanding of the constraints facing policy-makers.

6.2.3 Simulations

The base run of the dynamic model will be taken as a benchmark against which the results of the simulations will be compared. The base run shows the dynamics of the economy, as represented by the model, when no changes in exogenous variables and base year parameters occur. All external variables (such as world prices and world interest rates) are kept at their base year level, and the same holds for all policy variables (such as exchange rates). In the base run, government spending is allowed to increase by 7 per cent per year: to not allow for a rise in government spending would be to introduce a major deflationary shock to the system.

The base run is quite satisfactory in that it depicts familiar trends in the main variables. This inspires confidence in the model's ability to capture the main characteristics of the Thai economy well. It should be noted that the base year, 1989, was in many respects an exceptional year. The GDP growth rate in that year was far above the long-term average, at 12.4 per cent. The level of portfolio foreign investment was exceptionally high, and direct foreign investment was experiencing a boom. The base run and all the simulations show a sharp drop for many of the model variables in the first year of the run. For instance, GDP growth in the base run drops, and the inflation rate also drops from its relatively high base year level. These adjustments in the first year illustrate that the model is built more around the longer-term structural characteristics of the Thai economy than on the exceptional dynamics of the base year.

In the base run, total GDP increases by 6.6 per cent per year. This growth is mainly caused by the continued high level of private investment; the private investment to GDP ratio remains high, around 24 per cent. The volume of exports grows by 8.3 per cent and that of imports by 7.0 per cent per year, so that both export and import ratios further increase. Despite the faster growth of exports over imports, the current-account deficit grows continuously from 64 billion baht in the base year to 114 billion baht in year 10; this last figure is then equivalent to 4.3 per cent of GDP.

This shows that Thailand continues to depend on foreign capital to finance its growth. Domestic savings do not increase fast enough to reduce that dependence. The stock of total foreign liabilities (that is, foreign debt excluding stocks of direct and portfolio foreign investments) increases from a level around 24 per cent of GDP in the base year to 28 per cent in the last year.

The structural change in the production structure continues along the set pattern: the share of agriculture in GDP declines further and the share of manufacturing rises. The formalization of the economy continues; the capital income of unincorporated businesses declines from 40 per cent of total income in the base year to 34 per cent in the last year. The shares of corporate capital income and of wage labour increase.

Also, the financial deepening continues. The M3/GDP ratio increases from its base year level of 83 per cent to a level of 108 per cent by the end of the simulation period.

It can thus be concluded that the base run reproduces the historical trends of dynamic change in the Thai economy reasonably well. The growth rate is somewhat lower than, but comparable to, the long-run growth rate of the Thai economy over the last two decades. The comparatively high growth rate is combined with short-term stability, as reflected in the average inflation rate of only 2.3 per cent, another historical feature of Thai development. As in the past 15 years, economic growth is shown to depend on foreign capital inflows. The base run also reproduces, or continues, the recent trends of structural change that were already discussed in Chapter 2. The 'openness' of the economy, as reflected in its export and import ratios, continues to increase; the share of the industrial sector in GDP further increases and the process of financial deepening also continues.

However, the base run does not reproduce the rapid growth that actually occurred after 1989. The growth rates of output, exports and imports of the base run all lag behind actually observed trends. And private investment, external debt and the current-account deficit are all lower in the base run than they actually were in the period 1989–94. The main reason for this difference appears to be that the levels of important exogenous variables, such as government spending and capital inflows, were in reality higher than was assumed in the base run, while the international and domestic interest rates were in fact lower than was assumed in the base run simulation. Adjusting these exogenous model variables to the levels actually observed in the period 1989–94 would raise the growth rate in the base run to a level of over 8 per cent per year, quite comparable to the growth that in fact occurred.

The base run is used to compare the outcomes of the simulations. The simulations aim to further explore some of the questions that were analysed in Chapters 4 and 5. Three questions will be explored:

(a) What would have happened if at the end of the 1980s the economy had been hit by negative external shocks (as it had been at the end of the 1970s)? This is explored by simulating an increase in import prices and an increase in the world interest rate.

(b) How important are the inflows of DFI and PFI to the economic growth of Thailand? What would happen if, for instance, the levels of DFI and PFI inflows were to decrease sharply? This is explored by simulating a decline in the inflows of DFI and PFI.

(c) What is the impact of policy interventions? How important has the public sector financial reform been for the growth and stability of the economy? As argued in Chapter 5, the public sector surpluses of the last few years have helped to maintain stability during the growth boom. On the other hand, levels of public spending have dropped sharply and are generally considered to be inadequate for an economy that is growing so fast. It will thus be necessary to increase public spending to support the growing private sector. What will the effect of such an increase be? This will be explored in the simulation in which the levels of government investment and current spending are increased. Another issue discussed in Chapter 5 is the effectiveness of monetary policy. To pursue this issue further, an increase in the rate at which the Bank of Thailand lends to commercial banks is simulated.

In each simulation, only one exogenous variable is changed, and the effects of that change on the main endogenous variables are traced over the years. Three sets of simulations are described below. The first set of simulations aims to assess how vulnerable Thailand is to external conditions. Two types of external price shocks were introduced in the model: an increase in import prices and an increase in the world interest rate. In the second set of simulations the impact of the recent upsurge in DFI and PFI is tested by the simulation of a decrease in the level of direct foreign investment inflows and a decrease in the level of foreign portfolio inflows. The first two sets of simulations can be used to assess the impact of external trade and finance conditions on the Thai economy. The final simulation seeks to study the impact of domestic policy interventions: what are the effects of an increase in government spending and of monetary policy?

External price shocks

The first simulation to be described here is an increase in the level of import prices by 10 per cent (in year 1 all import prices rise by 10 per cent and in subsequent years they stay at that higher level). As can be expected in an open and import-dependent economy, the impact of such a price rise is contractionary. Figure 6.1 shows the level of GDP as a percentage deviation from the GDP in the base run of the model. Compared to the base run, GDP is lower in all years. The increase in import prices leads immediately to an increase in the domestic prices in the mark-up sectors. The acceleration of inflation (see Figure 6.4) leads to a decrease in the real wage and to a decrease in real income. Consumption and investment demand decline and unemployment rises. Gradually, with declining levels of economic activity and some substitution of imported consumption goods, import demand decreases and to a level lower than the base run levels.

The price level (Figure 6.4) first rises above the level of the base run, but with declining employment and demand, domestic prices gradually decrease to below the base run pattern. The growth in unemployment implies that the wage rate stays considerably below its base run level. It would thus appear that the increase in import cost is largely absorbed by lower wages and lower mark-up rates, and not so much by an increase in domestic prices. The effect of this is that exports are less affected by the import cost increase, so that the current-account deficit, which increases very strongly in the first year, subsequently decreases sharply when economic activity decreases (see Figure 6.7). In later years, when GDP recovers, the current-account deficit rises again as well, and it stays considerably above its base run level. External debt, however, does not increase compared to the base run (see Figure 6.10). The import price change does not affect the relative returns on assets or cost of liabilities very much, so that portfolio adjustments are small. The larger current account is financed by a slower accumulation of the central bank's foreign reserves (the model's overall closure).

Nidhiprabha (1984) conducts the same simulation, of an increase in import prices, with his econometric model. The outcomes are comparable, showing an increase in inflation, a decrease in GDP and, in his case, an increase in external indebtedness.

According to the CGE model, an increase in the import prices of 10 per cent would result in a decrease in the average GDP growth rate over the simulation period from 6.6 per cent per year in the base run to 6.3 per cent. It should be noted that around 1980 the import price index rose by more than 60 per cent within a three-year period. The present simulation suggests that the external shocks of that time are an important reason for the poor growth record of the early 1980s.

The second external shock to be simulated is an increase in the level of the world interest rate. In fact, in the simulation the world interest rate was set higher than the domestic interest rate of the base year: the world interest rate was increased in year 1 from its base level of 9.27 per cent to a new level of 15.27 per cent, and it stayed at that higher level for the rest of the simulation period. This increase is comparable to what happened around 1980.

Given the dependency of the Thai economy on foreign capital, one could expect that such a substantial increase in the cost of external loans would have a serious impact. There is, indeed, a contractionary impact on GDP, but only a very small one (see Figure 6.1). The contraction appears to result mainly from the negative impact of the interest rate increase on foreign borrowing. The reduction in foreign borrowing reduces the funds available to finance investment. The capital inflows from abroad decline in the short run, but in the later years of the simulation period they recover to levels similar to those in the base run, despite the continued higher level of the international interest rate.

It is somewhat surprising that the higher international interest rate is not translated into higher levels for the domestic interest rate. The role of the interest rate in the model is quite complex. Various rates of return are defined in the model, such as (i) the rate of return on foreign assets (determined by the world interest rate and the exchange rate); (ii) the rate of return on corporate capital; (iii) the rate of return on unincorporated capital (both are determined by the conditions in the productive sectors); (iv) the administered rate of return on government bonds; (v) the rate of return on the stock market (mainly determined by the fluctuations of the SET index); and (vi) the rate of return on domestic financial assets. This last rate of return is determined within the model. The rates of return are indexed (base year equal to 1). It should be noted that only two of these rates of return are sensitive to conditions on domestic financial markets: the rate of return on the stock market and the rate of return on other domestic financial markets. All other rates of return are determined either exogenously or by predominantly non-financial factors.

All these rates of return enter into the portfolio decisions of the economic agents. This implies that differences in the level of the rates of return do not lead to substitution processes, but that changes in the rate of return from one year to the next will lead to substitution among assets and liabilities. One given of the model is the very high rate of return on assets in the stock market in the base year, due to the sharp increase in the SET index caused by the inflow of portfolio foreign investment. In the dynamic run of the model this high level of the index is not repeated for subsequent years.[7] As a result, the index of the rate of return on the stock market drops sharply in the first year of the base run and of the simulations, and because of the interactions between the financial markets the rate of return on domestic financial assets also decreases rather sharply.

This interaction among the domestic financial markets dominates the trends of the domestic interest rate; the large increase in the world interest rate does not affect that underlying process. So, despite the large increase in the world interest rate, the interest rate on domestic financial markets decreases and the effects of the increase in the world interest rate on the rest of the economy are not very strong.

Vongpradhip (1988) runs the reverse simulation with her CGE model, testing the impact of a decrease in the world interest rate. In her model the decrease in the world interest rate would invite more external borrowing by corporations and financial institutions, with a downward effect on the domestic interest rate. This stimulates investment and leads to an increase of GDP. With GDP, exports and import also rise.

The current account improves, also because debt service on the external debt decreases with the drop in the global interest rate. In her model, the link between the international and the domestic interest rates is more direct, resulting in stronger effects of the interest rate shock on the real variables.

External finance shocks

A third external shock that was introduced was a decrease in the level of portfolio foreign investment. In the base run it was assumed that the high level of net inflows of the base year 1989 was maintained throughout the simulation period. Now it is assumed that the level of portfolio foreign investment would decrease by 20 billion baht compared to its base year level, remaining at that lower level throughout the simulation period.

One might have expected that changes in the level of portfolio investment inflows would be mainly felt at the stock market, where the trading volumes and prices would decrease with a drop in foreign investment. In fact, the effects of such a drop in inflows outside the stock market are quite substantial. This appears to be due to two effects: first, the wealth effects of fluctuations in the SET index, and second, the monetary effects of the inflows of portfolio funds.

A reduction of portfolio inflows first affects the SET index, which drops sharply, together with the rate of return on the stock market assets. The negative revaluation of stock market assets reduces the level of private wealth, which in turn reduces private consumption.

Another effect, somewhat unexpected, is a considerable rise in the domestic interest rate, compared to the base run. In the light of the analysis presented just above, such an increase would not be immediately obvious: should the drop in the rate of return on the stock market not also lead to a drop in the rate of return on other domestic financial assets? The fact that this does not occur is due to the monetary implications of the drop in portfolio investment. Portfolio foreign investment funds enter the Thai economy through commercial banks. Because the foreign funds form part of the base money of the monetary system, the inflows expand the reserves of the banks and their credit-creating capacity. Examination of the detailed liability structure of commercial banks reveals that the inflow of funds from abroad decreases substantially compared to the base run, largely due to the decrease in the inflow of portfolio funds. This has an immediate impact on the credit-creating capacity of the banks, and therefore a drop in the inflows results in a drop in the supply of credit. Indeed, in the simulation the credit extended by domestic financial institutions to the private sector decreased substantially. Credit availability has a direct effect on the availability of funds with which the private sector can finance desired investment. In the first year of the simulation, the budget constraint on investment tightens considerably, forcing, for example, the level of corporate investment down by 24 billion baht compared to the base year. In Chapter 5 it was argued that no direct link between portfolio investment flows and private corporate investment could be established. This simulation shows, however, that there is an important indirect link via the monetary system. This effect also helps to explain the complementarity between stock market activity and borrowing that was suggested in Chapter 5.

The decreases in private consumption and corporate investment lead to an increase in unemployment, a decrease in labour income and a decrease in household income. These lead to a decrease in household savings. This decrease in household savings, coupled with the decrease in credit received by households from banks, leads to a substantial decrease in household investment as well. All these effects on aggregate demand and employment are translated into a substantial decrease in GDP (see Figure 6.2) and in the price level (see Figure 6.5) compared to the base run.

The decline in portfolio investment further affects the balance of payments. The impact on exports is minor, but imports decrease with the decreases in investment and production. Current transfer payments also decrease substantially with the reduction of foreign share ownership. The result is a sharp improvement of the current-account deficit, which by the end of the simulation period is close to a balance (compared to the 4.3 per cent deficit in the base run, see Figure 6.8). This improvement leads to a decrease in the level of foreign debt relative to the level in the base run (see Figure 6.11).

Jansen's econometric model (1995) confirms that a decrease in PFI inflows would lead to a decrease in private consumption and investment and to a decrease in GDP. As inflation decreases and the real exchange rate improves, exports rise a bit and imports drop sharply with the decrease in expenditures. The current account improves. In this model, however, the external debt rises as financial markets compensate the loss of funds from PFI by increasing external borrowing.

The other financial external shock that is simulated is a decrease in the inflows of direct foreign investment by the same amount as in the simulation of decreased portfolio foreign investment (that is, a decline in the net inflow by 20 billion baht, i.e. from a level of 44 billion baht in the base year, to 24 billion baht in subsequent years). The outcomes of this simulation further show how dependent the Thai economy has become on foreign capital. The results are far more contractionary than those for the decline in portfolio investment. The GDP growth rate falls to a level of 6 per cent per year (compared to the 6.6 per cent of the base run) and the level of GDP falls considerably below the level of the base run (see Figure 6.2).

The drop in direct foreign investment has an immediate impact on the level of private investment. The level of corporate investment demand drops, not only because of the decrease of foreign investment (which is, of course, part of corporate investment), but also because of the knock-on effects of foreign investment on local investment demand. Household investments also decrease somewhat compared to the base run, but far less than in the previous simulation, where the decline in portfolio foreign investment had direct effects on household wealth and on households' access to credit. The decrease in direct foreign investment does not result in these wealth effects, and its monetary effects are also far less direct. The outcome is that in the first half of the simulation period, total private investment (corporate and household) remains higher than in the previous simulation, and so does GDP (see Figure 6.2). In the longer run, however, the impact of the continued lower level of DFI flows on private investment is a further decrease in investment and GDP, whereas Figure 6.2 shows that the economy had adjusted to the decline in PFI inflows after two years. At the end of the simulation period it is clear that the decrease in DFI has had effects far more contractionary than the decrease in PFI.

Another important effect of the decrease in foreign investment is a slower growth of exports. The foreign investment is strongly concentrated in export production, and the decline in these investments also leads, with a delay, to a slower growth of exports. The export/GDP ratio, which in the base run increases from 36.6 per cent to 42.5 per cent in the final year, reaches only 40.3 per cent in this simulation. Imports also decrease with the drop in investment and in production: the import/GDP ratio now reaches 39.2 per cent in the final year, compared to 40.8 per cent in the base run. Current transfer payments decrease with the drop in profit remittances. The current-account deficit initially decreases quite strongly, but when the decrease in export growth sets in, the difference with the base run becomes smaller again (see Figure 6.8). The net outcome is that, at the end of the period, the level of external debt is lower than it was in the base run (see Figure 6.11).

The monetary effects are much weaker in this simulation. The monetary system loses some foreign reserves, and so credit supply could decrease, but apparently the decrease in credit demand is enough to prevent tensions from rising on the financial markets. The domestic interest rate remains at the level of the base run. The difference with the decrease in portfolio investment is due to the fact that direct investment flows are not channelled through the monetary system; hence the monetary effects are less direct and less strong.

This simulation confirms that DFI has strong effects on the Thai economy. An increase in DFI leads to increases in investment, exports and GDP, but also in the external debt. Other studies support these findings (see Nidhiprabha et al. 1989 and Jansen 1995). Nidhiprabha et al. (1989) find that an increase in DFI increases manufacturing production capacity and thus increases exports of manufactures, but also leads to a Dutch disease effect which reduces the exports of non-manufactures. On balance, total exports decrease. It would appear that Nidhiprabha et al. underestimate the strong export orientation of recent DFI flows.

The last two simulations show some interesting contrasts. A decrease in PFI flows seems to be mildly contractionary, while it has a strong positive effect on the current account. On the other hand, a decrease in DFI inflows would have a strong contractionary impact without any sustained improvement in the current-account deficit. In both cases the price level drops to considerably below the base run value (see Figure 6.5). The changes in PFI inflows have quite strong monetary effects. The relatively short-lived impact of PFI flows on investment and economic activity, its strong effects on the price level and on the current-account deficit, together with its disturbing effects on domestic monetary balances might be reasons for the authorities not to encourage such inflows.

Policy interventions

Two policy shocks have been simulated: an expansionary fiscal policy and a contractionary monetary policy.

The first policy shock introduced to the model is an expansionary fiscal policy. In the base run of the model, current government spending and government investment were allowed to increase by 7 per cent per year. As the GDP growth rate in the base run was 6.6 per cent per year, the result was a rather stable ratio of government spending to GDP. However, many commentators on the Thai economy have observed that government spending should increase faster. The rapid economic growth of the past has created bottlenecks in physical infrastructure, in the supply of educated manpower, and in the protection of the environment. It is felt that the government should assume a more active role to deal with these problems and to create the preconditions for further growth. To test the impact of such a change in public sector policy, a simulation was run in which both current and capital spending by the government were assumed to grow at 10 per cent per year (rather than 7 per cent as in the base run). No change was introduced in the tax rates: it was assumed that the present fiscal surplus could be used to finance the expansion. The result is that government savings and the fiscal surplus decrease, although they remain positive.

The outcome of this simulation is predictable. The fiscal impulse has a strongly expansionary effect. The level of GDP rises substantially above the base run value, and inflation also accelerates considerably. The current-account deficit increases. The inflation implies a decline in the real exchange rate, which causes exports to lag behind. Imports rise with the higher level of aggregate demand, and current transfer payments to abroad increase with the increase in foreign borrowing. The current-account deficit rises to a level of over 7 per cent of GDP at the end of the period (see Figure 6.9).

The higher government spending does not lead to the crowding-out of private investment. The income growth generates higher levels of private savings, and private corporations also increase their borrowing from banks and from abroad. There is no increase in the domestic interest rate.

Still, the simulation runs into a serious constraint towards the end of the period. The constraint is very much in line with the predictions of models which adopt a monetary approach to the balance of payments: the central bank runs out of foreign reserves. At the end of the simulation period, the level of foreign reserves of the central bank has dropped down to a level equivalent to only 1.5 months of imports, clearly too low. The level of foreign reserves of the central bank is determined as a residue of all current- and capital-account foreign exchange transactions by all agents in the model. Apparently, at a certain moment the level of the current-account deficit can no longer be compensated by the capital inflows, which are either exogenous (e.g. direct and portfolio investment flows) or determined in the portfolio decisions of the domestic institutions.

One version of the CGE model introduced a minimum level for the foreign exchange reserves of the central bank (MIRES). The reaction of the model to hitting the MIRES limit is very strong: there is an abrupt cut in domestic credit and, hence, a severe drop in private investment and in GDP. In reality other reactions may also occur. If the international financial markets saw the level of reserves of the Bank of Thailand decreasing, they would revise their assessment of the creditworthiness of the country, and access to foreign borrowing might be impaired. Thailand would also appear less attractive to foreign direct and portfolio investors, and the net inflows of these funds would decrease. It would thus appear that a fiscal expansion, as modelled here, is unsustainable.

Similar simulations conducted with other models broadly confirm the above findings. Ramangkura and Nidhiprabha (1991) and Taylor and Rosensweig (1990) simulate an increase in government spending financed by monetary expansion. In these cases the direct expansionary effect of the higher government spending is reinforced by the effect of the monetary expansion. The money growth reduces the interest rate and stimulates investment. As GDP grows, imports also increase. The increase in inflation, however, leads to an appreciation of the real exchange rate, which has a negative impact on exports. The current account deteriorates. In Taylor and Rosensweig (1990) the decrease in the interest rate also leads to a reduced capital inflow from abroad. The higher current-account deficit and the reduced capital inflows lead to a much lower level of foreign reserves, just as was observed above.

Ramangkura and Nidhiprabha (1991) also run a simulation in which the growth of government spending is financed by higher taxes. In that case, the contractionary impact of the higher taxes neutralizes the expansionary effect of higher government spending. There is also no interest-rate effect in this case. In the CGE simulation above, no attention was paid to the financing of the increase in government spending, as it was assumed that the increase could be financed from the existing government surplus. A similar assumption was made in Jansen (1995). In that model the increase in government spending leads to a growing demand-supply gap, which is filled by external borrowing, quickly leading to unacceptable levels of external debt.

The monetary policy simulated is an increase in the bank rate at which commercial banks and government borrow from the central bank. The bank rate is increased by 3 percentage points. The reactions of the real variables of the model to this change are very small. GDP, inflation, the current account, and the external debt differ only marginally from their outcomes in the base run (see Figures 6.3, 6.6, 6.9, and 6.12). GDP is marginally higher, inflation marginally lower, and the current-account deficit and external debt are marginally higher.

This outcome confirms the comments in Chapter 5 about the diminishing effectiveness of monetary policy. The increase in the bank rate primarily affects the portfolio behaviour of the commercial banks: they borrow less from the central bank, and in consequence give less credit to the private sector. This has a negative effect on household investment, but not on the investment by private corporations. Corporate investment even increases slightly. The companies compensate the decrease in bank credit by borrowing somewhat more from abroad and by obtaining more funds from the stock market, but mainly by increasing their own retained savings. On balance, total private investment improves.

The increase in the bank rate has no effect on the interest rate on financial markets. This can be explained by the fact that banks obtain only a small part of their funds from central bank credit. But it may also be due to the particular interest-rate mechanism built into the model and the particular conditions of the base year, that were already discussed above (see comments on the world interest-rate simulation). As the domestic interest rate does not change, there is also hardly any change, in the private sector portfolios.

Another effect occurs through the fiscal balances. As borrowing from the central bank becomes more expensive, the government has to pay more on its debt with the central bank, so that total government spending increases, the government surplus decreases, and the government domestic debt remains higher compared to the base run. It is probably this fiscal effect that stimulates the economy and is responsible for the tiny increase in private investment. With the increase in investment, production capacity grows, so that exports increase and inflation drops. The decrease in inflation helps to improve the real exchange rate, which further stimulates exports.

Once again, it should be emphasized that the effects listed above are all very marginal. Still, the processes identified provide some clues about the past. In the early 1980s, the attempt to use high-interest rate policies to curb excess spending and improve the current account were not effective. The analysis above suggests that the higher interest rate then increased government spending (remember that at that time the government debt was still much higher than it was in 1989). The higher government spending may have more than compensated any contractionary effect of the high interest rate on private spending.

Taylor and Rosensweig (1990) use their model to simulate the effects of a more direct monetary policy: the limitation of the level of central bank credit to commercial banks. The outcome is that the domestic interest rate rises, which depresses investment and production. But these monetary effects are neutralized by two processes: firstly, the drop in GDP leads to lower imports and a smaller current-account deficit. Secondly, the higher domestic interest rate invites capital inflow from abroad. The resulting increase in foreign reserves largely neutralizes the initial impact of the monetary policy. This last mechanism seems to have dominated in the late 1980s. As the capital markets become more integrated, any tendency for the local interest rate to rise induces capital inflows.

6.3   Conclusions

The previous section reported on the construction and application of the CGE model for Thailand. The distinguishing characteristic of the model

is its emphasis on the capital accounts: the investment and saving behaviour of the various institutions, their financial portfolio behaviour
and the international capital flows are all explicitly modelled. The base
run of the dynamic model suggests that the model captures the underlying long-term dynamics of the Thai economy quite well in terms of
growth rates and the directions of structural change.

The model simulations have provided further insights into the questions that were raised in Chapters 4 and 5 about the impact of external
factors on Thai economic development. Section 6.1 noted the differences between the first foreign finance boom – the loan boom of 1975–85
– and the second foreign investment boom after 1987. The simulations
suggest four reasons for these differences:

(1) The adverse external shocks around 1980s had a strong impact on
the economic growth record. The first simulation reported above
assessed the impact of a sudden increase in import prices of 10 per
cent. Such an increase lowered the growth rate by 0.28 percentage
points per year. In reality, import prices increased by more than 60
per cent around 1980. Moreover, the growth of world trade stagnated in these years.

(2) The negative impact of the trade shocks was compensated by expansionary fiscal policy in the early 1980s. In the late 1980s, fiscal
policy became contractionary. The model simulation showed that
an increase in the growth rate of government spending, from 7 per
cent per year in the base run to 10 per cent, increased the growth
rate by 0.53 percentage points per year. In reality, the growth rate
of government spending (at constant prices) was 8.6 per cent per
year in the period 1979–84, against 4.6 per cent per year in the
period 1986–90.

(3) The growth boom of the second period received an important stimu-
lus from the DFI and PFI inflows. The simulations showed that, if
these inflows had been at about half their 1989 level, the growth
rate would have declined by 0.82 percentage points per year. Even
at half their 1989 levels, the DFI and PFI flows would have been
far in excess of their levels in the early 1980s.

(4) In the early 1980s the bank rate and the world interest rate were
higher than in 1989, but the simulation suggests that this would not
have affected the growth rate. Furthermore, in the early 1980s the

exchange rate was seriously overvalued, whereas in the late 1980s it was at a more appropriate level. Another study used the CGE model presented here to simulate the effects of a devaluation (see Jemio & Jansen 1993). The results show that a devaluation would be contractionary, that is, the growth rate would decrease. The higher exchange rate increases the cost of imports and of debt servicing, and leads to inflation. The positive effects on exports are only short-lived, as the accelerating inflation quickly erodes the real exchange rate gain of the devaluation (this is reflected in the movements of the real exchange rate in Figure 4.3, where the real exchange rate index dropped back quickly after the devaluation of 1984). This finding helps to explain the dismal performance of the economy in 1985 and 1986. The contractionary effect of the devaluation of 1984 combined with the tightening fiscal policies resulted in low growth rates. In reality the erosion of the devaluation did not occur in the second half of the 1980s, because the re-alignment of the main world currencies led to a depreciation of the Thai trade-weighted real exchange rate (see also Figure 4.3, which shows the difference between the real exchange rate and the trade-weighted real exchange rate).

The growth boom of the late 1970s gave way to the recession of the early 1980s, and the boom of the late 1980s was stronger. To a considerable extent this can be explained by the usual cyclical patterns. But the fact that the recession was so prolonged and the boom so exceptional may be explained by the factors listed above. The adverse external trade shocks provided a strongly negative impulse which the expansionary fiscal policy could not compensate. The late 1980s were blessed with a much more stable external situation (in 1986 oil prices even dropped). The strong expansionary effects of the DFI and PFI inflows in these years were only partially corrected by the contractionary fiscal policy.

These findings confirm that the Thai economy is very dependent on external conditions. The simulations also confirm and elaborate on the analysis of the impact of external finance as presented in Chapters 4 and 5. The DFI simulation produced all the main effects discussed in Chapter 5, thus confirming that these effects are the result of the DFI flows and not of particular policy interventions or other factors. With the increase in DFI, total investment increased by more than the DFI, and growth accelerated. The DFI inflow did increase inflation and appreciated the real exchange rate. But the capacity-creating effect of the export-oriented DFI was stronger, so that exports increased. Imports also increased. In the simulation, the impact on the current account was not so strong, perhaps because the model did not fully capture the increase in import intensity that accompanied DFI.[8] The PFI simulation showed that an increase in PFI flows has important effects beyond the SET. In particular, its effects on private wealth and on monetary balances are strong, and they have direct repercussions on the real side of the economy.

The fiscal policy simulation contains elements of the loan boom period of 1975–85. Government spending, or, more generally speaking, public sector spending, increased in that period as well. The simulation showed that such an increase stimulated domestic demand, investment and imports. On the other hand, the resulting appreciation of the real exchange rate discouraged exports. Unlike in the case of DFI-financed investment, the increase in investment did nothing to increase export capacity, because the investments were in the non-export-oriented sectors of the economy. Thus, in the fiscal policy simulation, the export/GDP ratio remained lower than the base run level, whereas the import/GDP ratio exceeded its base run level.

Comparison of these simulations confirms the conclusion of Chapters 4 and 5 that the foreign loan boom contained elements that were unsustainable. In Chapter 4 it could not be ascertained whether the poor outcomes in the early 1980s were due to the inherent inconsistencies of the strategy, or to the unfavourable external conditions. The results of the simulation indicate that, even under more favourable external conditions, the expansionary impulse generated by public sector expenditures leads to unsustainable outcomes. The sectoral allocation of the investments, and thus the production capacity that is created, and the real exchange rate effect create a strong anti-export bias, while the expenditure impulse increases import demand. The growing current-account deficit results in a rapidly growing external debt and, eventually, in a debt crisis.[9] Of course, it is possible to design policies to avoid these negative outcomes – for instance, a fully flexible exchange rate to correct for the inflation or investment allocation policies – but in the period 1975–85 such policies were not implemented.

The foreign investment boom of the late 1980s appears more sustainable. Again, there was a strong expansionary effect on the economy, so that investment, GDP and imports increased. Inflation also accelerated and the real exchange rate appreciated. But this time the allocation of investment was quite different, with a much greater share going to export-oriented sectors. The outcome was that exports grew rapidly, and that the current-account deficit, and the external debt, remained more manageable. In fact, according to the simulations, the increase in DFI would increase exports by more than the external debt, so that the external debt/export ratio, which worsened severely in the case of increased government spending, now improved.

The analysis of Chapters 4 and 5 and the model simulations confirm the dependence of the Thai economy on external finance. The Thai economy can grow fast when (i) there are positive exogenous impulses, such as an increase in DFI inflows, or when (ii) domestic demand impulses, for instance, from government spending or private investment, can be financed by external borrowing. Such expansionary impulses increase investment and income, but domestic savings do not rise very much, so that the dependence on external finance is prolonged.

Throughout this study, references have been made to the literature on the impact of external capital flows on developing economies. The effects of capital inflows have been discussed in detail. However, empirical studies of these effects have generally failed to lead to clear-cut conclusions. The present study provides some further insights. Before listing these, however, two general points need to be made.

Chapters 4 and 5, together with the model simulations reported here, show that different types of capital inflows have quite different macroeconomic impacts. Thus, any analysis of the impact of external finance that lumps all types of capital flows together is rather useless.

Furthermore, when one is analysing the effects of external capital inflows on the economy, one is implicitly assuming that the levels of these inflows are exogenously determined, and that the receiving economy adjusts to them. These adjustments are then the 'effects' of the capital inflows. In the analyses of Chapters 4 and 5 the increase in capital inflows was indeed viewed as an exogenous 'shock' to the economy. It was probably realistic to view the capital flows of the past as largely exogenously determined. Flows of aid and DFI were determined more on the supply side than by actions of the host country. In the mid-1970s developing countries rather suddenly obtained more access to foreign borrowing, due to factors beyond their control, and in the late 1980s, again suddenly, DFI and PFI flows increased.

However, it is no longer justified to consider all capital flows exogenously determined. The growing integration of financial markets, and the economic and financial development in Thailand necessitate a more subtle approach. Important elements of international financial flows remain largely exogenous. This is particularly the case with DFI and PFI flows. It is also the case with aid flows, but these are rapidly becoming unimportant in Thailand. But international commercial borrowing can no longer be considered an exogenous variable. As shown in Chapter 5, Thai corporations and financial institutions interact with international financial markets to finance desired levels of spending and to compose optimal portfolios of financial assets and liabilities.

When analysing the impact of foreign finance on the receiving economy, one needs to distinguish between exogenous and endogenous flows. Exogenous capital flows, such as DFI and PFI, have a macroeconomic impact on the receiving economy and pose adjustment policy challenges, some of which have been discussed in Chapter 5. However, it is more realistic to view other types of capital flows (long-term and short-term borrowing by private and public sector) as endogenous capital flows that are accommodating the internal (im)balances of the various agents in the Thai economy, rather than as exogenous flows to which the economy has to adjust. These new institutional realities were incorporated into the CGE model.

The literature has been concerned with the effects of external finance on investment, savings, growth and the balance of payments. The analysis in this study divided the effect on investment into the effect on the sector receiving the foreign funds and the effect on the other sectors in the economy. The effect of an increase in capital inflows on the investment of the sector towards which the inflows are directed, is unambiguously positive. In the 1970s the capital inflows led to an increased level of public investment and in the 1980s to an increase in corporate investment. The secondary impact on the investments of other sectors have been discussed in terms of crowding in or out. It was argued that crowding out – of private by public investment and of local by foreign investment – would occur mainly through domestic financial markets.

In the case of Thailand, with its well-developed financial markets and its access to foreign financial markets, no such crowding out occurred. But the same need not apply to other countries with less-developed financial markets. However, the international borrowing that helps prevent crowding out, builds up into a debt burden which may, in the end, undermine investors' confidence. This is what happened in the early 1980s.

The impact of external finance on domestic savings is mixed. The loan boom of the 1970s was associated with a decrease in public sector savings. The DFI boom led to a mild increase in the private corporate savings ratio. In recent years, however, the household savings ratio shows a worrisome downward trend. In both periods the increase in investment exceeded the change in savings by much more than the initial increase in capital inflows, so that the dependence on external finance increased.

The impact of external finance on growth appears to be strong. In the 1970s and the 1980s the increase in capital inflows was accompanied by growth booms. But in both cases these booms subsided after a few years, even though capital inflows remained high.

Exports and imports react differently to the capital inflows, depending on the type of capital. The public sector loan boom did not change the import propensity, but had a strong anti-export bias. The DFI boom stimulated exports considerably, but also increased the import intensity strongly. In both cases, the increased level of capital inflows led to an appreciation of the real exchange rate (Dutch disease), hence the main reason for the difference in export performance lies in the allocation of investment. Public investment was concentrated in the non-traded sectors, and DFI and private investment in the traded-goods sector.

The differences in the outcomes of the two foreign finance booms discussed in Chapters 4 and 5 are the result of (i) the inherent characteristics of the different types of international capital flows, (ii) the differences in external conditions in the two periods, and (iii) the differences in economic policies dealing with the two booms. Still, the comparison of the two periods and the model simulations made it possible to determine the distinct impact of each type of capital flow, showing clearly that different types of international finance have quite different effects on the receiving economy.

Figure 6.1 GDP behaviour after price shocks (% change from base run)

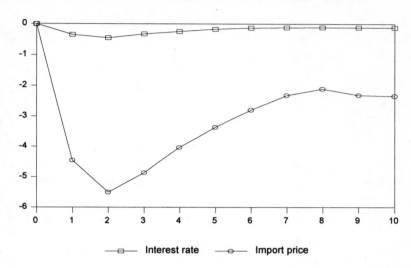

Figure 6.2 GDP behaviour following flow shocks (% change from base run)

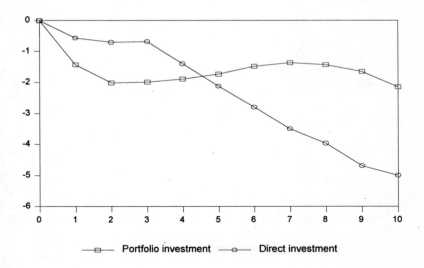

Figure 6.3 GDP behaviour following policy (% change from base run)

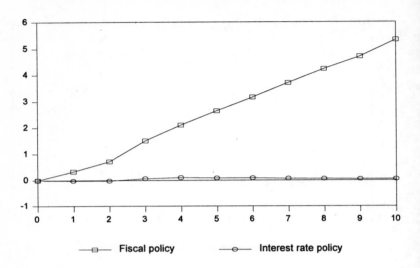

Figure 6.4 CPI behaviour following price shocks (% change from base run)

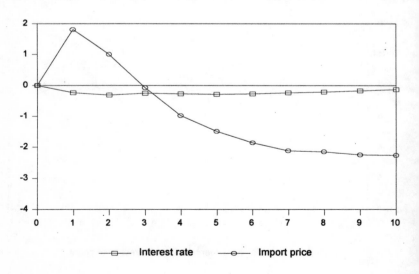

Figure 6.5 CPI behaviour following flow shocks (% change from base run)

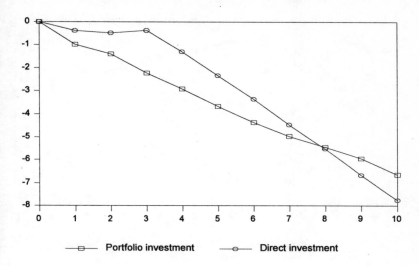

Figure 6.6 CPI behaviour following policy (% change from base run)

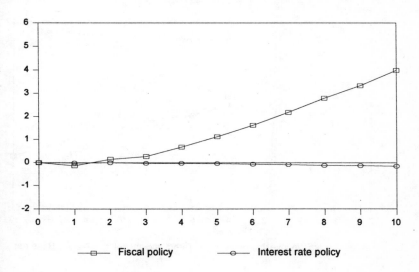

Figure 6.7 Current-account deficit after price shock (% of GDP)

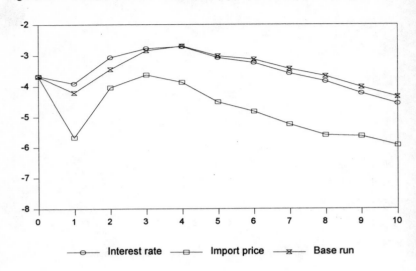

Figure 6.8 Current-account deficit after flow shocks (% of GDP)

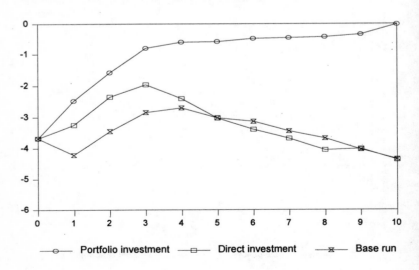

Figure 6.9 Current-account deficit after policy (% of GDP)

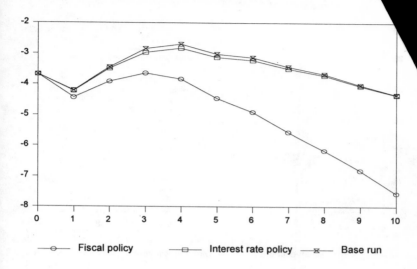

Figure 6.10 Debt outstanding for the non-financial sector after price shocks (% of GDP)

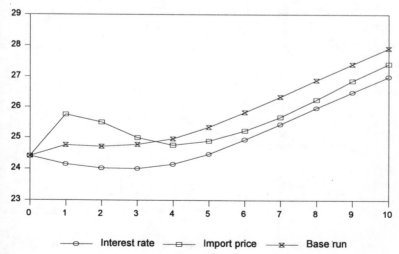

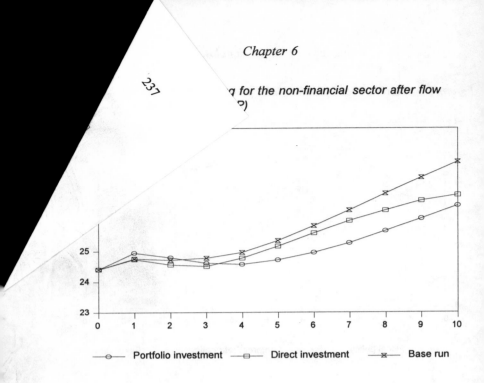

*...q for the non-financial sector after flow
...²)*

237

*Figure 6.12 Debt outstanding for the non-financial sector after policy
(% of GDP)*

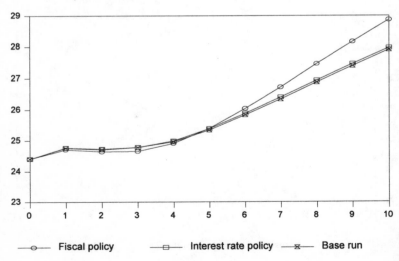

Appendices

Appendices

A2 Appendix to Chapter 2 Concepts and Compilation of the Social Accounting Matrix

The Social Accounting Matrix (SAM) is a popular tool in socio-economic analysis. It brings together economic data on production, expenditure, income generation, saving and investment with information about the distribution of these activities over the various sectors and institutions in the economy. As such, it allows analysis beyond the superficial level of macro-economic aggregates, and indicates the distribution of activities and incomes over the various social groups. For a full introduction to the issues relating to construction of Social Accounting Matrices and to their use in economic analysis see Alarcón et al. (1991)

In Table A2.1 the outline of the Social Accounting Matrix is presented. It can be observed that the SAM has two major components: a sub-matrix of current transactions (row/columns 11 to 24) and a sub-matrix of capital transactions (row/columns 25 to 34). Within the SAM some blocks can be identified.

In the matrix of current transactions, four blocks can be distinguished. Block 1 (row/columns 11 to 16) contains the domestic input-output relationships among the sectors of production, while imported intermediate inputs are recorded in row 24; together they describe the technical production structure and the interdependencies among the productive sectors.

Block 2 is the value added block (rows 17 to 19, columns 11 to 16). Value added at factor costs is broken down into wages (row 17) and profits (the latter is further disaggregated into the gross operating surplus of the unincorporated sector (row 18) and that of (private and state) corporations (row 19)). Adding row 23 (indirect taxes) leads to value added at market

241

prices. Adding vertically leads to total output or supply. Taking agriculture as an example (column 11):

- rows 11 to 16 add up to total intermediate inputs into agriculture;
- rows 17 to 19 add the value added produced in the sector;
- row 23 adds the indirect taxes;
- and row 24 adds the imports of intermediates for the agricultural sector.

The grand total is the total supply of agricultural commodities, which, of course, must be equal to the total demand, i.e. the total of row 11.

Block 3 shows how the current income is distributed and redistributed. First, there is the distribution of the income of the factors of production (as was given in the value added block) among the economic agents or institutions (rows 20 to 22, columns 17 to 19). The other element in this block is the current transfers among these institutions, such as interest and dividend payments, direct tax payments, government subsidies and current transfers with the rest of the world (row/columns 20 to 24).

Block 4 is the last block in the current transaction sub-matrix. It includes domestic consumption demand for the commodities of the six sectors (divided into household (rows 11 to 16, column 20), and government (rows 11 to 16, column 23) consumption). Part of the consumption demand is satisfied by the import of consumption goods (cells 24, 20 and 24, 23). The foreign demand for domestic commodities (export of goods and services) is included in column 24. This block shows how current income is spent on current consumption. The difference between current income and current spending is the savings.

These savings provide the link to the sub-matrix of capital transactions. In the matrix of capital transaction three blocks have been separated. Savings of the various institutions are given in block 5, (rows 26 to 29, columns 20 to 24) including foreign savings (cell 34, 24). These savings are used to finance investments. In block 6 capital formation of each institution is given (rows 11 to 16, columns 25 to 29).

Together with block 4, block 6 also adds up to total final demand, which is composed of consumption by households (column 20), consumption by government (column 23), exports (column 24), and investments (columns 25 to 29). Together with the intermediate demand of block 1, final demand adds up to total demand. For example, for agriculture (row 11) total demand is made up of:

- total intermediate deliveries (columns 11 to 16);
- household consumption of agricultural commodities (column 20);
- government consumption of agricultural commodities (column 23);

- exports of agricultural commodities (column 24);
- investments in agricultural commodities (columns 26 to 29).

This is where most other SAMs stop. The present SAM tries to make more explicit the financial linkages within the Thai economy, and the linkages of the economy with the rest of the world. It is clear that for each individual agent, investments and savings do not match. This gap has to be filled. The flow-of-fund block of the SAM (block 7) shows how this is done. In block 7 there is a sub-block of direct capital transactions among institutions (row/columns 26 to 29). For example, households provide share capital to private corporations (cell 27, 26) or buy government securities (cell 29, 26). Corporations may provide credit to each other and to state enterprises, and so on. The rest of the flow-of-funds block shows the patterns of financial intermediation, that is, the flows of funds that occur through financial institutions. Adding block 5 and block 7 horizontally results in the total sources of funds for each of the institutions; adding up vertically results in the total uses of these funds. For example, private corporations (row 27) obtain funds from:

- own savings (column 21);
- capital transfers from households (share capital, column 26);
- capital transfers from private enterprises and state enterprises and government (e.g. trade credit, columns 27, 28 and 29);
- credit from commercial banks (column 31) and from other domestic financial institutions (column 32);
- funds raised at the stock market (column 33);
- funds from abroad in the form of DFI or loans (column 34).

To see how the private corporations use these funds, we can add up vertically, i.e. column 27:

- own investments (rows 11 to 16), including the imports of capital goods (row 24);
- investing in inventories (row 25);
- giving credit to households (row 26);
- obtaining financial assets with other private corporations, e.g. through trade credit or purchase of shares (row 27);
- purchasing government securities (row 29);
- increasing holdings of currency (row 30), of bank deposits (row 31), and of deposits with other financial institutions (row 32);

The compilation of the SAM is a complex task involving the integration of information from various, often inconsistent, data sources consisting of (i) the National Accounts as published annually by the National Economic and Social Development Board (NESDB, annual); (ii) the Input-Output Table 1985 (NESDB 1991); (iii) Flow-of-Funds Accounts (published by the NESDB and the Bank of Thailand, 1982, 1983, 1986 & 1991); and (iv) the financial statistics as published by the Bank of Thailand (Bank of Thailand, quarterly).

There are discrepancies, first of all because of revisions in the national accounts estimates in 1987 and 1991, but also because the various sources use different concepts and definitions, and different estimation methods.

In the SAM89, the new National Accounts estimates provide references for the macroeconomic aggregates (value added, consumption, investment, exports, imports), and other sources (such as the Input-Output Table and surveys) are used to estimate the sectoral and institutional breakdown of these aggregates. The Input-Output Table was the main source for blocks 1, 2, 4 and 6 of the SAM89. The Input-Output Table for 1985 was updated to 1989 by correcting the 1985 table for changes in the sectoral composition of output between 1985 and 1989, and by correcting for changes in relative prices. The figures in block 3 were derived from the National Accounts and from household and labour force surveys, and blocks 5 and 7 were based on National Accounts, Flow-of-Funds Accounts and financial statistics. The statistical discrepancies that remained after this were relatively small and acceptable; they were eliminated using statistical methods.

Table A2.1 Social Accounting Matrix: The Concepts

				CURRENT ACCOUNTS															CAPITAL ACCOUNTS									GRAND TOTAL
		11	12	13	14	15	16	17	18	19	20	21	22	23	24	25	26	27	28	29	30	31	32	33	34	
C U R R E N T	11 Agriculture																									
	12 Mining																									
	13 Light Manufacturing			Block 1							Block 4									Block 6						
	14 Other Manufacturing																									
	15 Construction & Publ. Utilities																									
	16 Services & Others																									
A C C O U N T S	17 Wages																									
	18 Unincorporated Profits			Block 2							Block 3															
	19 Corporate Profits																									
	20 Households																									
	21 Private Corporations																									
	22 State Enterprises																									
	23 Government																									
	24 Rest of the World																									
	25 Changes in Stock																									
C A P I T A L	26 Households																									
	27 Private Corporations											Block 5									Block 7					
	28 State Enterprises																									
	29 Government																									
	30 Central Bank																									
A C C T S	31 Commercial Banks																									
	32 Other Financial Institutions																									
	33 Stock Market																									
	34 Rest of the World																									
GRAND TOTAL																										

A3 Appendix to Chapter 3
Data Sources and Definitions

The main data source is the National Accounts (NESDB, annual). The National Accounts of Thailand disaggregates gross savings into

(a) savings of households and unincorporated enterprises,
(b) net savings of private corporations and state enterprises,
(c) savings of general government, and
(d) depreciation allowance.

The same source disaggregates gross fixed capital formation into

(a) private (households *and* corporations), and
(b) public (state enterprises *and* government).

The basic data series for the period 1970–94 for savings and investments of the four agents were constructed as follows:

(a) 'Savings of households and private non-profit institutions' as reported in the new series of the National Accounts are taken as 'household savings'. These savings include savings of households and of unincorporated (family) enterprises; these are 'household savings' (S_h).

(b) 'Savings of general government' as reported in the new series of the National Accounts are taken as 'government savings' (S_g).

(c) (Net) 'savings of corporations and government enterprises' are given separately and the 'provision for the consumption of fixed capital' as reported in the new series of the National Accounts refers to both sectors. To estimate the gross savings of the two sectors, the depreciation allowance is divided between private corporations and state enterprises in proportion to the value of their capital stock. It is assumed that both sectors have the same rate of depreciation.

This approach results in estimates of gross savings of state enterprises (S_s) and gross savings of private corporations (S_c).

(d) In the Flow-of-Funds Accounts 'household investments' are estimated as the sum of the National Accounts categories 'private residential construction' and 'investment in new lands'. This practice is followed to calculate 'household investments' from the National Accounts. It should be noted that the household sector includes household businesses, and that this definition of household investments certainly underestimates the investments made by such firms (I_h).

(e) 'Private corporations investments' are obtained by deducting the household investment defined under (d) from total private investments as given in the National Accounts (I_c).

(f) 'Government investment' is set equal to 'government capital expenditure' as reported in budget data (Bank of Thailand, quarterly) (I_g).

(g) 'State enterprise investment' is obtained by deducting government investment as defined under (f) from total public sector investments as given in the National Accounts (I_s).

The resulting time series, as percentages of GDP, are presented in Table A3.1.

The estimates of capital inflow present some problems. In many studies, capital inflows are measured by the current-account balance of the balance of payments (with reversed sign: a current-account deficit means a positive capital inflow). The balance-of-payments equation can be written as:

(current account balance) + (capital account balance)
+ (monetary movements) + (errors & omissions) = 0

One could thus also take the capital-account balance as a direct estimate of the net capital flows. The difference between capital inflows measured from the current account and those measured from the capital account is explained by accumulation of monetary reserves and by the errors and omissions.

A third way of measuring capital inflows arises from the National Accounts: the national resource balance (investment-savings) should be covered by capital inflows.

The three measures of capital inflow give different results. The estimates from the current account, from the capital account and from the national resource balance do not coincide. Differences are explained by monetary movements and errors and omissions (for the two balance-of-payments estimates) and by the statistical discrepancy of the National Accounts.

It was decided to use the estimates from the capital account of the balance of payments, as these can be disaggregated according to the institutions receiving the inflows. In Table 3.1 of Chapter 3 the capital account of the balance of payments of Thailand is used to define capital flows to the different economic agents:

(a) the total net capital flow, defined as the net balance of the capital account (F);

(b) the capital inflow to the private corporate sector is defined as 'direct investments', plus 'portfolio investments in securities', plus 'net long-term loans and credits to private enterprises' plus 'private short-term loans' and 'trade credit' $(F_c$ or $F_{pr})$;

(c) the net flows received by government enterprises is defined as 'net long-term loans and credits to government enterprises', plus 'net short-term loans and credits to government enterprises' (F_s);

(d) the capital flow received by the government is defined as 'net government loans' and changes in long-term assets of the government (F_g);

With the liberalization of the foreign exchange transactions in the 1990s, the Bank of Thailand also changed its reporting of capital flows, so that for recent years the loans under categories (b) and (c) can no longer be disaggregated.

In Chapter 3 it was noted that, in principle, for each sector the sources of finance should equal its uses of funds. The sources of funds are:

- own savings,
- increase in credit from financial institutions,
- increase in other domestic liabilities, and
- foreign liabilities incurred.

And the uses of these funds can be divided into:

- own investments,
- acquisition of financial assets with financial institutions,
- acquisition of other domestic financial assets, and
- acquisition of foreign financial assets.

For the sectors household and unincorporated business *(h)*, private corporations *(c)*, central and local government *(g)*, state enterprises *(s)* and the domestic financial sector *(f)*, one can write:

HH: $$S_h + FLF_h + OFL_h + WFL_h = I_h + FAF_h + OFA_h + WFA_h \qquad (1)$$

CORP: $$S_c + FLF_c + OFL_c + WFL_c = I_c + FAF_c + OFA_c + WFA_c \qquad (2)$$

GVT: $$S_g + FLF_g + OFL_g + WFL_g = I_g + FAF_g + OFA_g + WFA_g \qquad (3)$$

SE: $$S_s + FLF_s + OFL_s + WFL_s = I_s + FAF_s + OFA_s + WFA_s \qquad (4)$$

FI: $$S_f + FAF_h + FAF_c + FAF_g + FAF_s + OFL_f + WFL_f =$$
$$I_f + FLF_h + FLF_c + FLF_g + FLF_s + OFA_f + WFA_f \qquad (5)$$

In these equations:

S_i = own savings of sector: $i = h, c, g, s$ and f;

I_i = own investment of each sector;

FLF_i = financial liabilities incurred with financial institutions, i.e. funds obtained by the sector from domestic financial institutions (e.g. loans from banks);

OFL_i = other financial liabilities incurred, i.e. funds obtained by the sector from domestic non-financial sectors (e.g. share capital acquired by corporations or government transfers to state enterprises);

WFL_i = financial liabilities incurred with the rest of the world (e.g. foreign loans);

FAF_i = financial assets acquired with financial institutions (e.g. deposits or promissory notes);

OFA_i = other domestic financial assets acquired (e.g. equity shares); and

WFA_i = foreign financial assets acquired.

Equations 1 to 5 can be directly traced back to the SAM89 of Chapter 2 (see Table 2.9). For instance, the left-hand side of equation 1 includes, at a slightly higher level of aggregation, the elements of row 26 of the SAM89, while the right-hand side includes the elements of column 26. The same applies to the other equations. The SAM89 provides more detail than the equations; e.g. the FLF_h of equation 1 combines liabilities incurred from commerical banks and from other financial institutions. The simplifications and aggregations of the present equations are necessary to construct consistent time series.

These equations can be simplified by netting out the other financial assets and liabilities and the foreign assets and liabilities.

$$NOFL_i = OFL_i - OFA_i \qquad (6)$$

$$NWFL_i = WFL_i - WFA_i \qquad (7)$$

Introducing equations 6 and 7 into 1 to 5 leads to:

HH: $\qquad S_h + FLF_h + NOFL_h + NWFL_h = I_h + FAF_h \qquad (8)$

CORP: $\quad S_c + FLF_c + NOFL_c + NWFL_c = I_c + FAF_c \qquad (9)$

GVT: $\quad S_g + FLF_g + NOFL_g + NWFL_g = I_g + FAF_g \qquad (10)$

SE: $\qquad S_s + FLF_s + NOFL_s + NWFL_s = I_s + FAF_s \qquad (11)$

FI: $\qquad S_f + FAF_h + FAF_c + FAF_g + FAF_s + NOFL_f + NWFL_f =$
$$I_f + FLF_h + FLF_c + FLF_g + FLF_s \qquad (12)$$

When the five equations 8 to 12 are added up, the domestic financial intermediation variables disappear, because the domestic assets acquired by one sector *(FAF* and *OFA)* are equal to the domestic liabilities *(FLF* and *OFL)* incurred by another sector. Summing up gives:

$$S_h + S_c + S_g + S_s + NWFL_h + NWFL_c + NWFL_g + NWFL_s =$$
$$I_h + I_c + I_g + I_s \qquad (13)$$

which is the familiar accumulation balance equation, equivalent to equation 3.3 of Chapter 3.

The equation system 8 to 12 juxtaposes the main sources of each sector against the uses. To establish the main sources and uses of funds of the various agents for the period 1970–94, it is necessary to use different data sources. The combination of different data sources creates problems of discrepancies, differences in concepts and definitions, and differences in estimation methods.

In principle the best source for the sectoral sources and uses of funds is the Flow-of-Funds Accounts of Thailand (see NESDB/BoT 1982, 1983,

1986 and 1991). Unfortunately these accounts suffer from a number of shortcomings that make them less appropriate for the present study.

The first drawback is that the Accounts do not cover the entire period of our analysis. Complete accounts are available up to 1983, and for the years 1984–90 accounts are incomplete. A second problem is that the Flow-of-Funds Accounts are still based on the old National Accounts, while the revision of the National Accounts that was published in 1987 showed considerable adjustments, particularly in the estimates of savings. The estimates of sectoral savings as obtained from the Flow-of-Funds Accounts are, therefore, not fully comparable with the estimates we used in Table A3.1. A similar problem is found in the estimates of foreign capital flows. The Flow-of-Funds Accounts measure changes in assets and in liabilities, whereas Table 3.1 used balance-of-payments estimates of the flows of foreign finance. There can be substantial differences between the two concepts. Some of the capital inflows do not create a liability (e.g. direct foreign investment), and the value of foreign assets or liabilities may change without any related capital flow (e.g. as result of exchange rate variations). It was, therefore, decided to use the estimates of sectoral savings and investment as derived from the new series of National Accounts and the estimates of sectoral capital inflows as derived from the capital account of the balance-of-payments statistics for the steps followed in the calculations.

The Flow-of-Funds Accounts were used to derive the estimates of the 'financial liabilities through the financial system' of the four sectors; this represents the funds raised by these sectors from the financial institutions. The Flow-of-Funds data have also been used to provide the disaggregated estimates of the sources of the financial system's liabilities: this provided the estimates for FAF_h, FAF_c, FAF_s and FAF_g; these are the assets (deposits, etc.) that these four institutions obtained with the financial institutions. The estimates of the net other domestic financial liabilities was then obtained as a residue.

The equation 12 for the financial system cannot be fully filled in. The savings and investment by private financial institutions are included in the National Accounts estimates of private corporations, and those of public financial institutions in the public sector estimates. The Flow-of-Funds Accounts give some separate estimates for the period 1970–86, but these suffer from the problems related to the flow of funds discussed above. Anyway, own savings and investments of financial institutions are a relatively small part of their sources and uses of funds, since their main business is intermediation.

The results are represented in Tables 3.3 and 3.4. As there are no Flow-of-Funds Accounts available for recent years, data for the last period are incomplete. The financial survey from the *Quarterly Bulletin* of the Bank of Thailand has been used to fill in some of the entries.

Table A3.1 Sectoral accumulation balances (% of GDP)

	I_h	S_h	I_c	S_c	I_{priv}	S_{priv}	I_g	S_g	I_{se}	S_{se}	I_{publ}	S_{publ}
1970	2.9	8.8	13.7	6.0	16.7	14.8	5.4	1.7	1.7	3.1	7.1	4.8
1971	2.9	10.0	13.7	6.5	16.6	16.5	5.5	1.2	1.3	3.0	6.7	4.1
1972	3.0	8.9	13.0	7.2	16.0	16.1	4.6	1.4	2.1	2.9	6.7	4.2
1973	3.3	12.1	14.0	7.5	17.3	19.6	3.5	1.9	1.6	2.6	5.1	4.5
1974	4.1	10.6	15.4	7.3	19.6	17.9	2.3	4.2	1.5	2.2	3.7	6.5
1975	3.2	8.6	14.5	7.6	17.7	16.2	3.3	2.6	1.8	1.8	5.2	4.4
1976	3.3	9.5	12.8	8.1	16.1	17.6	4.4	1.3	2.3	1.5	6.8	2.8
1977	3.7	10.1	14.9	7.8	18.6	17.9	4.2	2.4	3.2	1.7	7.4	4.6
1978	3.4	12.6	14.2	7.6	17.6	20.2	3.9	2.0	3.8	1.7	7.7	3.7
1979	3.2	10.8	14.8	7.9	18.0	18.7	3.5	1.8	4.1	1.6	7.6	3.5
1980	4.2	11.4	14.8	7.8	18.9	19.1	4.0	1.6	4.8	1.5	8.8	3.0
1981	5.2	10.4	13.8	7.7	19.0	18.1	3.7	1.2	5.2	1.7	8.9	2.9
1982	5.8	13.4	13.2	7.4	19.1	20.9	3.7	-0.4	4.2	2.0	7.9	1.6
1983	6.7	10.4	13.8	7.9	20.5	18.4	3.2	1.1	4.8	2.6	8.0	3.7
1984	6.8	10.7	13.5	8.1	20.3	18.8	2.8	0.6	5.5	3.1	8.3	3.7
1985	6.5	11.8	11.9	8.1	18.5	20.0	3.1	-0.3	5.6	3.5	8.7	3.2
1986	7.1	11.9	11.3	8.4	18.4	20.3	2.7	0.4	4.7	3.7	7.4	4.1
1987	7.8	12.4	13.9	9.1	21.7	21.5	2.4	2.3	3.6	3.8	6.0	6.0
1988	7.5	13.5	18.2	9.2	25.6	22.8	1.9	5.5	3.2	3.8	5.0	9.2
1989	8.6	14.4	20.9	9.9	29.6	24.3	2.0	6.1	2.5	3.7	4.5	9.8
1990	9.2	10.5	24.9	11.3	34.1	21.8	2.5	8.2	3.1	3.6	5.6	11.9
1991	9.7	10.5	24.5	11.8	34.2	22.3	3.1	9.1	3.5	3.3	6.7	12.4
1992	7.6	9.8	23.6	13.6	31.2	23.4	4.1	7.7	3.7	3.2	7.8	10.9
1993	7.3	8.9	24.9	13.5	32.2	22.4	5.0	8.8	3.2	3.1	8.1	11.9
1994	7.4	7.6	24.5	13.8	31.9	21.4	5.1	10.3	3.2	3.0	8.3	13.3

A4 Appendix to Chapter 4 Decomposition of External Shocks

Developing countries were subject to many severe shocks during the 1970s and 1980s. To measure the severity of these shocks an indicator is calculated, starting from the balance-of-payments identity, which states that the value of imports is equal to:

$$p_m M = p_x X + WR - NFP + CT + F - RES$$

or

$$M = \frac{p_x X}{p_m} + \frac{WR}{p_m} - \frac{NFP}{p_m} + \frac{CT}{p_m} + \frac{F}{p_m} - \frac{RES}{p_m}$$

where:

p_m and p_x	=	import and export prices in local currency,
M and X	=	volumes of imports and exports of goods and services,
WR	=	workers' remittances,
NFP	=	net factor payments, consisting of $NFP = i_w{}^* D + NOFP$ where:

$$i_w{}^* D \ = \ \text{interest payments on external debt;}$$
$$NOFP = \text{net other factor payments,}$$

CT	=	current transfers,
F	=	net flows of foreign capital, i.e. the balance of the capital account of the balance of payments, and
RES	=	change in international reserves of the monetary system.

Define:

$$X = \frac{X}{X_w} * X_w$$

so that

$$\Delta X = \left[\Delta\frac{X}{X_w}\right] X_{w,0} + \left[\frac{X_1}{X_{w,1}}\right] \Delta X_w$$

where X_w is the volume of world exports. The change in the import volume can now be decomposed:

$$\Delta M =$$

$$\left[\Delta\frac{p_x}{p_m}\right] X_0 + \frac{p_{x,1}}{p_{m,1}}\left[\Delta\frac{X}{X_w}\right] X_{w,0} + \frac{p_{x,1}}{p_{m,1}}\left[\frac{X_1}{X_{w,1}}\right] \Delta X_w$$

$$+ \frac{WR_0}{\Delta p_m} + \frac{\Delta WR}{p_{m,1}} - \left[\Delta\frac{i_w}{p_m}\right] D_0 - \frac{i_{w,1}}{p_{m,1}}\Delta D - \frac{NOFP_0}{\Delta p_m} - \frac{\Delta NOFP}{p_{m,1}}$$

$$+ \frac{CT_0}{\Delta p_m} + \frac{\Delta CT}{p_{m,1}} + \frac{\Delta F}{p_{m,1}} + \frac{F_0}{\Delta p_m} - \frac{\Delta RES}{p_{m,1}} - \frac{RES_0}{\Delta p_m}$$

The terms can be re-arranged as follows:

$$\Delta M =$$

$$\left[\Delta\frac{p_x}{p_m}\right] X_0 + \frac{WR_0}{\Delta p_m} - \left[\Delta\frac{i_w}{p_m}\right] D_0 - \frac{NOFP_0}{\Delta p_m} + \frac{CT_0}{\Delta p_m} + \frac{F_0}{\Delta p_m} - \frac{RES_0}{\Delta p_m}$$

$$+ \frac{\Delta WR}{p_{m,1}} - \frac{\Delta NOFP}{p_{m,1}} + \frac{\Delta CT}{p_{m,1}}$$

$$+ \frac{p_{x,1}}{p_{m,1}}\left[\frac{X_1}{X_{w,1}}\right] \Delta X_w$$

$$- \frac{i_{w,1}}{p_{m,1}}\Delta D + \frac{\Delta F}{p_{m,1}} - \frac{\Delta RES}{p_{m,1}}$$

$$+ \frac{p_{x,1}}{p_{m,1}}\left[\Delta\frac{X}{X_w}\right] X_{w,0}$$

In this last equation, the change in the import volume is decomposed into five effects. The first line of the right-hand side of the equation contains terms reflecting changes in the terms of trade, i.e. changes in export and import prices and in the international interest rate. The second line contains the changes in workers' remittances and other factor payments and current transfers, while the third line reflects the change due to the growth of world exports. All the effects contained in these three lines are largely exogenous.

In line four the financial variables are brought together. They reflect the outcomes of monetary policy and debt management. The last line reflects the change in export penetration, an indicator of the success or failure of trade policies.

All data for this equation have been obtained from Bank of Thailand data and from the International Financial Statistics of the IMF. The results are presented in Figure 4.1 of Chapter 4.

A6 Appendix to Chapter 6 Outline of the CGE Model for Thailand

The presentation here focuses on the main characteristics of the model, on the main behavioural patterns included, and on the closure rules. A complete presentation of the model can be found in Jemio and Jansen (1993).

The model is based on the Social Accounting Matrix for 1989 (SAM89) that was introduced in Chapter 2. The SAM89 presents a consistent picture of the economic structure of Thailand in 1989, including all real and financial linkages among sectors and institutions. The SAM89 reflects the *ex post* general equilibrium of all flows of income and expenditure, savings and investments for that year. The CGE model extends the SAM89 by introducing behavioural equations and parameters. For instance, the level of investment observed in the SAM is explained by the underlying investment function, and the level of consumption by the underlying consumption function.

In the simulations, shocks are introduced to the equilibrium of the base year SAM in the form of changes in the values of the exogenous variables (such as world prices, exogenous capital flows, or policy variables). The adjustments to these shocks in the model are determined by the behavioural equations and by the structural relationships of the SAM. Adjustments continue until a new general equilibrium is found, that is, until a new, fully balanced SAM is reached for each year of the simulation period.

The main behavioural patterns included in the model refer to production and income generation, production factor demand and supply, price and wage formation, consumption, saving and investment, and optimal portfolio adjustment for real and financial assets and liabilities for all institutions.

Domestic output is absorbed domestically or is exported. The level of domestic output is determined by a CES production function in the cases of the agricultural and mining sectors. The prices in these two sectors are assumed to follow world market prices, and any gap between demand and supply is filled by exports (or imports). The CES production function also determines the demand for capital, labour and imported intermediate inputs in these sectors.

The other four sectors are dominated by modern, oligopolistic firms that engage in mark-up pricing. These sectors are characterized by excess capacity, so that supply can adjust to demand. Prices in these sectors are set by a fixed mark-up over variable cost (labour and intermediate inputs). The demand for labour and for imported intermediate inputs is assumed to be in a fixed relationship to the level of output. The model allows for the possibility that the level of supply may be constrained by either the availability of foreign exchange to finance the imports of intermediate inputs or by a shortage of labour. If any of these limits is encountered, prices (and mark-up rates) will adjust to close the demand-supply gap.

The very dynamic behaviour of manufactured exports was captured by a special function that was econometrically established, in which the level of exports was seen to increase with the level of output of the sector, the level of (export-oriented) direct foreign investment and relative price changes. Since the 1970s, foreign investment has become increasingly export oriented, and there is a clear link between foreign investment inflows and the growth (after a delay) of exports.

Factorial income (labour income and incomes of corporate and unincorporated capital) is distributed to the institutions. All income from labour and from unincorporated profits is allocated to households, and corporate profits are distributed among private corporations and state enterprises according to their capital stocks.

Total labour demand can now be established as the sum of the demand of the six production sectors, and can be contrasted with the supply of labour, which is assumed to grow at a fixed rate. Wage formation in Thailand is segmented by sub-markets for labour, and by region, but sufficient data to model the various segments of the market separately are not available. In recent years pressures on the labour market have been relatively high, due to the rapid economic growth, and this has been reflected in upward pressures on the wage level. It is assumed that the average wage rate follows the changes in the price level, but is also sensitive to the rate of economic growth; at times of rapid growth the demand pressures increase on at least some of the sub-markets for labour and this results in wage increases that tend to become generalized.

The distinguishing characteristic of this CGE model is its detailed treatment of saving, investment and portfolio behaviour of each of the institutional agents. This behaviour is encapsulated in the simple accounting identity, embodied in the SAM capital account of each agent, according to which for each institutional agent (k):

$$ASS_k = LBT_k + WTH_k \qquad (A6.1)$$

or: *total assets = total liabilities + net wealth*

Such accumulation balances hold for each agent (households, corporations, state enterprises, government), but also for financial institutions (central bank, commercial banks, other financial institutions). Assets include physical capital, government bonds, bank deposits and foreign assets; liabilities include share capital, bonds, bank credit and foreign credit. For each of these assets and liabilities the model defines and allocates rates of return (or cost), and it defines the revaluations that may occur in the stocks of assets and liabilities (of physical capital due to depreciation; of foreign assets/liabilities due to changes in the exchange rate; and of stock values due to changes in the stock market index). Subsequent sections then describe the institutional portfolio behaviour.

The accumulation balance adjustment of the household sector follows the 'prior savings' approach. Household savings are determined by the level of disposable household income and the level of net wealth (including any asset revaluation). Increases in wealth lead to a decrease in savings. Total household consumption is then derived as the difference between income and savings, and total consumption is distributed over the various commodities (including imported consumption goods) with the help of a Linear Expenditures System (LES-functions).

Households can add liabilities to their savings, liabilities obtained from domestic financial institutions. Households cannot borrow abroad and even the credit they can obtain from domestic financial institutions may be rationed by the portfolio decisions of the financial institutions.

Households and unincorporated firms allocate the available funds (i.e. their wealth, augmented by current savings, and their liabilities) to the various assets through CES-type stock-adjustment functions, which describe the changes in the initial asset structure, changes that are made in response to changes in relative profitability of the various assets. Such functions are generally used in structuralist CGE models; for instance, they are also applied in Taylor and Rosensweig (1990) and Vongpradhip (1987, 1988). The function determines the holdings of asset AA_K as follows:

$$AA_{k,K} = a_{k,K} * \left[\frac{rf_{k,K}}{rf_k} \right]^{\sigma_k} * ASS_k \qquad (A6.2)$$

where $a_{k,K}$ is the share of financial asset K in agent k's total asset portfolio, $rf_{k,K}$ the return on this asset, rf_k the average return on agent k's assets, σ_k the elasticity of substitution for the agent's portfolio and ASS_k the size of the total portfolio of assets.

It is assumed that households do not hold foreign assets. In many other developing countries, the demand for foreign assets by households (i.e. capital flight) has become a serious matter of concern, but in the case of Thailand such outflows of funds have been very small throughout the years, if they exist at all, and they are ignored in the model. Household investments in real assets are, implicitly, derived as a residue.

The other real sector institutions (corporations, government, state enterprises) are less financially constrained than the households are. In the private corporate sector, savings are obtained by deducting transfer payments (e.g. dividends), interest payments on domestic and foreign liabilities and tax payments from the gross operating surplus.

Corporate investment is, in principle, determined by demand. The investment demand equation was estimated econometrically. The accelerator mechanism is strong, but it was also found that the level of direct foreign investment inflows and the real rate of interest do have a significant impact on investment demand. The impact of foreign investment is interesting. Obviously, foreign investment is part of corporate investment, but it was found that the changes in the flows of foreign investment have an additional impact on total investment demand which is captured neither by its inclusion in total investment, nor by the accelerator effect. The level of actual investment can fall below the level of investment demand due to foreign exchange shortages or due to the budget constraint. Any disequilibrium between investment demand and the budget-constrained investment finance function or the foreign exchange-constrained investment function is solved by determining the *realized* level of investment as the minimum of the three functions, thus:

$$IR_c = min \; (IRF_c, \; IRE_c, \; IRB_c) \tag{A6.3}$$

where *IR* is the realized level of investment and *IRF*, *IRE* and *IRB* are investment demand, and the maximum levels of investment that are possible given the foreign exchange-constraint and the budget-constraint of the corporate sector, respectively.

The foreign exchange-constrained level of investment is determined by the import capacity, which follows from the external balance and from other claims on the import capacity. The budget constraint of corporations is derived from its asset and wealth balance (see equation A6.1 above). The liabilities available to firms are dependent on foreign capital inflows and on the portfolio decisions of corporations and domestic financial institutions. As Thai corporations have close contacts with local financial institutions and with free access to external credit, the constraints on corporate investment are not severe, and they were not binding in the simulations performed. Corporations can always borrow (domestically or abroad) to release any constraint. Therefore, the level of corporate investment tends to follow investment demand.

Corporations decide on their financial assets and liabilities portfolio using the same type of CES-functions as the household sector (see equation A6.2). The closure in this sector will be the corporate borrowing from commercial banks. The close links between major corporations and the financial institutions make it realistic to assume that banks will satisfy any credit demand that corporations will have.

State enterprises have an investment demand function not unlike the one of private corporations. The level of desired investment is determined by an accelerator term and by the level of foreign finance that is available. A constant term is added to the state enterprise investment demand function; variations in its value can be used to simulate policy changes. State enterprises make portfolio decisions about the level of financial assets and liabilities, in which their borrowing from commercial banks acts as the closure.

In the government sector the level of investment is an exogenous (policy) variable, as is the level of government consumption expenditure. As in the case of private corporations, state enterprise and government investment could, in principle, be constrained by the foreign exchange or the budget constraint. The closure for the government balance is the credit from the Bank of Thailand, but, in fact, the government has been running surpluses in recent years and has been paying back to its creditors.

The accumulation balances and the budget constraints of the various institutional agents are interconnected through the process of financial intermediation. For instance, corporations borrow from banks, but the credit-creating capacity of banks is dependent on, among other things, the deposits households are willing to put in the bank, and the amounts that banks can borrow from the central bank. The ability of the central bank to provide reserves for the banks is, in turn, determined by the level of foreign exchange reserves and by the claims on central bank resources by the government. If the financing of the fiscal deficit would result in excess claims on the central bank, it would have to reduce its credit to banks (and thus reduce credit supply for the private sector, i.e. crowding out) or reduce its foreign reserves. To the latter process there is a clear limit. However, in the base year of the present model, the government had a budget surplus and was paying back its debt. The financial markets were thus relatively liquid and there was no danger of crowding out private credit demand.

Financial intermediation occurs through the central bank, commercial banks, other financial institutions (mainly finance companies) and the stock markets (SET).

The central bank (Bank of Thailand) extends credit to the government and to commercial banks and other financial institutions. In principle, the credit extended to government, banks, and non-bank financial institutions is determined by their demand. The central bank has, however, two instruments of monetary policy: it can increase the interest charged on its loans, and it can limit the amount of credit it makes available.[1]

Commercial banks and other financial institutions meet the demand for credit from households, corporations, state enterprises and government. They derive their funds from deposits and from borrowing abroad or from the central bank. The adjustment of their asset and liability portfolio follows the same portfolio adjustment functions as the other sectors do. The domestic interest rate fluctuates to clear any gap between the demand for and supply of credit.

The Security Exchange of Thailand (SET) was included as a separate channel of financial intermediation. The SET is modelled as a price-clearing market. The SET is not a channel for (hostile) take-overs of firms. Most large corporations with shares listed on the SET are still controlled by families that hold controlling shares of the listed capital. The flows of funds into and out of the SET are thus not determined by strategic corporate plans, but more by the returns and cost of funds compared to alternative assets and liabilities. Listed corporations 'offer' new shares to the SET as part of their portfolio decisions, based on relative cost of sources of funds. The households and corporations demand shares, again, as part of their asset portfolio decisions, based on relative returns. Another category of demand that is exogenous, is the inflows of portfolio investment funds from abroad. These inflows are channelled through commercial banks to reflect the actual practice in Thailand whereby foreign investors deposit their funds with banks, which, in turn, use these funds to purchase the desired shares and, generally, also hold these shares as custodians, on behalf of the foreign investors.

At the SET, the price of shares (i.e. the SET index) moves to equilibrate demand and supply. Fluctuations in the SET index are an important source for revaluations of private wealth.

The balance of payments largely follows from the previous processes. Exports follow from the summation of sectoral export functions. Import demand is assumed to be largely income or output related with limited price substitution. Demand for intermediate imports is part of the CES production function in the sectors with production functions, and holds a fixed relation to output in the mark-up sectors. Imports of investment goods are a fixed proportion of total investment, the proportion being determined by the base year SAM. The imports of consumer goods is determined through the LES system and dependent on income and relative prices.

The various elements of current transfer payments follow either the patterns established in the base year SAM, or are determined by portfolio adjustments (e.g. interest payments on external debt). The capital account transactions are partly exogenous (e.g. direct and portfolio foreign investment) and partly endogenous (e.g. corporate borrowing abroad).

The balance of the current account and the capital account transactions of the balance of payments and of the foreign exchange transactions of financial institutions ends up as changes of foreign reserve holdings by the central bank, which act, in principle, as the closure of the whole model (at least, when the budget or foreign exchange constraints are not active).

The nominal exchange rate is fixed and used as a policy instrument. Officially, the baht is linked to a basket of currencies, but the precise composition of the basket is not disclosed and this gives some flexibility to the nominal exchange rate. As a matter of fact, the baht has, over the years, shown a remarkable stability with respect to the US dollar. The real exchange rate is defined as

$$RER = \frac{P_w e}{P_d} \tag{A6.4}$$

where P_w is the level of world prices, e the nominal exchange rate and P_d the domestic price level. The real exchange rate plays a role in the export functions and in the function explaining the imports of consumer goods.

The import capacity is determined by export earnings, net current transfer payments, net foreign asset acquisition by the various institutions as determined by their portfolio functions, and net inflow of autonomous direct and portfolio foreign investment. If import demand exceeds the import capacity, the level of output will decrease (due to reductions in the import of intermediate inputs) and the level of investment will decrease (due to the reduction in the import of capital goods).

Another constraint on the model is the budget constraint, which works mainly through the domestic financial system, where the central bank decides on the credit to financial institutions; these decisions, in turn, influence the extent to which the financial institutions can expand their credit to the non-financial sector. The availability of credit may restrict the level of investment that households and private and public corporations can realize.

Policy variables

The model system described above defines an economic system characterized by institutions, each with their own behavioural rules, and by a set of markets, some of which are imperfect. The effectiveness of policy interventions will be influenced by this institutional context and by the assumed sectoral adjustment behaviour. Key policy instruments in the model are: the nominal exchange rate; the minimum level of central bank reserves (MIRES), which will determine the amount of credit the central bank will make available to domestic financial institutions; the interest rate charged by the central bank; the level of government consumption and investment expenditure; and tax rates.

Parameter values and model calibration

Most of the parameters of the model are defined by base-year SAM. For instance, the main spending propensities, direct and indirect tax rates, initial composition of asset and liability portfolios of the various agents and the sectoral allocation of labour in the base year are all implicitly defined in the SAM and are adopted in the model. Elasticities of production functions, export functions and financial portfolio functions were either estimated econometrically or pitched at levels that were also used in other, comparable studies.

The base-year calibration procedure follows that common to CGE models: initial prices and quantities are combined with the parameters and elasticities to calculate the share parameters and exogenous constants that validate the base-year values in the SAM. The presence of (stocks of) assets in the model complicates calibration since income flows (and hence also savings decisions) depend on incomes earned from assets. The structure of the SAM, showing beginning-of-period and end-of-period stocks of assets and liabilities, already recognized this complication. We calibrate for the end-of-period portfolio holdings of all institutions as reported in the South-East block of the SAM (rows 37 to 47, columns 26 to 35 of Table 2.9, Chapter 2).

Once the model was calibrated, the dynamic model was used to produce a base run of the model over a period of 10 years. In this base run policy variables (such as exchange rate, tax rates, administered interest rate) and external variables (such as import prices and world interest rate) were kept constant. The only change from base year values of exogenous variables that was allowed in the base run, was the growth of exogenous government current and capital spending by 7 per cent per year. This was considered necessary to generate a base run in which the government spending ratios would remain more or less constant. The base run generated, over the 10-year period, a GDP growth rate of 6.6 per cent and an average rate of inflation of 2.3 per cent per year, figures that are quite close to the long-term rates that Thailand has experienced over the last three decades. The base run serves as a benchmark in the analysis of the outcomes of the simulations.

Notes

Chapter 1

1. Japan, Hong Kong and Taiwan used to rely on own savings to finance investment. South Korea and Singapore used to run large current account deficits, indicating the use of external finance. In the 1980s these countries also reduced or eliminated their dependence on foreign funding (see James et al. 1989).

2. Hong Kong and Singapore could be added to this list, but are not covered in the analysis that follows. As trade-based city-states without significant agricultural sectors, their industrialization experiences are of a different nature and offer less comparative information.

Chapter 2

1. Data in the Production Yearbook of the Food and Agriculture Organization of the UN show that, at 2004 kg per ha, rice yields in Thailand are much lower than yields in countries like China, India, Indonesia, Malaysia, Pakistan, Philippines, Sri Lanka and Vietnam. It is also clear that Thailand's performance in rice production is particularly poor. Comparison of Thailand's yields in other crops to yields in other countries in the same group of nine shows better rankings for Thailand for maize (ranked 2), cassava (3), sugar (6) and tobacco (6). See FAO (1992).

2. For instance, tuna canneries started to emerge in the 1980s, and by 1987 Thailand had become the world's biggest exporter of canned tuna. By that time it was also the biggest exporter of canned pineapple. The export of frozen prawns doubled between 1984 and 1987 (*Far Eastern Economic Review*, 29 December 1988).

3. See Hewison and Brown (1994) for a historical account of the repression and fragmentation of the labour movement in Thailand.

4. Even in a comparative perspective, Thailand's income distribution is very unequal. Krongkaew (1994) compares data for four Asian NICs, four ASEAN countries and China, and concludes that Thailand has the most unequal income distribution in this group.

5. Chenery estimates patterns of development from the experience of a large group of countries. Countries at the level of Thailand's 1992 *per capita* income would have, on average, an export/GDP ratio of 24 per cent (Chenery 1979: 16). Thailand's export ratio in 1992 was 36 per cent. As early as 1965, Thailand had a relatively high export ratio compared to other countries of a similar size that also followed a balanced development strategy (Chenery 1979: 30).

6. This approach is taken in Akrasanee, Jansen and Pongpisanupichit (1993), Chapter 2, where SAMs were constructed for 1975 and 1985. The comparison of the coefficients of the two SAMs, together with time series data on some main variables, were then used to analyse the patterns of structural change in the Thai economy.

Chapter 3

1. The increase in the investment ratio in 1980 is due to the revision of the National Accounts. In 1992 the NESDB published a new, rebased series of National Accounts, with estimates going back to 1980. In this series, the estimates of investment are somewhat higher than in the old series.

2. In fact, the balance-of-payments identity is:

$$CAB + F + \Delta RES + E\&O = 0$$

where RES are the foreign reserves of the monetary system and $E\&O$ the measurement errors and omissions. In equation 3.2, the ΔRES and the $E\&O$ are ignored.

3. For a fuller discussion of data sources, see the appendix to this chapter. In 1992 the classification in the published balance-of-payments accounts changed, and loans to private and state corporations were no longer noted separately.

4. Grants have been relatively unimportant in the period under study. In the early 1970s they were equivalent to around 0.5 per cent of GDP, but they rapidly decreased afterwards. This was the result of the decrease in transfers from the USA after the end of the Vietnam War and of the reduction in highly concessional aid as Thailand grew richer.

5. The *F*-variable in equation 3.5 is measured, in Table 3.1, from the capital account of the balance of payments, because this source gives the inflows by the various receiving institutions. In equation 3.1 above, based on the National Accounting system, the difference between investment and savings is equal to the current account. As indicated already in note 2 above, the current-account balance need not be equal to the capital-account balance; the difference may arise from two other entries of the balance of payments, changes in reserves *(RES)* and errors & omissions *(E&O)*. To make the identity consistent, equation 3.5 should read:

$$I_h + I_c + I_{se} + I_g = S_h + S_c + S_{se} + S_g + F_c + F_{se} + F_g - \Delta RES + E\&O$$

6. The early years of the SET were characterized by volatility and speculation. This led to a crisis in 1979, when a large finance and securities company collapsed and the SET crashed. As a result, many other finance and securities companies also experienced serious financial problems. The SET index fell from 258 at the end of 1978 to 149 in 1979, and slid down further to 106 at the end of 1981. The crisis invited intervention by the central bank to restore the stability of the SET and to monitor more closely the activities of the finance and securities companies.

Chapter 4

1. In some countries the 'errors and omissions' can be quite substantial, as they include not only measurement errors, but also systematic errors in the reporting of items, for instance due to smuggling, over- or under-invoicing or capital flight. The instabilities of the 1970s and 1980s have led, in many developing countries, to private sector reactions. Where external conditions were adverse and domestic policies unconvincing, the private sector reacted by reducing investment and by moving savings abroad to more stable financial markets. In cases where capital controls prevented these capital transfers, illegal

channels were found for this 'capital flight'. The account 'errors & omissions' of the balance of payments is sometimes used as an estimate of capital flight, i.e. unrecorded transfers of funds by the private sector to foreign financial markets. It should be noted that the entry 'errors & omissions' is, at best, only a very indirect, narrow and unsatisfactory statistical proxy for capital flight, and that more elaborate methods to estimate capital flight have been designed (see e.g. Vos 1992).

In the case of Thailand, there is no reason to assume that such systematic factors play a role: the E&O are relatively small, rarely over 1 per cent of GDP, and are, in the various years, either positive or negative. Since Thailand has not had any serious internal and external socio-economic and political unrest, and given the fact that, in general, economic growth has been rapid and domestic financial market relatively free, one would not expect that there were substantial incentives for such a capital flight. The *International Banking Statistics* collected by the IMF recorded as deposits held by non-bank Thai residents with banks outside Thailand in 1990 an amount of 0.9 billion US dollars; this was less than 4 per cent of the total outstanding external debt of Thailand in that year.

2. The *World Development Report 1994* of the World Bank gives estimates for 1992 of the central government expenditures as percentages of GNP for 54 developing countries: only four of these countries had lower ratios than Thailand (World Bank 1994, Table 10). The same report also gives information on general government consumption expenditures as percentages of GDP in 1992. Of the 89 developing countries listed, 17 had lower ratios than Thailand and 7 had a similar ratio (World Bank 1994, Table 9). It also appears that in Thailand the growth of the ratio in the period from the early 1970s to 1992 was less rapid than elsewhere.

   The *International Financial Statistics* (published by the International Monetary Fund) gives the average ratio of central government expenditure to GDP in developing countries in 1988 as 28.5 per cent; for the Asian developing countries the average ratio is 20.5 per cent. In Thailand the ratio of national government expenditure to GDP was 16.9 per cent in 1988.

3. In the literature this effect is called 'Dutch disease', referring to events that took place in the Dutch economy when external earnings

suddenly increased after the discovery and exploitation of large reserves of natural gas.

4. The real exchange rate is defined as:

$$RER = NER * \frac{P_w}{P_{tha}}$$

where *RER* is the real exchange rate; *NER* the nominal exchange rate (bahts per US dollar); P_w the changes in international price and P_{tha} the changes in domestic prices. The *RER* in Figure 4.3 is an index with the base 1970 = 100.

5. A simple regression illustrates this fact:

$$p = \underset{(16.37)}{1.03\ p_w} + \underset{(4.55)}{0.41\ F/Y_{(t-1)}}$$

$$R^2(adj) = 0.89; \quad D.W. = 1.85$$

where:

p = Thai inflation, rate of change CPI;
p_w = world inflation; and
F/Y = total capital inflows as percentage of GDP.

A similar correlation can be established between inflation and other indicators of demand pressures, such as the growth rate of GDP or the domestic credit growth, but the link between inflation and capital inflows is much stronger (as reflected in the size and significance of the coefficients) than that between inflation and other indicators of domestic aggregate demand.

6. The trade-weighted real exchange rate is defined as:

$$TWRER = \frac{\Sigma\ w_i * NER_i * P_i}{P_{tha}}$$

where NER_i are the bilateral nominal exchange rates between the baht and the currencies of Thailand's major trading partners; P_i the changes in the domestic prices of Thailand's trading partners; and w_i the weights that the various trading partners have in Thailand's foreign trade. For currency weights in Thailand's trade see Nijathaworn and Senivongs (1994).

7. Wattananukit and Bhongmakapat (1989) run a regression to explain the growth rate of exports over the period 1970–87. They conclude that 57 per cent of the export growth can be explained by the growth of world trade, and about 19 per cent by the level of export prices relative to the export prices of main competitors: the remaining 24 per cent of export growth is explained by other factors. Their analysis looks at the growth rate and not at the export ratio, but it confirms the important role of relative prices. Although they do not directly include the real exchange rate, it is clear that their relative export price is a concept similar to the trade-weighted real exchange rate.

8. Such concerns existed already at an earlier stage, however. *The Far Eastern Economic Review* reports on an aid donor meeting in Paris in 1981, where aid donors, including the World Bank, expressed concern about Thailand getting deeper into debt to finance the economy's large current-account deficit (*Far Eastern Economic Review*, 13 December 1981).

9. The revision of the National Accounts, published in 1992, included a significant increase in household investment over the earlier National Accounts estimates. Apparently better methods were used to estimate residential construction. This revision makes it difficult to compare trends in household investment, and thus in total private investment, before and after 1980.

10. Their results are based on pooled data (Blejer & Khan 1984) from a sample of 24 developing countries (all variables in real terms). Their equation is:

$$I_{pr,t} = 0.319\,\Delta Y_{t-1} - 0.091\,GAP + 0.257\Delta DCR + 0.574\,I_{pr,t-1}$$
$$\quad\quad (5.82)\quad\quad\quad (1.41)\quad\quad\quad (4.23)\quad\quad\quad\quad (8.80)$$

$$\quad\quad + 0.158\,TGIR - 0.191\,(GIR - TGIR)$$
$$\quad\quad\quad (2.09)\quad\quad\quad\quad (2.64)$$

$$R^2\,(adj) = 0.934$$

TGIR is the trend value of public investment and *GIR* is the total level of public investment, so that *GIR* – *TGIR* is the deviation from the trend value. A regression in which only the total level of (real) public investment *(GIR)* was included failed to lead to significant coefficients, while the above equation, in which trend and non-trend elements were separated, did give a significant positive coefficient for the trend and a significant negative coefficient for the deviation variable. The accelerator variables $(\Delta Y_{t-1}$ and $I_{pr,t-1})$ are highly significant, as is the financial constraint variable (ΔDCR). Of course, this financial variable may also capture part of the crowding out, if the financing of additional public investment reduces credit availability for the private sector. The variable *GAP* is an indirect indicator of capacity utilization.

11. Their regression, based on pooled time series data (Greene & Villanueva 1991) of a sample of 23 developing countries over the period 1975–87 is:

$$I_{pr}/Y = -0.083\,RI + 0.249\,g_{t-1} + 0.080\,I_{pu}/Y - 0.004\,p$$
$$\quad\quad (3.06)\quad\quad (6.50)\quad\quad\quad (2.03)\quad\quad\quad (4.02)$$

$$\quad\quad + 0.084\,Y^{pc}_{t-1} - 0.031\,DSR_{t-1} - 0.033\,D/Y_{t-1}$$
$$\quad\quad\quad (0.32)\quad\quad\quad (2.55)\quad\quad\quad (2.99)$$

$$R^2 = 0.81$$

where:

I_{pr}/Y = the private investment ratio,
I_{pu}/Y = the public investment ratio,
RI = the real deposit rate of interest,
g = the growth rate of GDP *per capita,*
Y^{pc} = the level of GDP *per capita*
DSR = the debt-service ratio, and
D/Y = the debt/GDP ratio.

12. Jansen (1995) contains a macroeconometric model which also includes a private investment demand equation. According to this equation, private investment is stimulated by public investment, by growth of aggregate demand, and by an appreciation of the real exchange rate (which makes imported capital goods cheaper). It is discouraged by the external-debt burden.

13. The *Far Eastern Economic Review* (24 March 1983) reported that, although not all the conditions of the first SAL had been implemented, still a second SAL had been signed. In particular, the first SAL failed to reform state enterprise pricing to the extent intended. Consequently, the second SAL gave high priority to fiscal reform, in-

cluding state enterprise price reform. It has been suggested that the SALs helped to create an international commitment among Thai officials and politicians: many measures in SALs that were unpopular among politicians were implemented in subsequent years because of this commitment (see Sahasakul et al. 1989: 47).

14. Another illustration of the difficulties in fiscal adjustment is the fact that the IMF Stand-by Facility, that had been approved in mid-1985, was terminated by the Thai after about half of the funds had been withdrawn. Many of the targets of that agreement had been achieved for 1986, but there was disagreement about the budget deficit and about desirable fiscal policy for 1987 (see *Far Eastern Economic Review*, 26 February 1987).

15. In the years between 1980 and 1986 actual revenue had always been lower than budget targets. In 1987 actual revenue exceeded budget targets, thanks to the rapid economic growth. This experience was repeated in the years after 1987 and contributed to the budget surpluses of these years.

16. See *Far Eastern Economic Review*, 27 September 1984.

17. For instance, investments in gas and lignite development contributed to a reduction of the imported energy dependency from 70 per cent in 1980 to 50 per cent in 1986 (*Far Eastern Economic Review*, 25 June 1987).

Chapter 5

1. See, for instance, some of the contributions in Cable and Persaud (1987). In addition to this financial advantage of DFI, many other possible advantages are suggested. Foreign investment might bring in new technologies, operate in export production, increase competition on domestic markets and thus increase efficiency, etc. The inflow of PFI might stimulate the development of the stock market and thus generate more funds for corporate investment. The *World Development Report 1991* (World Bank 1991b: 94–95) points out that DFI, when accompanied by appropriate domestic macroeconomic policies, may raise the productivity of investment, transfer technology and stimulate exports. The *World Development Report 1989* (World Bank 1989: 110–11) argues that PFI helps to increase demand for stocks on

the stock markets which, in most developing countries, are still very small. In this way, PFI may stimulate the development of these markets.

2. See Page (1987). A summary of the various arguments for and against DFI in developing countries may be found in e.g. Grieco (1986) or Helleiner (1989).

3. Dunning (1995) gives data on the stock of outstanding DFI. In 1967, 69 per cent of the total stock was in developed market economies, and 31 per cent was in developing countries (of which 7.8 per cent was in Asia). By 1992, the share of developing countries had dropped to 22 per cent, but the share of Asia had increased to 11.4 per cent.

4. The World Bank's *Quarterly Review on Financial Flows to the Developing Countries* (March 1991: 8) lists the 20 main recipient countries. These 20 countries received 90 per cent of total DFI flows to all developing countries over the period 1981–90. Among these, the six main recipients accounted for 60 per cent of all DFI flows to LDCs, and the ten main recipients for 74 per cent. Thailand has always been one of the main recipient countries. In the 1970s and early 1980s it ranked eighth or ninth in the listing of host countries; after 1986 it moved up to sixth place.

5. The 1992 GDP of developing countries is listed in the *World Development Report 1994* of the World Bank (World Bank 1994: 166; Russia and the former Soviet Republics as well as the Eastern European countries have not been included among developing countries). China could be added to the list of twelve – not so much as receiver of flows of PFI but as a major destination for DFI flows.

6. Over the period 1980–90 the growth in *per capita* GDP was positive in Brazil and Chile, and negative in the other three Latin American countries. The average rate of inflation over those years was very high for Argentina, Brazil and Mexico, and lower, but still considerable, for Chile and Venezuela, where it was around 20 per cent per year.

7. The exception in this group is the Philippines, which seems to follow a more Latin American pattern in terms of economic performance, with a negative growth rate and substantial inflation throughout the 1980s.

8. The data on DFI, based on the balance-of-payments statistics of the Bank of Thailand, underestimate the actual DFI levels. According to IMF rules, profits reinvested by TNCs should (i) be included in the repatriation of profits by TNCs and (ii) then be added to new DFI inflows to give the total of foreign investment, but this is not done by the Bank of Thailand, which does not report reinvested profits separately. Figure 5.2 gives the inflows of DFI. Historically, outflows of DFI from Thailand had been negligible, but in 1987 they suddenly rose to a substantial level (170 million US dollars) due to the establishment of foreign branches by Thai banks. In subsequent years outflows of DFI from Thailand also remained at levels far above historical experience.

9. The drop in DFI flows, as recorded in Figure 5.2, may be exaggerated. As mentioned in note 8, DFI flows to Thailand are underestimated because reinvested profits are not recorded and included. It should be noted that, whereas DFI inflows rose to very high levels after 1986 and thus profits from such investments also must have risen, the recorded repatriation of profits and dividends, as percentages of GDP, have remained stable, at around 1 per cent of GDP since 1986. This suggests that a growing share of DFI profits is retained for reinvestment in Thailand.

10. Data from the *International Financial Statistics* allow a comparison between Thailand and other ASEAN countries. They show that the net DFI inflows started to increase in 1986 and 1987 in Thailand and in the Philippines. In the Philippines they dropped sharply after 1988, while in Thailand they continued to increase and then stabilized at a high level. DFI inflows in Indonesia and Malaysia started to rise only in 1988 and then increased rapidly (see also Jha 1994).

11. According to the central bank, the rise in private investment was caused by (i) the recovery of the economy which encouraged capacity expansion; (ii) the increased inflows of DFI that were attracted to Thailand by low-cost labour; (iii) government policies supporting private investment and (iv) the relatively low interest rates (see Bank of Thailand, *Annual Economic Report 1987*, p. 31).

12. The mechanism leading to this result appears to be the demand-supply balance on the (protected) domestic market for manufactures. DFI in this sector increases the supply of manufactured goods. Demand will

also increase with income, but as part of the income will accrue to the foreign firm and be repatriated, it is quite possible that the increase in supply will exceed the increase in demand, so that output prices and profitability of the sector will decline and domestic investment will fall. Such demand-supply imbalances will not occur in the export-oriented sectors.

13. Khan and Reinhart (1990) use a growth equation which makes the rate of growth a function of the investment ratio, the growth rate of the labour force and the growth rate of exports. They subdivide total investment into private and public investment. They run the regression of cross-section data for 24 developing countries. The data are the averages of the variables for each country over the period 1970–79. They also run regressions with the growth rate of imports rather than exports.

They conclude that the impact of private investment on growth is stronger than that of public investment, because its coefficient in the growth equation is larger and significant, while the public investment variable fails to obtain a significant coefficient. Sarmad (1990) shows that their results are sensitive to period and country selection. He did obtain the same results as Khan and Reinhart when he restricted himself to the same database, but not when he looked at a broader country group and at data for a more recent period.

14. Husain and Jun (1992) also run the regression for a group of South Asian countries (Bangladesh, India, Pakistan and Sri Lanka). For this sample the DFI variable did *not* obtain a significant coefficient.

15. In Chapter 6 the CGE model is used to simulate the effects of a decrease in the level of DFI inflows to about half of the level of 1989. With such a drastic decrease, private investment and growth would indeed drop. There would be less inflation and thus less appreciation of the real exchange rate. This positive effect on exports is countered, however, by the drop in export-oriented DFI, and the export/GDP ratio declines. However, all effects are relatively mild. The substantial decrease in DFI (equivalent to about 1 per cent of GDP) results in a decline in the GDP growth rate of 0.6 per cent per year. These outcomes support the claim that the growth of DFI during 1986–90 cannot in itself account for the double-digit growth, although it did make a significant contribution.

16. In the 'loan boom' period discussed in the previous chapter there was a modest increase in the import ratio. Table 2.7 of Chapter 2 has shown that the ratio of merchandise imports to GDP increased from 19 per cent in 1973 to over 28 per cent in 1980–81. The table also shows that most of that increase was due to the increasing cost of oil imports. Imports of intermediate goods or of capital goods, as percentages of GDP, did not change much in these years.

17. According to Bank of Thailand data, the outward remittances of technical fees and copyright and patent royalties amounted, in 1992, to more than 11 billion baht, equivalent to 0.43 per cent of GDP. In 1986 this share had been 0.19 per cent.

18. Figure 5.3 shows that since 1990 the real interbank rate and the real LIBOR rate have approached each other more closely. This is a sign of the increasing integration of the Thai and the international financial markets. Banks can now more easily borrow and lend on off-shore markets, and this forces the interbank rate to follow the international interest rate more closely. However, the gap between the international interest rates and the domestic lending rates appears to have widened somewhat in recent years (see the analysis in the Bank of Thailand *Annual Economic Report 1994*, pp. 44–45).

19. A very simple regression illustrates this point:

$$SET_t = 0.99\ SET_{t-1} + 107.17\ PFI/Y$$
$$(17.39) \qquad\qquad (3.71)$$

$$R^2(adj) = 0.94;\ D.W. = 1.99$$

where:

SET_t = average value of SET index for the year,
SET_{t-1} = value of SET index at the end of the previous year, and
PFI/Y = net inflows of PFI as a proportion of GDP.

20. The study by Demirguc-Kunt (1992) analyses the capital structure of major listed companies in a sample of nine developing countries with emerging stock markets, including Thailand. In a regression explaining the leverage ratio (i.e. the ratio of long-term debt to equity) the variable indicating stock market activity has a significant positive impact, suggesting that equity and debt are complements rather than substitutes.

21. In the period 1986–94, the inflows of PFI were equivalent to 3.8 per cent of private corporate investment on average, but there were substantial variations from year to year.

22. See the regression in endnote 5 of Chapter 4. This relationship also remained strong in the most recent period. Further confirmation of this relationship will be given in Chapter 6, where the CGE model is used to simulate the effects of a decrease in PFI inflows. Two effects dominate. One is that a drop in PFI flows leads to a drop in the SET index, which is translated into a decrease in private wealth and private consumption. The second effect is monetary: the reduced PFI inflows mean a drop in the monetary base and a sharp rise in domestic interest rates, which results in a decrease in private investment. The reduced levels of private consumption and investment, and the reduced growth rate of the money supply all contribute to a lower rate of inflation.

Chapter 6

1. For a brief review of early econometric models see Nijathaworn and Arya (1987).

2. The model contains 28 behavioural equations. Seventeen of these relate to the real part of the economy: three functions to explain the various categories of imports, three to explain three categories of exports, two production functions, a private consumption and a private investment function, and a taxation function. Furthermore, there are five price equations. The main link between the financial and the real block is that portfolio asset choices of the private sector and the inflows of external finance determine the availability of funds to finance private investment. More indirectly, growth of the money supply will lead to domestic price increases which will have an impact on the levels of exports and imports.

3. The book which includes this chapter was published in 1990. The model, however, was constructed in 1984 and was based on a 1980 SAM.

4. For instance, Keijzers et al. (1983) presents an elaborate CGE model, called the SIAMESI model, based on a 1975 SAM. Hutaserani and Jitchuson (1988) apply the Thailand Agricultural Model (THAM-2)

to study trends in income distribution and poverty. The THAM-2 is a dynamic CGE model focusing on food production and distribution. Sussangkarn (1991) uses an elaborate CGE model to analyse labour market problems.

5. See, for instance, Taylor (1990) for a more detailed characterization of this tradition and for a number of applications. See also Jemio (1993).

6. See Vos (1991) for a review and discussion of this aspect.

7. In this respect the model reflects reality: after attaining its high level at the end of 1989, the SET index first continued to rise in the first half of 1990, but subsequently fell and only very gradually and haltingly recovered in 1991 and 1992.

8. The econometric model in Jansen (1995) specified the interaction between DFI and imports in more detail. In the simulation it was shown that an increase in DFI would lead to a sharp deterioration of the current account.

9. In the simulation reported above, the external debt did not grow so rapidly, as the expansion started from a fiscal surplus situation. It should also be noted that in the early 1980s the government itself did not borrow much abroad. However, the increase in domestic borrowing by the government forces corporations and financial institutions to borrow abroad.

Appendix to Chapter 6

1. In the model, credit rationing by the central bank is captured by an indirect mechanism. The Bank of Thailand decides on the minimum level of its foreign exchange reserves required (MIRES). If that level becomes binding, it will ration credit by giving credit to the government according to demand and making only the residue available to financial institutions. By varying the level of MIRES, the model can thus simulate monetary policy. It must be noted, however, that such a policy may not be very effective in cutting back domestic spending since banks, and corporations, can also borrow abroad.

References

Ajanant, Juanjai, Supote Chunanuntathum & Sorrayuth Meenaphant(1986) *Trade and Industrialization of Thailand*. Bangkok: Social Science Association of Thailand.

Akrasanee, Narongchai, K. Jansen & Jeerasak Pongpisanupichit (1993) *International Capital Flows and Economic Adjustment in Thailand*. Research Monograph No. 101, Bangkok: Thailand Development Research Institute (TDRI).

Alarcón, J., J. van Heemst, S. Keuning, W. de Ruijter & R. Vos (1991) *The Social Accounting Framework for Development. Concepts, Construction and Applications*. Aldershot: Avebury.

Amranand, Piyasvasti & W. Grais (1984) 'Macroeconomic and Distributional Implications of Sectoral Policy Interventions: An Application to Thailand', World Bank Staff Working Papers, No. 627, Washington DC: World Bank.

Amsden, A. (1989) *Asia's Next Giant: South Korea and Late Industrialisation*. New York: Oxford University Press.

Bank of Thailand (annual) *Annual Economic Report*. Bangkok: Bank of Thailand.

Bank of Thailand (quarterly) *Quarterly Bulletin*. Bangkok: Bank of Thailand.

Bank of Thailand (1992) *50 Years of the Bank of Thailand, 1942–1992*. Bangkok: Bank of Thailand.

Bank of Thailand (1994) *Papers on Policy Analysis and Assessment*. Bangkok: Bank of Thailand.

Barro, R.J. (1991) 'Economic Growth in a Cross Section of Countries', *The Quarterly Journal of Economics*. 106(2): 407–43.

Blejer, M.I. & M.S. Khan (1984) 'Government Policy and Private Investment in Developing Countries', *IMF Staff Papers*. 31: 379–403.

Borensztein, E. (1990) 'Debt Overhang, Credit Rationing and Investment', *Journal of Development Economics*. 32: 315–35.

281

Borrmann, A. & R. Jungnickel (1992) 'Foreign Investment as a Factor in Asian Pacific Integration', *Intereconomics*. 27(6): 282–88.

Bos, H.C, M. Sanders & C. Secchi (1974) *Private Foreign Investment in Developing Countries*. Dordrecht: Reidel Publishing Company.

Bowles, P. (1987) 'Foreign Aid and Domestic Savings in Less Developed Countries: Some Tests for Causality', *World Development*. 15(6): 789–96.

Brewer, T.L. (1991) 'Foreign Direct Investment in Developing Countries: Patterns, Policies and Prospects', Working Paper (WPS 712), Washington DC: International Economics Department, World Bank.

Brummitt, W.E. & F. Flatters (1992) *Exports, Structural Change and Thailand's Rapid Growth*. Bangkok: Thailand Development Research Institute.

Buffie, E.F. (1993) 'Direct Foreign Investment, Crowding Out, and Underemployment in the Dualistic Economy', *Oxford Economic Papers*. 45(4): 639–67.

Cable, V. & B. Persaud (eds) (1987) *Developing with Foreign Investment*. London: Croom Helm.

Calderón, A. & E.V.K. FitzGerald (1994) *Private Response to Public Policy: Financial Flows and Economic Adjustment in Mexico since 1982*. The Hague: Institute of Social Studies.

Campbell, B.O., A. Mason & E.M. Pernia (eds) (1993) *The Economic Impact of Demographic Change in Thailand, 1980–2015: An Application of the HOMES Household Forecasting Model*. Honolulu: East-West Center, University of Hawaii.

Chaipravat, O., K. Meesook & S. Garnjarerndee (1979) 'Bank of Thailand Model of the Thai Economy', Discussion Paper No. 79/25, Bangkok: Department of Economic Research, Bank of Thailand.

Chalamwong, Yongyuth (1993) *A Study of Infrastructure Problems Experienced by Thai Manufacturing Industries*. Bangkok: Thailand Development Research Institute.

Chan, S. (ed.) (1995) *Foreign Direct Investment in a Changing Global Political Economy*. London: Macmillan.

Charoensin-o-larn, Chairat (1988) *Understanding Post-war Reformism in Thailand*. Bangkok: DK Publishers.

Chenery, H.B. (1979) *Structural Change and Development Policy*. London: Oxford University Press.

Chenery, H.B. & T.N. Srinivasan (eds) (1989) *Handbook of Development Economics, Vol. II*. Amsterdam: North Holland.

Chenery, H.B. & A.M. Strout (1966) 'Foreign Assistance and Economic Development', *American Economic Review*. 56(4): 679–733.

Chhibber, A., M. Dailami & N. Shafik (eds) (1992) *Reviving Private Investment in Developing Countries: Empirical Studies and Policy Lessons*. Amsterdam: North Holland.

Dahlman, C.J. & P. Brimble (1991) 'Technology Strategy and Policy for Industrial Competitiveness: A Case Study of Thailand' in World Bank (1991c).

Das, D.K. (1993) *The Yen Appreciation and the International Economy*. London: Macmillan.

Das, D.K. (ed.) (1993) *International Finance: Contemporary Issues*. London: Routledge.

De Melo, J. (1988) 'The Macro-economic Effects of Foreign Aid: Issues and Evidence' in Jepma (ed.), pp. 187–206.

Demirguc-Kunt, A. (1992) 'Developing Country Capital Structures and Emerging Stock Markets', Working Paper (WPS 933), Washington DC: Country Economics Department, World Bank.

Douglass, M. (1984) *Regional Integration on the Capitalist Periphery: The Central Plains of Thailand*, Institute of Social Studies, Research Report Series, No. 15, The Hague.

Dunning, J.H. (1995) 'The Role of Foreign Direct Investment in a Globalizing Economy', *BNL Quarterly Review*. 193: 125–44.

Dutta, M. (ed.) (1987) *Asia-Pacific Economies: Promises and Challenges*. Greenwich (CT): JAI Press.

Embree, J.F. (1950) 'Thailand: A "Loosely Structured" Social System', *American Anthropologist*. 52: 181–93.

Evans, M.K. (1969) *Macroeconomic Activity, Theory, Forecasting and Control: An Econometric Approach*. New York: Harper & Row.

Falkus, M. (1995) 'Thai Industrialization: An Overview' in Krongkaew (ed.), pp. 13–32.

FAO (1992) *Production Yearbook*. Rome: FAO.

Fazzari, S.M., R.G. Hubbard & B.C. Petersen (1988) 'Financing Constraints and Corporate Investment', *Brookings Papers on Economic Activity*. 1: 141–206.

FitzGerald, E.V.K., K. Jansen & R. Vos (1994) 'External Constraints on Private Investment Decisions in Developing Countries' in Gunning et al. (eds), pp. 185–220.

Fres-Felix, M.L. (ed.) (1992) *Public Sector and Monetary Policy in the SEACEN Countries*. Kuala Lumpur: Southeast Asian Central Banks Research and Training Centre.

Fry, M.J. (1993) 'Unstable Current Account Behaviour and Capital Flows in Developing Countries' in Das (ed.), pp. 54–71.

GATT (1991) *Trade Policy. Country Report Thailand.* Geneva: GATT.

Girling, J. (1981) *Thailand: Society and Politics.* Ithaca & London: Cornell University Press.

Greene, J. & D. Villanueva (1991) 'Private Investment in Developing Countries. An Empirical Analysis', *IMF Staff Papers.* 38: 33–58.

Grieco, J.M. (1986) 'Foreign Investment and Development: Theories and Evidence' in Moran et al., pp. 35–60.

Griffin, K. (1970) 'Foreign Capital, Domestic Savings and Economic Development', *Oxford Bulletin of Economics and Statistics.* 32(2): 99–112.

Gunning, J.W., H. Kox, W. Tims & Y. de Wit (eds) (1994) *Trade, Aid and Development: Essays in Honour of Hans Linneman.* Basingstoke: Macmillan.

Gupta, K.L. & M.A. Islam (1983) *Foreign Capital, Savings and Growth: An International Cross-section Study.* Dordrecht: Reidel Publishing.

Haggard, S. & R.R. Kaufman (eds) (1992) *The Politics of Economic Adjustment. International Constraints, Distributive Conflicts, and the State.* Princeton (NJ): Princeton University Press.

Healey, D. (1991) *Japanese Capital Exports and Asian Economic Development.* Paris: OECD.

Helleiner, G. (1987) 'Direct Foreign Investment and Manufacturing for Export in Developing Countries: A Review of the Issues' in Cable & Persaud (eds), pp. 67–83.

Helleiner, G. (1989) 'Transnational Corporations and Direct Foreign Investment' in Chenery & Srinivasan (eds), pp. 1441–80.

Heller, P.S. (1975) ' A Model of Public Fiscal Behavior in Developing Countries: Aid, Investment and Taxation', *American Economic Review.* 65(3): 429–45.

Hewison, K. & A. Brown (1994) 'Labour and Unions in an Industrialising Thailand', *Journal of Contemporary Asia.* 24(4): 483–514.

Hughes, H. & G.S. Dorrance (1987) 'Foreign Investment in East Asia' in Cable & Persaud (eds), pp. 44–66.

Husain, I. & K.W. Jun (1992) 'Capital Flows to South Asian and ASEAN Countries: Trends, Determinants and Policy Implications', Working Paper (WPS 842), Washington DC: International Economics Department, World Bank.

Hutaserani, Suganya & Somchai Jitchuson (1988) *Thailand's Income Distribution and Poverty Profile and their Current Situation,* 1988 TDRI

Year-End Conference, Bangkok: Thailand Development Research Institute.

Ichikawa, N. (1990) *Foreign Investment in Thai Development: Special Focus on Japanese Investment*. Bangkok: Thailand Development Research Institute.

Ingram, J. (1971) *Economic Change in Thailand, 1850–1970*. Stanford: Stanford University Press.

International Monetary Fund (1992) *World Economic Outlook. October 1992*. Washington DC: IMF.

James, W.E., S. Naya & G.M. Meier (1989) *Asian Development: Economic Success and Policy Lessons*. Madison: University of Wisconsin Press.

Jansen, K. (1989) 'Financial Development and the Intersectoral Transfer of Resources: The Case of Thailand', *Development and Change*. 20: 5–34.

Jansen, K. (1990) *Finance, Growth and Stability: Financing Economic Development in Thailand, 1960–86*. Aldershot: Avebury.

Jansen, K. (1991) 'Thailand, the Next NIC?', *Journal of Contemporary Asia*. 21(1): 13–30.

Jansen, K. (1995) 'The Macroeconomic Effects of Direct Foreign Investment: The Case of Thailand', *World Development*. 23(2): 193-210.

Jansen, K. & R. Vos (eds) (forthcoming) *External Finance and Adjustment: Failure and Success in the Developing World*. London: Macmillan.

Jemio, L.C. (1993) 'Micro- and Macroeconomic Adjustment in Bolivia (1970–89), A Neostructuralist Analysis of External Shocks, Adjustment and Stabilization Policies'. PhD thesis, Institute of Social Studies, The Hague.

Jemio, L. & K. Jansen (1993) 'External Finance, Growth and Adjustment: A Computable General Equilibrium Model for Thailand', Institute of Social Studies Working Paper, subseries on Money, Finance and Development, No. 46, The Hague.

Jepma, C.J. (ed.) (1988) *North-South Cooperation in Retrospect and Prospect*. London: Routledge.

Jha, S.C. (1994) 'Resource Mobilization in Developing Asia: Changing Patterns and Emerging Issues', *Journal of Contemporary Asia*. 24(4): 459–81.

Kangwanpornsiri, Kanjanee (1993) *Portfolio Investment in Thailand and Asia-Pacific Economic Cooperation*. Bangkok: National Institute of Development Administration.

Kantachai, N. et al. (1987) *Technology and Skills in Thailand*. Singapore: Institute of Southeast Asian Studies.

Keijzers, G.H.J., E.M.J. Hoogteijling & A.J. Mathot (1983) *The SIAMESI Model for Thailand*. Amsterdam: Economic and Social Institute, Free University of Amsterdam.

Khan, M.S. & C.M. Reinhart (1990) 'Private Investment and Economic Growth in Developing Countries', *World Development*. 18(1): 19–27.

Kirakul, Suchada (1986) 'Mobilisation of Informal Sector Savings in Thailand', Bangkok: Department of Economic Research, Bank of Thailand.

Kitchen, R.L. (1986) *Finance for the Developing Countries*. Chichester: John Wiley & Sons.

Klausner, W.J. (1987) *Reflections on Thai Culture*. Bangkok: Siam Society.

Krongkaew, Medhi (1985) 'Agricultural Development, Rural Poverty and Income Distribution in Thailand', *Developing Economies*. 23(4): 325–46.

Krongkaew, Medhi (1993) 'Poverty and Income Distribution' in Warr (ed.), pp. 401–37.

Krongkaew, Medhi (1994) 'Income Distribution in East Asian Developing Countries: An Update', *Asian-Pacific Economic Literature*. 8(2): 58–73.

Krongkaew, Medhi (ed.) (1980) *Current Development in Thai-Japanese Economic Relations: Trade and Investment*. Bangkok: Thammasat University Press.

Krongkaew, Medhi (ed.) (1995) *Thailand's Industrialization and its Consequences*. London: Macmillan, New York: St. Martin's Press.

Kwan, C.H. (1994) *Economic Interdependence in the Asia-Pacific Region: Towards a Yen Bloc*. London: Routledge.

Lall, S. & P. Streeten (1977) *Foreign Investment, Transnationals and Developing Countries*. London: Macmillan.

Lau, L.J. (ed.) (1986) *Models of Development. A Comparative Study of Economic Growth in South Korea and Taiwan*. San Francisco: ICS Press.

Leeahtam, Pisit (1991) *Thailand's Economic Adjustment in the 1980s: From Crisis to Double Digit Growth*. Bangkok: Dokya Publishing House.

Lucas, R.E.B. (1993) 'On the Determinants of Direct Foreign Investment: Evidence from East and Southeast Asia', *World Development*. 21: 391–406.

Machado, K.I. (1995) 'Japanese Foreign Direct Investment in East Asia: The Expanding Division of Labor and the Future of Regionalism' in Chan (ed.), pp. 39–66.

Moran, T.H. et al. (1986) *Investing in Development: New Roles for Private Capital?* New Brunswick: Transaction Books.

Morishima, M. (1982) *Why Has Japan 'Succeeded'?: Western Technology and the Japanese Ethos*. Cambridge: Cambridge University Press.

Mosley, P. (1980) 'Aid, Savings and Growth Revisited', *Oxford Bulletin of Economics and Statistics*. 42(2): 79–95.

Mosley, P. (1987) *Overseas Aid: Its Defence and Reform*. Brighton: Wheatsheaf.

Mosley, P., J. Harrigan & J. Toye (1991) *Aid and Power: The World Bank and Policy-based Lending*. London: Routledge.

Mulder, N. (1979) *Everyday Life in Thailand, an Interpretation*. Bangkok: DK Publishers.

Naqvi, S.N.H. & K. Sarmad (1993) *External Shocks and Domestic Adjustment: Pakistan's Case, 1970–1990*. Islamabad: Pakistan Institute of Development Economics.

Nartsupha, Chattip & Suthy Prasartset (1981) *The Political Economy of Siam*. Bangkok: Social Science Association of Thailand.

NESDB (National Economic and Social Development Board) (annual) *National Income of Thailand*. Bangkok: NESDB.

NESDB (National Economic and Social Development Board) (1991) *Input-Output Table for Thailand 1985*. Bangkok: NESDB.

NESDB-BoT (National Economic and Social Development Board & Bank of Thailand) (1982) *Flow-of-Funds Accounts of Thailand*. 1982 edition. Bangkok: NESDB/BoT.

NESDB-BoT (National Economic and Social Development Board & Bank of Thailand) (1983) *Flow-of-Funds Accounts of Thailand*. 1983 edition. Bangkok: NESDB/BoT.

NESDB-BoT (National Economic and Social Development Board & Bank of Thailand) (1986) *Flow-of-Funds Accounts of Thailand*. 1986 edition. Bangkok: NESDB/BoT.

NESDB-BoT (National Economic and Social Development Board & Bank of Thailand) (1991) *Flow-of-Funds Accounts of Thailand, 1984–90*. Bangkok: NESDB-BoT.

Newlyn, W.T. (1977) *The Financing of Economic Development*. Oxford: Clarendon Press.

Nidhiprabha, Bhanupongse (1984) 'External Shocks and Adjustment Policies in Thailand'. PhD thesis, Johns Hopkins University, Baltimore (Md.).

Nidhiprabha, Bhanupongse (1987) 'The Role of Monetary Policy in Stabilizing the Thai Economy', paper for the International Conference of Thai Studies, Canberra: The Australian National University.

Nidhiprabha, Bhanupongse & D. Sawamiphakdi & C. Kamheangpatiyooth (1989) *Econometric Modelling of the International Influences on the Thai Economy*. Bangkok: Thailand Development Research Institute.

Nijathaworn, Bandid & Gosah Arya (1987) 'An Econometric Model for Thailand under the LINK System', paper presented at the Macroeconomic Research Conference, Bangkok: Thailand Development Research Institute.

Nijathaworn, Bandid & Thanisorn Dejthamrong (1994) 'Capital Flows, Exchange Rate and Monetary Policy: Thailand's recent experience' in Bank of Thailand, pp. 1–15.

Nijathaworn, Bandid & Chirathep Senivongs (1994) 'International Use of Currencies: An Evidence in the East Asia and Pacific region' in Bank of Thailand, pp. 30–39.

Noland, M. (1990) *Pacific Basin Developing Countries: Prospects for the Future*. Washington DC: Institute for International Economics.

Oman, C. (1984) *New Forms of International Investment in Developing Countries*. Paris: OECD.

Onchan, T., Y. Chalamwong & S. Aungsumalin (1974) *Agricultural Credit in Chainat Province in Thailand*, Research Report No. 9, Department of Agricultural Economics, Faculty of Economics and Business Administration, Kasertsat University, Bangkok.

Osotsapa, Somkiat (1987) 'Impact of Low Agricultural Prices on Asian Agriculture', Paper No. 3004, Faculty of Economics, Chulalongkorn University, Bangkok.

Page, S. (1987) 'Developing Country Attitudes Towards Foreign Investment' in Cable & Persaud (eds), pp. 28–43.

Panayotou, T. (ed.) (1985) *Food Policy Analysis in Thailand*. Bangkok: Agricultural Development Council.

Papanek, G.F. (1972) 'The Effect of Aid and Other Resource Transfers on Savings and Growth in Less Developed Countries', *Economic Journal*. 82: 934–50.

Papanek, G.F. (1973) 'Aid, Foreign Private Investment, Savings and Growth in Less Developed Countries', *Journal of Political Economy*. 81(1): 120–30.

Phipatseritham, K. & K. Yoshihara (1983) *Business Groups in Thailand*, Research Notes and Discussion Paper No. 41, Institute of Southeast Asian Studies, Singapore.

Pongphaichit, Pasuk (1982) *Employment, Income and the Mobilisation of Local Resources in Three Thai Villages*. Bangkok: ILO/ARTEP.

Pongphaichit, Pasuk (1990) *The New Wave of Japanese Investment in ASEAN*. Singapore: Institute of Southeast Asian Studies.

Pongpisanupichit, Jeerasak, Wisarn Pupphavesa, Somjai Phagaphasvivat, Pipat Pitayaachariyakul & Duangmanee Vongpradhip (1989) *Direct Foreign Investment and Capital Flow*, Background Paper No. 6, 1989 Year-End Conference, Thailand Development Research Institute, Bangkok.

Porter, M.E. (1990) *The Competitive Advantage of Nations*. London: Macmillan.

Potter, J.M. (1976) *Thai Peasant Social Structure*. Chicago: University of Chicago Press.

Ramangkura, Virabongse & Bhanupongse Nidhiprabha (1991) 'The Macroeconomics of the Public Sector Deficit', World Bank Policy, Research and External Affairs Working Papers Series (WPS 633), Washington DC.

Ratanakomut, Somchai (1995) 'Industrializing the Service Sector, with Special Emphasis on Tourism', in Krongkaew (ed.), pp. 85–98.

Robinson, D., Y. Byeon & R. Teja with W. Tseng (1991). *Thailand: Adjusting to Success, Current Policy Issues*, IMF Occasional Paper No. 85, Washington DC.

Sahasakul, C., N. Thongpakde & K. Kraisoraphong (1989) *Lessons from the World Bank's Experience of Structural Adjustment Loans (SALs): A Case Study of Thailand*. Bangkok: Thailand Development Research Institute.

Sarmad, K. (1990) 'Public and Private Investment and Economic Growth', Institute of Social Studies Working Paper, subseries on Money, Finance and Development, No. 34, The Hague.

Savvides, A. (1992) 'Investment Slowdown in Developing Countries during the 1980s: Debt Overhang or Foreign Capital Inflows?', *KYKLOS*. 45(3): 363–78.

Sawamiphakdi, Damkirng & Chanin Kamheangpatiyooth (1991) *Responses of Thai Economy to External Economic Shocks*. Bangkok: Thailand Development Research Institute,

Scitovsky, T. (1986) 'Economic Development in Taiwan and South Korea, 1965–1981' in Lau (ed.), pp. 135–95.

Serven, L. & A. Solimano (1992) 'Private Investment and Macroeconomic Adjustment: A Survey', *World Bank Research Observer*. 7(1): 95–114.

Siamwalla, Ammar (1975) 'Stability, Growth and Distribution in the Thai Economy', in Ungphakorn et al., pp. 25-48.

Siamwalla, Ammar (1991) *Land-abundant Agricultural Growth and Some of Its Consequences: The Case of Thailand*. Bangkok: Thailand Development Research Institute.

Siamwalla, Ammar & Suthad Setboonsarng (1987) *Agricultural Pricing Policies in Thailand: 1960–1985*. Bangkok: Thailand Development Research Institute.

Sibunruang, Atchaka (1984) 'Foreign Direct Investment and Manufactured Exports in Thailand'. PhD thesis, University of Sussex.

Sibunruang, Atchaka (1992) 'Changing Patterns of Foreign Direct Investment in Thailand', paper presented at the Pacific Economic Outlook Specialists Meeting, Osaka, March 1992.

Singhaumpai, Yootaphol & Suchart Sakkankosone (1992) 'Public Sector and Monetary Policy in Thailand' in Fres-Felix (ed.), pp. 391–432.

Skinner, G.W. (1958) *Leadership and Power in the Chinese Community in Thailand*. Ithaca: Cornell University Press.

Snyder, D. (1990) 'Foreign Aid and Domestic Savings: A Spurious Correlation?', *Economic Development and Cultural Change*. 39(1): 175–81.

Suehiro, A. (1989) *Capital Accumulation in Thailand, 1855–1985*. Tokyo: Centre for East Asian Cultural Studies,

Sundararajan, V. & S. Thakur (1980) 'Public Investment, Crowding Out, and Growth: a Dynamic Model Applied to India and Korea', *IMF Staff Papers*. 27: 814–55.

Supapongae, Mathee & Rungsun Hataiseree (1993) 'Monetary Policy in Thailand: An Update' in Talib (ed.), pp. 503–37.

Sussangkarn, Chalongphob (1991) 'Labour Market and Macroeconomic Performance', paper presented at the annual seminar of the project 'Promotion of Analysis and Consideration of Population Consequences of Development Planning and Policy in Thailand', Thailand Development Research Institute, Bangkok.

Sussangkarn, Chalongphob, Jere Behrman, Yongyuth Chalamwong, Mathana Phananiramai & Prapon Pattamakitsakul (1991) *Population and Economic Development in Thailand: Some Critical Household Behavioural Relations*, Research Monograph 7, Thailand Development Research Institute, Bangkok.

Talib, A. (ed.) (1993) *Monetary Policy in the SEACEN Countries. An Update*. Kuala Lumpur: The SEACEN Centre.

Tambunlertchai, S. (1980) 'Attitude and Experience in Japanese-Thai Joint Venture Investment' in Krongkaew (ed.).

Taylor, L. (1988) *Varieties of Stabilization Experience: Towards Sensible Macroeconomics in the Third World*. Oxford: Clarendon Press.

Taylor, L. & J.A. Rosensweig (1990) 'Devaluation, Capital Flows and Crowding-out: A CGE Model with Portfolio Choice for Thailand' in Taylor (ed.), pp. 302–32.

Taylor, L. (ed.) (1990) *Socially Relevant Policy Analysis: Structuralist Computable General Equilibrium Models for the Developing World.* Cambridge (Mass.): MIT Press.

Taylor, L. (ed.) (1993) *The Rocky Road to Reform. Adjustment, Income Distribution and Growth in the Developing World.* Cambridge (Mass.): MIT Press.

TDRI (Thailand Development Research Institute) (1987) *Productivity Changes and International Competitiveness of Thai Industries.* 1987 TDRI Year-End Conference, Bangkok: TDRI.

TDRI (Thailand Development Research Institute) (1990) *Industrializing Thailand and its Impact on the Environment.* 1990 TDRI Year-End Conference, Bangkok: TDRI.

TRDI (Thailand Development Research Institute) (1991) *Educational Options for the Future of Thailand.* 1991 TDRI Year-End Conference, Bangkok: TDRI.

TDRI (Thailand Development Research Institute) (1993) *Thai Economic Outlook, Highlighting the Differences.* Bangkok: TDRI.

Tejima, S. (1993) 'Future Prospects of Japanese Foreign Direct Investment in the 1990s and Its Implications in Asia' (mimeo).

Thisyamondol, P., V. Arromdee & M.F. Long (1965) *Agricultural Credit in Thailand, Theory, Data, Policy.* Bangkok: Kasertsat University.

Tiralap, Anupap et al. (1993) *Private Sector Research & Development, 'Lessons from Success'.* Bangkok: Thailand Development Research Institute.

Tseng, W. & R. Corker (1991) *Financial Liberalization, Money Demand and Monetary Policy in Asian Countries,* IMF Occasional Paper No. 84, Washington DC.

Uathavikul, Phaichitr, Direk Patmasiriwat & Chanin Kamheangpatiyooth (1987) *Economic Policy Management in Thailand: Response to Changes in the World Economy 1973–1987,* 1987 TDRI Year-End Conference, Bangkok: TDRI.

UNIDO (1992) *Thailand, Coping with the Strains of Success.* Oxford: Blackwell Publishers.

United Nations (1992) *World Investment Directory 1992,* Vol. 1: Asia and the Pacific. New York: United Nations.

Ungphakorn, Puey et al. (1975) *Finance, Trade and Economic Development in Thailand: Essays in Honour of Khunying Suparb Yossundara.* Bangkok: Sompong Press.

Verbruggen, H. (1985) *Gains from Export-oriented Industrialization in Developing Countries, with Special Reference to South-East Asia.* Amsterdam: Free University Press,

Visser, A.P.R. (1978) 'Een Dorp in de Centrale Vlakte van Thailand'. PhD thesis, University of Utrecht.

Vongpanitlerd, Sumeth (1992) *The Development of Thailand's Technological Capability in Industry*, Research Monograph 9, Thailand Development Research Institute, Bangkok.

Vongpradhip, Duangmanee (1987) 'A CGE Model with Real and Financial Sector Linkages', paper presented at the Macroeconomic Research Conference, October 1987, Thailand Development Research Institute, Bangkok.

Vongpradhip, Duangmanee (1988) 'Short-run Effects of Monetary Measures on the Economy: Comparative Static Analysis Based on a Thai CGE Model with Real and Financial Linkages' (mimeo).

Vongvipanond, Pairoj (1980) *Finance in Thailand's Industrial Development Context.* Report for NESDB, Bangkok: TURA.

Vos, R. (1991) 'Social Accounting, Flow-of-Funds and Capital Accumulation', in Alarcón et al., pp. 165–90.

Vos, R. (1992) 'Private Foreign Asset Accumulation, Not Just Capital Flight: Evidence from the Philippines', *Journal of Development Studies.* 28(3): 500–37.

Vos, R. (1994) *Debt and Adjustment in The World Economy, Structural Asymmetries in North-South Interactions.* London: Macmillan; New York: St. Martin's Press.

Vos, R. & J. Yap (1996) *The Philippine Economy: East Asia's Stray Cat? Structure, Finance and Adjustment.* Basingstoke, etc.: Macmillan; New York: St. Martin's Press.

Wade, R. (1990) *Governing the Market: Economic Theory and the Role of Government in East Asian Industrialization.* Princeton: Princeton University Press.

Warr, P.G. (ed.) (1993) *The Thai Economy in Transition.* Cambridge, UK: Cambridge University Press.

Wattananukit, Atchana & Teerana Bhongmakapat (1989) *The Impact of the External Sector on the Thai Economy and its Determinants.* 1989 TDRI

Year-End Conference. Bangkok: Thailand Development Research Institute.

White, H. (1992) 'The Macroeconomic Impact of Development Aid: A Critical Survey', *Journal of Development Studies*. 28: 163–240.

White, H. (1993) 'Aid and Government: A Dynamic Model of Aid, Income and Fiscal Behaviour', *Journal of International Development*. 5(3): 305–12.

Wiboonchutikula, Paitoon (1987) 'Total Factor Productivity Growth of Manufacturing in Thailand' in TDRI, pp. 4–36.

Wiboonchutikula, Paitoon (1993) 'Thailand's Trade in Manufactured Goods in the Asia-Pacific Region', Thailand Development Research Institute, Bangkok.

Wijnbergen, S. van (1986) 'Macroeconomic Aspects of the Effectiveness of Foreign Aid: The Two Gap Model, Home Goods Disequilibrium and Real Exchange Rate Misalignment', *Journal of International Economics*. 21: 123–36.

Wong, J. (1979) *ASEAN Economies in Perspective. A Comparative Study of Indonesia, Malaysia, the Philippines, Singapore and Thailand*. London: Macmillan.

Wonghanchao, Warin & Jeerasak Pongpisanupichit (1987) 'Contribution of Direct US Investment to the Thai Economy' in Dutta (ed.), pp. 225–52.

World Bank (1982) *Thailand, Program and Policy Priorities for an Agricultural Economy in Transition*. Washington DC: World Bank.

World Bank (1983) *Thailand, Perspectives for Financial Reform*. Washington DC: World Bank.

World Bank (1984) *Thailand, Managing Public Resources for Structural Adjustment*. Washington DC: World Bank.

World Bank (1987) *World Development Report 1987, Industrialisation and Foreign Trade*. Oxford: Oxford University Press, for the World Bank.

World Bank (1988) *World Development Report 1988 Public Finance in Development*. Oxford: Oxford University Press, for the World Bank.

World Bank (1989) *World Development Report 1989, Financial Systems and Development*. Oxford: Oxford University Press, for the World Bank.

World Bank (1990) 'Report on Adjustment Lending II: Policies for Recovery of Growth', Document R 90–99, the World Bank, Washington D.C. (March).

World Bank (1991a) 'Thailand, Country Economic Memorandum', the World Bank, Washington DC.

World Bank (1991b) *World Development Report 1991, The Challenge of Development*. Oxford: Oxford University Press, for the World Bank.

World Bank (1991c) *Three Studies in Support of the Seventh Plan*. Washington DC: Asia Country Department, World Bank.

World Bank (1992) *World Development Report 1992, Development and the Environment*. Oxford: Oxford University Press, for the World Bank.

World Bank (1993) *Global Prospects and the Developing Countries*. Washington DC: World Bank.

World Bank (1994) *World Development Report 1994, Infrastructure for Development*. New York: Oxford University Press.

Index

295